P9-BBM-803

Facing the Brink

FACING THE BRINK

an intimate study of crisis diplomacy

EDWARD WEINTAL

CHARLES BARTLETT

Charles Scribner's Sons   New York

COPYRIGHT © 1967 CHARLES L. BARTLETT AND EDWARD WEINTAL

This book published simultaneously in the United States of America and in Canada—Copyright under the Berne Convention

All rights reserved. No part of this book may be reproduced in any form without the permission of Charles Scribner's Sons.

B–3.67[V]

Printed in the United States of America
Library of Congress Catalog Card Number 67-15494

Foreword

In the course of their regular reportorial assignments over two decades and in gathering material for this book, the authors, between them, have interviewed literally every key official involved in foreign affairs, from Presidents and Secretaries of State down. We have had many frank discussions with them. We should like to thank them for the infinite patience and generosity they have shown even when they knew we were often critical of the official line they represented.

To list them all would not be practical but we would like to single out two whose job it was to deal with us *ex-officio*. Ex-Assistant Secretary of State for Public Affairs, James Greenfield, and his deputy, Richard I. Phillips, may well serve as models for their profession. They never tried to "sell" us a line but were invariably helpful in opening up sources without concern for the "image" that might result from the encounters.

Mr. Charles Scribner, Jr., and Mr. Burroughs Mitchell of Charles Scribner's Sons gave us encouragement and assistance when things looked darkest. Their enthusiasm for the book helped us overcome the difficulties of writing history as it unfolds.

To James Hurd of the State Department go our deepest

thanks for removing bureaucratic road blocks from our paths and for tirelessly snipping away at red tape.

We are deeply obligated to our friend and colleague Tom Lambert, of the *Los Angeles Times,* who volunteered to help with marshalling and writing up some of the vast material we collected in the course of our research. Without him, the book would have been much longer in the making.

Our researchers, Steven Crane and Katharine Gresham, have done yeoman work in checking facts, dates and spelling.

Finally, Mrs. Teresa Oehmann and Mrs. Colleen Woodard, who have plodded patiently through illegible handwriting and mumbled dictation in order to produce a readable manuscript, deserve our grateful appreciation of their proficiency and accuracy.

The authors have approached their task with clinical detachment. There are no heroes or villains in this book. We have described each participant as we saw him, scoring in some cases, failing in others. Like most people, statesmen and diplomats have their haloes as well as their clay feet.

We are under no illusion that the record cited in this book is complete in each case. Some of it is still highly classified. The motivations of such volatile characters as Khrushchev, Castro, Nasser and De Gaulle could only be surmised. All that can be claimed for the book is that it gives the reader an intimate glimpse of history in the making.

E. W.
C. B.

Contents

Foreword   v

ONE   Crisis diplomacy   1

TWO   Aux armes, citoyens!   16

THREE   "Komer's war"   37

FOUR   Challenge on the doorstep   54

FIVE   Sonic booms over Hanoi   70

SIX   Self-made crises   93

SEVEN   Diplomat in Chief   112

EIGHT   —But not the Secretary of State   138

NINE   The devil's advocate   167

TEN   The astrologers   181

ELEVEN   The ultimate crisis   206

Appendix   221

Index   235

O ✦ N ✦ E

Crisis diplomacy

In the days immediately following the assassination of President Kennedy, Mr. Johnson confided to General Eisenhower that he felt completely at home with domestic affairs but did not know enough about foreign policy or have a staff good enough to handle it. Eisenhower suggested some of his former advisers might help the new President, but Johnson failed to respond and until the 1964 election concentrated on the Great Society and left foreign affairs almost entirely to Secretary Rusk and McGeorge Bundy, his assistant for National Security Affairs.

A few weeks before his 1964 re-election, Johnson had been urged by several prominent foreign affairs specialists to seize the initiative in foreign affairs for the United States. Such men as Dean Acheson, Robert Lovett and John McCloy had been pressing him, in effect, to move boldly on NATO's problems instead of handing over their solutions, by default, to General de Gaulle. But the President was cautious, replying that more study was needed before the United States could make a new move.

As the election approached, John McCone, then the director of the CIA, told the President:

"In a few weeks you are bound to win the election with the greatest majority any President ever had. I believe that will

1

be the time to take a global look at our foreign policy and review it in all its aspects."

Mr. Johnson agreed, and early in 1965 a foreign policy review meeting was called at the White House. The Secretaries of State and Defense, Presidential Assistant McGeorge Bundy and the President's sixteen-member advisory panel on foreign affairs were invited to the session, held in the Cabinet room. Many of the panel members were well known—Acheson, McCloy, Lovett—but the group, appointed by the President on September 9, 1964, also included some strangers to the foreign affairs community.

The meeting started briskly as the President described to the gathering the difficulties he would have to face taking initiatives in foreign affairs, especially those requiring new appropriations from Congress. He concluded his talk with the usual Johnsonian appeal to the patriotism of his listeners. "These are my foreign problems," he told the group in effect. "You, as some of the wisest men in the nation, must help me solve them."

To everyone's astonishment, Mr. Morris Liebman, a Chicago lawyer who was also a member of the presidential foreign policy panel, then began a long-winded and spirited discussion on ways to help the President. There were Americans, he said, who simply did not comprehend their country's foreign affairs problems, and had to be awakened to them. That was particularly true of the Middle West, he continued, and Washington must alert and heed the Midwest. As Mr. Liebman later explained, he intended to "goose the establishment" and to break down "the rigidities which have been guiding foreign policy since the war."

The "establishment" did not know what to make of Liebman's remarks. At one point while he was talking, Dean Acheson exploded a blunt behind-the-hand profanity to John McCloy, another member of the foreign policy "establishment."

The effect of Mr. Liebman's interjection was to break up the meeting. McCone's well-meant initiative collapsed. As far as is known, this was President Johnson's only attempt to take a global look at the foreign policy of his own administration.

Sometime later, McGeorge Bundy dispatched a circular letter to government departments, universities, foreign policy centers and research organizations, asking for new foreign policy ideas. Very few came from the government agencies. "I never get any ideas from the departments," the President complained. "Why can't we have more ideas?"

Bundy received a wide array of foreign policy proposals, however, from the universities and institutes, many staffed with experts bearing doctorates and reputations for expounding ideas differing from government policies. But the universities' and institutes' prosposals, some obviously contrived to stress differences with current policies, proved of little or no use.

Meantime, crisis has succeeded crisis and Lyndon Johnson—a thorough pragmatist reluctant to institute major changes in foreign policy—has been reacting to international troubles created by others but taking no long-range initiatives of his own. "He is afraid of the unknown," a former aide observed, "and will not move in a new situation unless he is forced to move by events."

To make matters worse, there was virtually no formal machinery available to Johnson for coordinating national security affairs. It has remained almost non-existent since the Eisenhower administration.

Shortly after Kennedy entered the White House, Professor Walt Rostow and McGeorge Bundy, two key presidential aides, decided the national security mechanism on which Eisenhower had relied was cumbersome and unnecessary. It consisted primarily of the National Security Council, established in 1947 on the recommendation of James Forrestal, who believed President Truman urgently needed an advisory body to assimilate and digest the views and proposals of all the government agencies involved in foreign affairs.

Wary of intrusion upon its preserves in foreign policy, the State Department initially balked at the NSC. President Truman was not immediately attracted by it, and stayed away from its meetings until the outbreak of the Korean War.

However, the NSC, with a small staff, in the ornate old State-War-Navy Building next to the White House, gradually became a focal point of foreign policy deliberations from 1950 until Bundy and Rostow decided to scuttle it in January, 1961.

President Eisenhower, who wanted his papers fully "staffed out," relied on the NSC to a greater extent than either his predecessor or successor in office. But even he found the NSC machinery too unwieldy for effective handling of some of the crises occurring in his administration.

Thus the Lebanon crisis of 1958 was not even discussed in the NSC. The decision to land a U.S. force was made by a small group who met in the President's office after a formal NSC meeting. Secretary Dulles in a thirty-minute presentation described the problem, summarized intelligence reports, the extent of our commitment under the CENTO treaty and concluded by recommending that the commitment be fulfilled.

Surprisingly, only the Deputy Defense Secretary, the late Donald Quarles, raised diplomatic objections and feared UN reaction to U.S. intervention in the Middle East. Chairman of the Joint Chiefs of Staff, General Nathan Twining, warned that once we go in "we may be there for ten years or longer."

But once the decision had been made, the military planners were ready. Within a few hours the entire operation was backed up all the way to Norfolk. The operation was so thorough that an army division lifted from Germany was ready to land in Beirut with its atomic missiles. It was only at the last minute that someone in the Pentagon realized what the introduction of atomic weapons into the explosive Middle East situation would mean politically and ordered the Navy to leave the missiles on board ship while the division disembarked.

The diplomatic planning that accompanied the landing of U.S. troops on July 15–17, 1958, was also adequate. A day after the first landing, heads of state of other CENTO powers, Turkey, Iran and Pakistan, meeting in Ankara expressed their "satisfaction and thanks" for U.S. intervention. By August 13, a special UN assembly was summoned to deal with the crisis and to hear a six-point peace program for the Middle East presented by President Eisenhower.

Similarly, the question of inviting Soviet Chairman Khrushchev to the United States never went to the NSC: the decision was made by a small group in the President's immediate entourage.

But on the whole the NSC served its purpose in the Eisenhower days. It debated the Quemoy and Matsu issue and, although no formal decision to defend the offshore islands was ever made within the NSC, the lengthy debates on the weapons to be used and the logistics to be applied *in case* the decisions should be made were regarded at the time as equivalent to a commitment.

The NSC also conducted a thorough examination of U.S. policy toward Nasser and the United Arab Republic, after Dulles' abrupt refusal to finance the construction of the Aswan Dam. The State-Pentagon-CIA paper laid before the NSC described Nasser as the "wave of the future" and advocated offering him economic and political support ahead of the Soviets. The decision went against the paper's authors but only after the proposal was fully considered by President Eisenhower and Secretary Dulles.

In a little-known incident, the NSC at one time also recommended giving General de Gaulle nuclear weapons, but not the know-how for manufacturing them. However, this recommendation was quickly withdrawn at a subsequent meeting. It would be interesting to speculate on the course of U.S. relations with De Gaulle if that decision had been allowed to stand.

Under the procedure followed in the Eisenhower days, every statutory member of the NSC had to have his say. Eisenhower used to say that plans by themselves were less important than planning. Situations never developed according to plans but the process of planning served to acquaint officials with the problems they would have to face should the contingency arise. It also enabled the President to listen to all sides of a given problem.

As soon as the President expressed his own views, his decision was recorded and subsequently every participant was given an opportunity to see the minutes and to make sure that he agreed with the recorded interpretation of the President's views. This procedure, at least, provided a record of the crucial issues debated before the NSC.

In typical Washington fashion, attendance at NSC meetings soon became a status symbol. There were times when sixty people or more were present at the top-secret meetings. Admiral Lewis Strauss, who had a seat on the council as chairman of the Atomic Energy Commission, insisted he should retain it after his nomination to be Secretary of Commerce. When the matter was laid before Eisenhower, the President turned down the admiral's request with the offhand remark that "next thing you know we'll have [Secretary of Agriculture] Benson on the council." The request died a natural death when the Senate refused to confirm the admiral's nomination to the Commerce Department.

The advance guard of the incoming Kennedy administration registered two prime complaints about the NSC.

The first was that the plans and proposals it approved were consistently strained of content to meet the objections and qualifications of all the governmental agencies and departments involved. One career official, a Kennedy holdover from the Eisenhower administration, told Bundy and Rostow the NSC once had wasted six weeks debating whether the United States should commit vast resources to take the lead in space or merely spend enough to match the pace of the Russians.

The second complaint was aimed at the Operations Coordinating Board, an arm of the NSC which Eisenhower's aides created in 1953 to follow up decisions by the council and to insure that they were carried out. The OCB had enlarged its assignments to direct task forces engaged in drafting massive papers that were designed to assert the United States' policy objective in every nation of the world. These "country papers," as they were called, were composed at the price of bickering and compromise among the agencies which had a voice in them and the activity had caused the OCB to become criticized as "a paper mill."

Bundy and Rostow took the view that the over-all mechanism was too elaborate to meet President Kennedy's less formal needs and that the initiative of the State Department was being sapped by all the planning and follow-up activity in the White House. The two professors argued that the desk officers in the department should serve as the focal figures in drafting country plans and that the White House should not attempt to control their deliberations. Bundy felt the coordinating could be accomplished by the departments, aided by a small White House staff of men with keen, sensitive minds who would struggle to establish an informal network of responsive officials throughout the government. They abolished the OCB and pulled together their staff from the universities, Manhattan law firms and the talent they found in the government.

The demise of the OCB caused President Kennedy some wry amusement. Informed the OCB had been swept away, Kennedy remarked to Rostow: "You are a fine politician, Walt. You have just abolished sixty patronage jobs."

Seemingly indifferent about the abolition of the OCB, Kennedy was dismayed by the NSC itself. He apparently believed the weight of officialdom at these sessions might mute some of his most trusted advisers, and that the presence of so many persons at the meetings was conducive to newspaper "leaks." He tried at first to hold formal NSC meetings every two weeks, gradually extended the period to three weeks, then determined to convene the council only when necessary.

In the agonizing days of self-examination after the Bay of Pigs, Kennedy repeatedly asked himself and others if more formalized staffing would have disclosed his crucial error in believing the invasion could succeed after he cancelled the air cover for the landing force. Many argued at the time and later that if Bundy had done what NSC staff members had done before him—elicit all the viewpoints and dissents within the government—the serious doubts of the Pentagon's military officers would have come to the surface.

Kennedy recognized that he and his staff had not functioned effectively in the Bay of Pigs crisis. Some efforts were made soon after that debacle to re-establish a coordinating committee somewhat resembling the OCB. But Kennedy favored informal meetings with a few advisers, preferring to deal with specialists and shrinking from the advice of those who had not been intimately involved in the problem at hand.

When Johnson was Vice-President, an aide suggested the Texan's morale would be improved if Kennedy occasionally asked his advice on foreign policy issues. President Eisenhower and Secretary of State John Foster Dulles had rarely made an important foreign policy move without consulting Johnson when he was Senate Majority Leader.

Kennedy shook his head when he heard the suggestion. "I know," he said, "I feel bad about Lyndon because he is miserable in that job. But when a problem blows up, I never think of calling him because he hasn't read the cables."

Although a great deal can be said for the Kennedy-Johnson trend toward informality in shaping foreign policy—it is less laborious and disputatious, decisions can be reached more quickly, the lesser number of people involved insures greater control over and therefore a lesser danger of "leaks" about their deliberations—some kind of formalized procedure is necessary for the orderly conduct of foreign affairs.

It is true the NSC of Eisenhower's time tended to become a debating society, with too many officials assuming they had the right and duty to attend and take part in policy-making meetings. It is true, also, that the minutes of the Eisenhower NSC meetings, carefully perused by Kennedy aides after they reached the White House, were found to be intensely dull. One New Frontiersman described them as an infallible cure for insomnia. Even loyal veterans of the Eisenhower days have conceded that the NSC discussions frequently bogged down. The focus would freeze on one aspect of a large issue and the session would end without time to consider the over-all policy. Presidential Assistant Robert Cutler's preoccupation with semantics often seemed excessive to men who had to sit still as he drove at specifics: "What exactly do you mean by preserving democracy in South Korea?" At one meeting, Dulles studied a Cutler paper which had painstakingly defined the issue, with left and right columns listing the differences, and declared breezily, "I can take either the left or the right."

But occasional boredom is not too high a price to pay for an apparatus which is capable of performing effectively as a safety net under the high-wire act. To the extent that the regular NSC meetings served to pull the government together, to insure that the President heard every side of an issue before he acted, and to examine danger spots before they erupted into crises, their omission is a risk in the operations of the Johnson administration.

President Johnson has employed the NSC as little more than a rubber stamp. "Approved by the NSC" has sounded impressive in Congressional hearing rooms and in newspaper stories. In fact, the NSC under Johnson has seldom debated foreign policy problems. Instead, as in the Dominican and Vietnam crises, it has supplied ratification of decisions already made which, for one reason or another, have caused trouble.

Some movement toward better employment of the NSC and, generally, toward a more formalized decision-making process began with the return to the White House in 1966 of Walt Rostow who, according to a former Cabinet officer, is "the only man in the government who looks over the horizon." Rostow, an incorrigible optimist, has been struggling manfully to provide a formalized channel for foreign policy decision-making. According to Rostow, the President was definitely interested and has even complained that there are not enough foreign policy meetings to occupy his time.

To satisfy the President's appetite for foreign policy discussions, the National Security Council meetings are now held intermittently to inform and alert the President without compelling him to make immediate decisions.

Under the latest dispensation, the 45-minute sessions held every other Thursday have been taking up only those problems or crises which may require presidential decisions at a later date. One such meeting, for instance, was devoted to the problem of food, with Secretary Rusk, former AID Chief David Bell and Agriculture Secretary Orville Freeman discussing foreign needs as well as domestic availabilities. At the end of the discussion it was recorded that the President approved the general lines of the Rusk-Freeman proposals with the usual admonition that "we must have Congress with us."

Thus, at least the bureaucracy now obtains guidance to the President's thinking, even though it may have to come back with additional arguments before the final decisions are made.

There have been objections to the new method, notably from Defense Secretary McNamara, who has felt that "you don't go to the President until you are ready for a decision." But the President seems to like the system and has been a regular attendant at the sessions.

The argument as to the best way of decision-making in crises will undoubtedly go on through this and following administrations. There is obviously no one answer and no guaranteed method. Some of the recent crises have been handled successfully by improvisations; others remained unsolved and even deteriorated in spite of advance planning.

The timing, the circumstances, the personalities involved, the intentions and capabilities of the adversary differ in each crisis. The storm clouds come in different shapes at varying speeds from every portion of the sky. As Secretary McNamara pointed out, there were 164 significant outbreaks of violence between 1958 and 1966. None was a formally declared war but each represented a threat to an established government and was therefore a matter of concern to the United States.

In a thoughtful review of international affairs written in 1903, Britain's late Lord Salisbury asserted that "the victories of diplomacy are won by a series of microscopic advantages—a judicious suggestion here, an opportune civility there, a wise concession at one moment and a far-sighted persistence at another—of sleepless tact, immovable calmness and patience that no folly, no provocation, no blunder can shake."

Thus, the ingredients that go into the making of foreign policy are almost limitless. The factors that fit one problem are totally inapplicable to another; the imperatives of one issue are irrelevant to a second.

But the danger is persistent that the ingredients which make foreign policy will be injected according to whim or impulse. A President may be tempted to let sympathy with one ally or impatience with another shape his decisions. He is often led to ignore the planners, whose long-range considerations are not always pertinent to his political needs. His preoccupations with the immediate can cause him to neglect the future. Badgered by headlines and importuned from capitals around the world, an American President can easily fall into a posture of reacting instead of guiding, responding instead of leading. He can become a captive of crises precipitated by others.

In a reflective speech to the American Society of International Law in April, 1966, ex-Undersecretary of State George Ball recalled the prediction of a friend who had recently finished reading Arnold Toynbee's works on the life cycles of nations and civilizations.

"When America has run its course," the friend prophesied, "I know what headstone will appear in the history books. It will be: 'The United States—a nation that died of a surfeit of pragmatism.' "

Americans are indeed a pragmatic people, Ball conceded, and pragmatism indeed characterizes many of their government's approaches to foreign policy, which often take "the course of least resistance."

"It is easy, and tempting, to become absorbed in the operational aspects of foreign relations, and to ignore the longer-term implications of policy," Ball went on.

"But if America is to survive as a civilization, if in fact the world is to survive as a healthy environment for human beings, then we have to remind ourselves of the larger framework of policy—something better than the habits, the improvisations, the expedients of years gone by," he said, "or we shall find ourselves repeating the old mistakes in a world where mistakes by great nations can mean world destruction."

It is distressingly true that American policy abroad in the Kennedy and Johnson administrations has concentrated on "the operational aspects of foreign relations," and that little attention has been paid to "the longer-term implications of policy." Perhaps the blame for this should not be saddled squarely either on Kennedy or Johnson, for the crises which have racked their administrations and demanded so many hasty "operational" responses stemmed in good part from the failure of some of their pragmatic predecessors to consider the "longer-term implications" of their foreign policies and policy moves abroad.

Kennedy was no less pragmatic than Johnson, but he was equipped with a wider horizon and wider interest in foreign affairs than his successor. His sensitive instincts for diplomatic dealings did not, however, avert some short-term mistakes with wrenching long-term consequences in foreign affairs.

He realized belatedly, for instance, that the hastily convoked Nassau conference with Macmillan in December, 1962, abruptly cancelling the Skybolt missile program and offering Polaris submarines to Britain but not to France, except as an afterthought, would plague our relationship with both allies in the future. "We did not even know the meaning of the words we were using at Nassau," Kennedy later confided to an associate.

Kennedy had been warned. In a memorandum dated December 17, 1962, and handed to Kennedy on the eve of his departure for Nassau, Walt Rostow, the newly appointed Policy Planning Chief, wrote:

> I understand you have heard all the arguments you wish to hear about the Polaris arrangement with Britain but let me leave these thoughts with you for the plane for I have rarely seen so dangerous a gap between a high-level decision and the judgment of junior subordinates.

The Polaris deal, Rostow wrote, could upset the Brussels negotiations from which Macmillan hoped to secure membership in the Common Market. He advised that the British public was reconciled to losing the Skybolt missile and that this problem should not take precedence over the priority objective of securing De Gaulle's assent to Britain's admission in the Common Market. He warned that De Gaulle, already sensitive about the special relations between Britain and the United States, would be infuriated by an enlargement of this relationship to include mutual ownership of Polaris missiles. Rostow's warning was sound. Less than a month after the meeting at Nassau, the French president proclaimed that Britain was not a European nation and could not become one without accepting profound changes in its traditions.

In spite of these mishaps, Kennedy apparently had hoped to inculcate some longer-term factors into American foreign policy. Before his inauguration, he commissioned a series of task forces to prepare a set of reviews and recommendations on a host of foreign policy issues, including defense, disarmament, the United Nations, NATO and De Gaulle, the organization of the State Department. Task force members quizzed at least two-score "senior Americans well informed on national security matters," the chiefs of half a dozen research institutes and various British, West German, Belgian, French and Canadian officials.

George Kennan contributed a series of foreign policy suggestions to Kennedy in an eight-page letter written August 17, 1960. The former chief planner in the State Department recommended a cut-back in some of this country's political and military commitments abroad, and a diplomatic campaign "to heighten the divisive tendencies within the Soviet bloc."

There is no doubt that had Kennedy lived he would have evolved a long-term Soviet policy of his own. He was fascinated by the problem. In his private talks he invariably expressed the hope of making an historic departure toward better relations with the Soviet Union.

Shortly after his inauguration in 1961, Kennedy summoned Llewellyn Thompson, the then ambassador to the Soviet Union, and his two predecessors, Charles E. Bohlen and George Kennan. "Now tell me about Russia," the young President asked, and listened for several hours. Later Kennedy spent more than eight hours in one week listening to Thompson's reports and suggestions.

However, Kennedy's curiosity also had its drawbacks. He was in the habit of bypassing the Secretary and Undersecretary to call Thompson directly, asking point blank: "What should I do about this problem?" The weakness of this system was that, with the best will in the world, Thompson could not always fill in his chiefs in time and was in constant fear of making his own policy rather than reflecting the Secretary's views.

Kennedy also saw Latin America as a likely field for U.S. initiatives. He put a new life into the Alliance for Progress, an idea conceived by the Eisenhower administration, though without the glamorous name. But Kennedy's greatest success in the field of foreign policy came to him not through advance planning but as an unpredictable byproduct of his courage, coolness and skill in handling the Cuban missile crisis.

Khrushchev's retreat from Cuba in the face of Kennedy's pressure showed the world on both sides of the Iron Curtain that the Russians were not ten feet tall and would back down when confronted by stern determination. Russian weakness was exposed and the Cuban example has ever since served as a stimulus to East European countries, such as Poland and Rumania, to seek greater freedom from the Soviets. It has opened the eyes of the uncommitted world. Another—and probably less desirable result—was Western Europe's, and especially De Gaulle's, confidence that the Soviets would not attack. This inspired Europe's demands for more "independence" from the United States.

But, all in all, looking back on the Kennedy period, it would seem that George Kennan's and other advisers' proposals for a thorough review of U.S. foreign policy went unheeded. American commitments abroad were not reduced. In fact, notably in Vietnam, they were increased. Had he not suffered reverses in the Bay of Pigs and in Laos, it may well be that President Kennedy would have thought twice before expanding the Vietnam commitment early in 1962 from 700 to 11,000 advisers. Had he followed a long-range policy plan rather than an understandable concern for his image as a result of the Bay of Pigs fiasco, he may have reduced rather than increased the Vietnam commitment.

Kennan had urged Kennedy "to regain the initiative" to "provide the impetus to change" in international matters with "a succession of carefully calculated steps timed in such a way as not only to throw the adversary off balance but to keep him off it." Instead, Kennedy's tenure in office was marked by a series of reactions to Communist initiatives—in Berlin, Cuba and Southeast Asia. It was Kennedy who was forced into reactions instead of eliciting them. The hasty planning for the Berlin, Cuban and some of the Southeast Asian emergencies was impressive. But it was pragmatic and operational, more in the nature of a fire-fighting exercise than a careful and long-range campaign for fire prevention.

Averting a policy of response demands a resumption of American initiative in foreign affairs. As Kennan wrote to Kennedy, this country "cannot exercise adequate control over a given international situation unless you act constantly on it— unless you yourself provide the impetus to change instead of just leaving it to others or to chance."

Equally, such a course demands more of what Lord Salisbury described as "immovable calmness and patience that no folly, no provocation, no blunder can shake." The crisis-ridden history of the Kennedy and Johnson administrations described in this book provides conclusive proof that impatience with a crisis situation coupled with the natural American tendency to "do it now" has involved the United States in crises where, with some pre-planning, involvement could have been avoided. There have been some crises, like Cuba, where it would have been impossible to make a unilateral decision *not* to be involved. But there were others where aloofness and ambiguity rather than "firm positions" could have prevented involvement or reduced the risks where it was inevitable.

T ☆ W ☆ O

Aux armes, citoyens!

President Kennedy once noted that the Chinese characters denoting the word "crisis" mean both "danger" and "opportunity."

Only a few of the crises involving the United States in the last three administrations faced the country with a sudden and direct threat to its security. But all presented an opportunity for a display of statesmanship and diplomacy.

It can always be assumed that the interest of a super-power like the United States is somehow involved in every crisis occurring anywhere in the world. But the wiser course is to consider in advance whether U.S. interests would best be served by getting into the crisis or by staying out.

In some cases, avoiding a commitment has proved to be more beneficial than getting into one. At the height of the 1965 India-Pakistan conflict over Kashmir President Johnson called in former Secretary of State Dean Acheson and asked what the United States should do about it. "Mr. President," Acheson archly replied, "have you ever thought of doing nothing?"

Presidential and Pentagon sympathies were with Ayub of Pakistan, a nominal ally. But by staying out of the fray the administration prevented the crisis from becoming an East-West issue. Though some U.S. officials were tempted to mediate, wiser counsel prevailed on the ground that, as an ally of

16

Pakistan, and a friend of India, the United States could not escape the charge of bias in favor of one side or another. There were also misgivings that U.S. aloofness would help the Soviets score a diplomatic victory. But the Soviet-sponsored Tashkent accord had come and gone without any visible damage to American prestige.

In diplomacy, "doing nothing" means sitting back and exercising political influence derived from military and economic power. Unfortunately, the ability to translate the overwhelming American power into political influence has been singularly absent in the U.S. diplomatic arsenal. The instinct has often been, as in Vietnam, to commit actual U.S. forces and materiel as the most effective form of crisis participation.

One of the few crises in which the United States somehow managed to avoid military commitment, using skills and influence instead, was the Cyprus episode of 1964.

It is inconceivable but nevertheless true that no advance planning for the predictable Cyprus crisis was ever done. For at least three years before the flare-up it had been quite obvious that the jerry-built London-Zurich agreements of 1959 establishing Cyprus independence could not last. It was also obvious that the British, bent on reducing or liquidating their overseas commitments, would have had to relinquish their peacekeeping role on the island.

It could also have been assumed that Cyprus would sooner or later be dropped into Washington's lap. The threats of a Soviet takeover, of military confrontation between two NATO allies, of a holy war between Moslems and Christians were all there for anyone to see. Yet when the denouement finally came, there were no contingency plans for handling the crisis and the entire scenario had to be improvised.

The basic causes of the Cyprus crisis have not been settled to this day. The Turks and the Greeks are still at each other's throats, but in trying to find an ad hoc "accommodation" the United States was fortunate enough to have found in those who handled the crisis some of the talents and skills which, according to the third Marquess of Salisbury, are essential ingredients of a successful diplomatic enterprise. Without them, war would have been inevitable and U.S. military involvement virtually certain.

This country's critical involvement in Cyprus began on January 25, 1964, when British Ambassador Sir David Ormsby-Gore called on Undersecretary George Ball, acting as Secretary of State in Rusk's absence, to announce the British were no longer prepared to keep peace on the island. Under the 1959 Zurich-London agreements, Britain was named as a guarantor of Cyprus independence.

"Her Majesty's government has concluded," the ambassador told Ball, "that it is best to establish an international force on Cyprus, and early rather than late." That force, the British ambassador suggested, should be "broadly based," but should include detachments only from NATO nations. The British urgently needed U. S. support and, more importantly, a sizable U. S. contingent with supplies and airlift for the proposed international force.

Ball's first reaction was to suggest ways for the British to carry on. But Ormsby-Gore was adamant. He said his government was no longer prepared to bear the burden alone. If there were no other solution, he continued, Britain was ready to drop the Cyprus issue in the UN's lap. Ormsby-Gore had seen a Chief of Staff paper calling for a force of 10,000 men, but he believed that Commonwealth Relations Secretary Duncan Sandys might trim that total to some degree.

The ambassador said he also had been instructed to urge the U.S. to order its mission in Ankara to reproach the Turks for their reluctance to cooperate with the British on Cyprus. What the British really were asking was American assumption of prime responsibility in an issue on which the United States had not been consulted and which, at the time, affected American interests only indirectly.

Ball subsequently reported the Ormsby-Gore meeting to Secretary Rusk. Then, with no more than a "Dean, let me handle this one," Ball proceeded to deal with the Cyprus crisis almost single-handedly. To be sure, he kept Rusk meticulously informed about every Cyprus development and about every American move in the crisis. But Ball was the American front-runner in each step as the turbulence swelled steadily and dangerously.

Never slow to take advantage of trouble in the West or to exacerbate a handy crisis, the Russians leaped into the Cyprus imbroglio a few days after Ormsby-Gore's démarche to Ball. On February 7, 1964, in almost identical notes, Soviet Premier Nikita Khrushchev warned the U.S., Britain, France, Greece and Turkey that any move against the island would be "the source of international complications fraught with grave consequences." As Soviet notes go, Khrushchev's was almost prosaic. But it inserted the Soviet Union into the Cyprus issue, and won some sympathy for Moscow on the troubled island.

With Johnson's and Rusk's approval, Ball swung into action. On February 10, he flew to Athens and Ankara to solicit Turkish and Greek support for a NATO peacekeeping force. He then flew to Cyprus to seek President Makarios' endorsement. The bearded archbishop previously had said "no" without even bothering to study the proposal.

Ball was deeply worried as he approached Makarios. He was travel-weary, uncertain whether his British, Greek and Turkish endorsements would hold up, but primarily uneasy about the archbishop. Reports from other American officials who had talked with him noted that their conversations often had a way of drifting into near-fantasies. Ball decided to be blunt.

The two met twice on February 12. The first session went quietly enough as the archbishop listened to the Undersecretary's forceful plea for restraint. But the second meeting was tumultuous.

After some questions about the proposed international force, Makarios blandly told Ball that the issue of such a unit could be decided later; that the crisis should be submitted to the UN Security Council with a demand for an endorsement of the political independence and territorial integrity of Cyprus. Such an endorsement, of course, would have precluded any intervention by the Zurich guarantor powers and would have left

Cyprus under the sole control of Makarios' armed Greek Cypriote majority. It could also have sparked a Turkish invasion.

Ball exploded. In a later message to President Johnson, he reported that for the next forty-five minutes he "told off" Makarios and his ministers "in a fashion remote from diplomatic exchanges," drawing a lurid forecast of the results that would ensue if the archbishop persisted on his "rash course." Outwardly, Makarios seemed unruffled.

Ball suspected, however, that he might have dented the archbishop's calm. As he left Makarios' office, Ball reported, even the archbishop's luxuriant beard "seemed pale." But the Undersecretary was grievously worried. He feared Makarios might be under the thumb of some of his more extremist Cabinet ministers, who seemed determined to put Cyprus to flames if they could not get it on their terms.

The Undersecretary told President Johnson that feelings were so high and passions so intense that "a blow-up is exceedingly possible." He suggested that overwhelming pressure be exerted on Makarios "to frighten him sufficiently to consider some move to halt the killing" which was mounting on the island, and daily inflaming the Turks.

Ball flew back from Cyprus to Ankara, with only one thought in mind: to restrain the Turks from invading Cyprus. The Turks agreed, but it was obvious their restraint was wearing paper-thin. Ball then flew to Athens to counsel moderation on the Greeks. This was the same message Greek officials had been receiving by telephone from prominent Americans of Greek extraction—a diplomatic side-effort Ball had concocted to reinforce his country's official pleas to Athens.

Meanwhile, fed up with Makarios' intransigence and the failure of their own efforts to restore order on Cyprus, the British tossed the island crisis to the UN with a request for a Security Council meeting. Angered at being beaten to this move, the Cyprus delegation rushed in an hour later with a similar request, shouting that the Turks were threatening to invade their island.

Ball now was involved in an offensive on several fronts.

Flying from Ankara to Athens, from Cyprus to London, New York and Washington, he touched bases with every participant in the island crisis who might help deflect the mounting storm.

In a last-minute effort to put the matter back in British hands, President Johnson urged British Prime Minister Sir Alec Douglas-Home to convoke a summit meeting of the guarantor powers under Article IV of the Treaty of Guarantee. In a letter written in mid-February, 1964, the President offered to strengthen the British by sending either George Ball or General Maxwell Taylor as observers.

The President's two-page letter was promptly answered by a brief message from Douglas-Home. The British prime minister thought the idea of a summit meeting was fine but warned that a meeting of this kind could be construed as (1) cutting across the peacekeeping efforts of the UN and (2) ganging up by the larger powers on the small Republic of Cyprus. The British were obviously determined to abandon their leadership in Cyprus.

A few days earlier, on instructions from Washington, Thomas Finletter, U.S. permanent representative to the NATO Council, urged NATO Secretary General Dirk Stikker to request fullest information from all parties concerned and to call an emergency NATO meeting as soon as it became obvious that peace between the two NATO members was seriously threatened. He had also been told by Washington to establish close liaison with other permanent representatives in order to have the latest and most accurate information available at all times.

But despite intensive diplomatic activity, Cyprus entered a stage of recurring crises with the outbreak of inter-communal fighting. The fighting spread from town to town and the Turkish Cypriotes were pushed into an increasingly difficult position. A Turkish invasion scare occurred on March 13. From then on, reports reaching the State Department described the situation on the island as "painful and on the verge of becoming catastrophic."

The crisis reached its climax on the evening of June 2,

1964, when a "critic" message flashed into Washington from
U.S. Ambassador Raymond Hare in Ankara. The message
informed the Johnson administration that the Turkish Security
Council had decided the night before to invade Cyprus.

The invasion was to be staged by forces already trained
for the seaborne move and now deployed in the Iskenderun
area on Turkey's southern Mediterranean coast. General Tagmac, Deputy Chief of Staff, had been secretly given command
of the invasion forces. Their mission was to establish a "political and military beachhead" on the island, in the hope of gaining for Turkey an advantage over the Greek and Cypriote governments in the negotiations that were expected to get under
way immediately after the landing.

The Turks had planned the invasion with the connivance
of Fazil Kutchuk, the Turkish Cypriote vice-president of
Cyprus. The Turk-Kutchuk scheme called for the latter to demand a meeting of the Cypriote Cabinet, which had not assembled for months. As soon as Kutchuk's request was turned
down by Archbishop Makarios—and it was taken for granted
he would reject the Kutchuk demand—the Turkish invasion
force was to have moved against the island.

The Turks had tried diligently to camouflage their invasion plans. Throughout the week of late May-early June,
Turkish staff officers made it a point to appear at all diplomatic functions. The deception was so successful that the
British ambassador in Ankara described the increased
Turkish military activities as "routine maneuvers" and "business
as usual." The ambassador, apparently unconcerned, went
off on a pleasure trip to Istanbul—but hastened back to Ankara
at the suggestion of his American colleague who later briefed
him on the true import of the "maneuvers."

If his wide-ranging and inquisitive staff had not suspected
something furtive was afoot, Ambassador Hare later reported, the Turkish invasion plan might have succeeded.

Ambassador Hare's "critic" message was relayed promptly
to the seventh-floor office of Undersecretary Ball, again acting
as Secretary while Rusk was on his way back from the Nehru
funeral via Saigon and Honolulu. Ball had previously been
scheduled to visit General de Gaulle in Paris and later to

attend the closing sessions of the UNCTAD conference in Geneva. After meetings with the Cyprus task force and the British ambassador, Ball left for Paris on schedule in the evening of June 4. Before leaving, Ball advised the President that only a personal appeal to Turkish Prime Minister Inonu could forestall an invasion.

Rusk's first task on his return to the department was to draft the letter for President Johnson's signature. Rusk's draft, described as the "bluntest document ever sent to an ally," was signed swiftly by President Johnson on June 5, 1964. The letter said: "I wish to emphasize in fullest friendship and frankness that I do not consider such course of action [a Cyprus invasion] by Turkey, fraught with such far-reaching consequences, as consistent with the commitment of your government to consult fully in advance with us."

Ambassador Hare has indicated that you have postponed decision for a few hours in order to obtain my views. I put it to you personally whether you really believe it is appropriate for your government, in effect, to present a unilateral decision of such consequences to an ally who has demonstrated such staunch support over the years as has the United States for Turkey. I must, therefore, urge you to accept the responsibility for complete consultation with the United States before any such action is taken.

Turkish military intervention, the letter continued, would lead to clashes with Greece. It would cause violent repercussions in the UN, and wreck any hope of UN assistance in settling the island crisis. It would "lead to the slaughter of tens of thousands of Turkish Cypriotes."

I hope [the President warned] you will understand that your NATO allies have not had a chance to consider whether they have an obligation to protect Turkey against the Soviet Union if Turkey takes a step which results in Soviet intervention, without the full consent and understanding of its NATO allies.

And unless I can have your assurance that you will not take such action without further and fullest consultation, I cannot accept your injunction to Ambassador Hare of secrecy, and I must immediately ask for emergency meetings of the NATO Council and the UN Security Council.

Johnson, Rusk and Ball were fully aware that only a tough U.S. stand could forestall a Turkish thrust at Cyprus. But they also feared that the proud, sensitive Turks, increasingly enraged about the developments on Cyprus, might react violently to excessive U.S. pressure. They tried to soften their harsh words, therefore, with appeals to Turkey's pride, citing the esteem in which Turkey was held in Washington.

We have considered you as a great ally with fundamental common interests. Your security and prosperity have been the deep concern of the American people, and we have expressed that concern in the most practical terms. We and you fought together to resist the ambitions of the Communist world revolution. This solidarity has meant a great deal to us, and I would hope it means a great deal to your government and your people.

We have no intention of lending any support to any solution of Cyprus which endangers the Turkish Cypriote community. We have not been able to find a final solution because this is, admittedly, one of the most complex problems on earth. But I wish to assure you that we have been deeply concerned about the interests of Turkey and the Turkish Cypriotes and will remain so.

You have your responsibilities as chief of the government of Turkey; I also have mine as President of the United States.

You may consider that what I have said is much too severe and that we are disregardful of Turkish interests in the Cyprus situation. I should like to assure you this is not the case. We have exerted ourselves privately and publicly to assure the safety of the Turkish Cypriotes and insist that a final solution of the Cyprus problem should rest on the consent of the parties most directly concerned. It is possible you feel in Ankara the United States has not been sufficiently active in your behalf. But surely you know that our policy has caused the liveliest resentment in Athens, and has led to a basic alienation between the United States and Makarios.

Johnson ended his letter by asking Prime Minister Inonu to come to Washington for a "full discussion" of the Cyprus crisis, and to hold off any thrust at the island until after the Washington meeting. Mr. Inonu later accepted the invitation.

While the presidential missive was being digested in Ankara, an Airforce KC-135 was ordered to Geneva to take

Ball to London and home after the United Nations conference on trade and development had concluded its final session.

As he was preparing his final report on the conference, Ball was called to the telephone. It was Secretary Rusk. "The President is worried about Cyprus and wants more action there," he told Ball. "I can't discuss it now because I am going out to dinner but I will call back after midnight." It was then past midnight in Geneva.

Ball went out for a snack and returned to his Geneva hotel, hoping for a nap. That hope went glimmering as the American embassy in Geneva began relaying a series of Washington messages. About 4:30 in the morning, the sleepless Ball was called to the embassy for a trans-Atlantic teleprinter conference with Rusk. The conference room was hot and stuffy and Ball dozed repeatedly during the ninety-minute exchange, which concluded with orders for the Undersecretary to shelve his London-Washington flight plan and proceed at once to Athens and Ankara.

Ball returned to his hotel at dawn and stretched out on a sofa under a large map of Europe. At 6:30, the KC-135 pilot was summoned to Ball's room and told of the flight-plan changes. Ball asked if the pilot needed additional crewmen or supplies, and was told "no." But as the pilot was leaving the room, he scratched his head and asked aloud: "Where the hell is Athens?" Somewhat nervously, Ball pointed out the Greek capital on the map over the sofa.

Arriving in Athens at 3:45 P.M. on June 10, Ball outlined the Cyprus situation to the Greeks in the starkest terms. Continuing trouble on the island, he told Premier Papandreou, was a major threat to world peace, and "it is imperative the matter be settled definitively." Ball reminded Papandreou he had talked with the British and General de Gaulle about Cyprus, had polled NATO's members on the crisis and "found everywhere a common anxiety to see the problem resolved rapidly." He summarized President Johnson's letter to the Turkish government—the contents of which were unknown then to the Greeks—and added:

"Disaster was avoided only by President Johnson's force-

ful intervention and his adamant insistence that there could be
no war between NATO allies."

Ball told Papandreou the United States had no formula
for a Cyprus settlement, was committed to no side in the crisis
and only insisted that some solution be worked out quickly.
This American insistence on "heavily involved neutrality"
perplexed the Greeks, and the Turks as well. They obviously
reasoned that if the United States was so interested in settling
the Cyprus crisis it should offer at least some outline for a
settlement. But Ball shied away from such a move, on grounds
that any American settlement would be rejected immediately
by one or another party in the crisis as "made in the United
States."

Continuing with Papandreou, Ball said the island crisis
was so tangled, so involved, that it required concessions from
both Greece and Turkey. And President Johnson felt, Ball declared, that only the Greek and Turkish prime ministers could
work out a satisfactory formula for a settlement. "If you, Mr.
Prime Minister, and the Turkish government, take no immediate and effective action," Ball said somberly, "the Cyprus crisis
can expand into war, or open the way to Communism in the
eastern Mediterranean."

Papandreou seemed unmoved. He told Ball the time was
not propitious for a Cyprus settlement, an appraisal the Undersecretary summarily rejected. Papandreou said Greece
wanted a Cyprus solution based on *enosis,* i.e., union with
Greece—an outcome Turkey was rejecting flatly. Ball replied
Turkey had to be considered in any settlement. Papandreou
then complained that the "turbulence" over Cyprus stemmed
only from Turkey's invasion threats.

Ball ripped into that argument. "I told him I knew that
one; then I said I believed he was too well grounded in philosophy to overlook the complexity of any inter-theory of causa-
tion," he reported later at the State Department.

"I told him nobody could determine how the threat of intervention contributed to the turbulence over Cyprus, nor how
the turbulence gave reality to the intervention threat. I said he
should acknowledge that the explanation he offered was over-
simplification."

Papandreou was evasive when Ball pressed for face-to-face talks with the Turks. He asked Ball again what kind of Cyprus settlement the United States favored, and the Undersecretary fell back again on his contention that the United States had no specific plan in mind. The meeting ended on a "friendly note," but the Greeks seemed unpersuaded of the menace of the Cyprus crisis, apparently reasoning that the United States would block any Turkish invasion attempt and playing for time in the hope that *enosis* would be theirs by default.

Ball left Athens the same day and arrived in Ankara at 1:45 A.M. on June 11. He was disappointed at his inability to move the Greeks but heartened by at least one development. He reported to President Johnson and the State Department that the Greek attitude on Archbishop Makarios had changed markedly, that the churchman's "flirtations with Moscow and Khrushchev" had finally alarmed Athens. Papandreou, Ball went on, had told him that Makarios had not been helpful in the Cyprus crisis, and had implied that the archbishop should be excluded from any role in settling it. Further, Ball said, Papandreou finally had acknowledged that Cyprus was an issue involving other nations besides Greece and Turkey, one "in which the major world powers must take a hand."

Before leaving Athens for Ankara, Ball invited Papandreou to visit President Johnson in Washington. He accepted. Both the Greek and Turkish prime ministers now were scheduled for White House talks.

In Ankara, Ball found the Turks seething over the Johnson letter. "We understand why it may have been necessary to administer a bitter pill," a high Turkish official told Ambassador Hare even before Ball's arrival, "but we cannot understand why it had to have a bitter coating as well."

The Undersecretary opened his talk with Inonu asserting again that the United States felt only close and warm friendship for Turkey. To show his confidence in the Turks, Ball then revealed to Inonu the substance of his meeting with Papandreou, and the latter's continued insistence on *enosis* as a Cyprus solution.

Inonu, still smarting from the lashes of Johnson's letter,

seemed somewhat mollified by Ball's presentation. The American attempt to promote a Cyprus settlement based on strong principles was a hopeful development in the crisis, he acknowledged. Of course, he added dryly, principles are liable to be abandoned when the time comes to translate them into concrete measures. However, Inonu was gratified by the Greek government's change in attitude toward Makarios, describing it as one of "the first rays of light in the dark situation."

As the meeting ended, Inonu took Ball aside and told him he thought President Johnson's letter included "all the juridical thunderbolts that could be assembled."

"And, of course, as a result, you have committed some errors and said some unjust things," he went on, adding: "Our foreign office will answer the thunderbolts."

Returning to Washington on June 11, Ball immediately plunged into a frantic round of diplomatic activity. The visits of Turkish Premier Inonu and Greek Premier Papandreou, scheduled for the 22nd and 24th, respectively, had to be prepared, the President briefed and communiques drafted.

The visits produced nothing new. A joint Johnson-Inonu communique on June 23 stated that the discussions proceeded from "the present binding effects of existing treaties," i.e., the Zurich-London agreements. This was a distinct concession to Turkey, which had been given a share in the control of the island as one of the guarantor powers under the treaties.

The Greek premier who came two days later promptly challenged the Johnson-Inonu assertion. In an open press conference he stated that the 1959 agreements had lost their validity and that Greece supported independence for Cyprus and its right to self-determination. He flatly rejected direct negotiations with Turkey because "no one is more competent to do that than the United Nations mediator."

While the two prime ministers were in New York attending the UN, Ball tried to obtain UN blessing for an American mediation effort.

At a June 26th New York meeting with Secretary General U Thant, he suggested that Greek and Turkish representatives meet with Dean Acheson, former Secretary of State, to try to work out a Cyprus solution. Acheson was warmly remembered in both countries for his work on the 1947 American aid program after the British had pulled out of Greece.

Ball suggested Camp David, President Johnson's Maryland retreat, as a site for the meeting. The Undersecretary made it plain to U Thant he did not want any Cypriotes there.

Because of its American overtones, U Thant was not at all enthused by Ball's proposal. He suggested Geneva instead of Camp David as a meeting site. Ball reluctantly agreed. U Thant then proposed that previously appointed UN mediator Sakari Tuomioja, a Finnish diplomat, rather than Acheson, ask Greek and Turkish representatives to meet with him at Geneva. If Acheson wished, U Thant conceded, he could take up quarters nearby, and Tuomioja could consult him if necessary. U Thant was obviously anticipating Russian charges in the Security Council that the United States was bossing Tuomioja and a possible Makarios demand for a Cypriote presence at the Geneva talks.

Ball balked, however, at the Thant-proposed role for Acheson, asserting the United States could be of little help if Acheson were kept at arm's length from the Greek-Turkish discussions.

In a summary to President Johnson and Secretary Rusk, Ball said the Secretary General would refuse UN sponsorship for a Geneva mediation meeting featuring Acheson. But even if Acheson were to remain in the wings, Ball continued, it was important to proceed with a Greek-Turkish meeting.

U Thant relayed the proposal to Papandreou. The Greek prime minister agreed to send a delegate to Geneva, but would not hear of having an American representative at the meeting. U Thant said Acheson could go to Geneva and set himself up "even in the next room or in the next building" so he would be available, if necessary. Papandreou grudgingly agreed to consider such a limited role for Acheson.

Meanwhile, Ball had discussed the Acheson role with Turkish Prime Minister Inonu, who was also at the UN. Inonu agreed to have the ex-Secretary meet with the Turkish and Greek delegates in Geneva. But he warned he could not guarantee what might happen if the Geneva talks failed. He obviously had little hope the Greeks would negotiate a Cyprus settlement.

Ball then called again on President Johnson to renew the pressure for negotiations through personal appeals to the Greeks and Turks. But this time the presidential intervention misfired.

Papandreou was enraged by a Johnson letter delivered to him in Athens July 2 by an American embassy official. "More of the same," the Greek leader snorted indignantly as he began a bitter tirade against the United States.

The Johnson letter was an "ultimatum," Papandreou sputtered, and Greece was no more prepared to accept such a fiat than it had been willing to accept commands from the Nazis in 1940. The United States professed to lead the free world, he went on, but where was its plan for a Cyprus settlement? The United States professed devotion to the principle of self-determination, he continued angrily, but why would it not support that principle on Cyprus?

Warming up to his subject, Papandreou said the United States seemed to imply it would "stand aside" if Greece and Turkey went to war over Cyprus. Only recently, he suggested, Defense Secretary Robert McNamara had indicated to him that Greece would lose such a war to the more heavily armed Turks.

Why did the United States not forbid Turkey as well as Greece to use their American-supplied weapons except in self-defense, Papandreou stormed. Why did NATO not forbid the Turks to take any military action that might trigger a war?

The Greek prime minister ignored the American embassy officer's protests that President Johnson's letter was not an "ultimatum," but was meant to be a message of conciliation. He ended the session by repeating a grudging agreement to send a delegate to Geneva, where Acheson was heading.

By this time, tension on Cyprus had reached the boiling point. Greek Cypriotes, fearful the American and other diplomatic moves and the Geneva meeting might produce a settlement distasteful to them, were becoming more violent. The

Greek Cypriote armed forces were estimated at 45,000 men, including some 5,000 Greek army soldiers believed to have sneaked onto the island. The Turkish Cypriotes had 10,000 men, including some 500 regular Turkish army soldiers. Infiltration of men and material for both sides was proceeding without effective hindrance.

Greece had alerted its armed forces, and moved some troops toward the Turkish border as a "defensive measure." Makarios barred UN troops from the Cypriote port of Limassol, believed to be the disembarkation point for soldiers and arms from Greece.

The Danes and Swedes were threatening to recall their UN peace force contingents on Cyprus unless the Greeks and Turks halted the arms race. Makarios further enraged Ankara by calling on the Cypriotes to "march toward *enosis*."

Against this ominous background came Geneva reports of an "Acheson plan" for Cyprus. The plan called for the island's union with Greece, cession of the Greek Dodecanese island of Kastellorizon to Turkey, re-settlement of Turkish Cypriotes wishing to emigrate, compensation for such emigrants, two enclaves on Cyprus for Turkish Cypriotes who wished to remain and establishment of a Turkish military base. The latter provision further enraged Makarios.

But the "Acheson plan" was getting nowhere, its author reported gloomily in early August.* The Geneva talks might collapse, he predicted, unless the Greeks began considering some imperative compromises. And if Greece did not do this, Acheson continued, it might find itself at war with Turkey, a war it probably would lose, thus weakening its defenses against its northern Communist neighbors.

While much of the Cyprus activity was conducted in the glare of publicity—Ball's flights and appointments were known, and some details of his various meetings were published—it also featured two clandestine forays into one of the most ticklish personal relationships in the Cyprus crisis: the antagonism between Makarios and General Grivas. Hostility

* See Appendix, p. 221.

between the two men dated back to pre-independence days and their disputes on strategy in the guerrilla campaign against the British. The prelate and the soldier made no effort to hide their dislike for one another. The possibility of a Grivas coup against Makarios was a constant element in all Cyprus equations.

With Ball's knowledge, an underground contact was established with Socrates Iliades, chief lieutenant to Grivas who was director of the defense of Cyprus.

In secret meetings held in July and August, Grivas, who had just returned to Cyprus after a self-imposed exile in Greece, outlined his plan to unite the island with Greece. The plan provided protection for Turkish Cypriotes remaining on the island, and compensation for those wishing to leave. The British base on Cyprus would be turned over to Turkey and staffed by Turkish personnel under a Turkish commander.

But the most important, though unexpressed, feature of the Grivas plan was the ouster of Makarios, who had repeatedly said "no" to any NATO base on Cyprus. The United States secretly relished this feature of the Grivas plan.

However, before anything could be done about the Grivas program, the Cyprus war broke out in earnest. On August 5, Makarios' Greek Cypriotes began a series of land and sea assaults on two Turkish Cypriote village strongpoints.

Retaliating two days later, four American-supplied Turkish Air Force jets strafed the Greek Cypriote-held town of Polis. The next day, thirty Turkish jets thundered down on Greek Cypriote towns on the island's north coast in what the Turkish government described as a "limited police action" to deter further Greek Cypriote assaults on Cypriote Turks. The following day, August 9, Turkey sent an armada of sixty-four jets on another strafing and bombing foray against northwest Cyprus. The conflict was escalating to what the diplomats called "alarming proportions."

From Athens, the Greek government notified Washington that it "would be forced to intervene" unless the United States "did something" to halt the hostilities. A squadron of Greek planes roared over Cyprus, fortunately at a time when no

Turkish jets were about. Makarios formally appealed for military help to the Soviet Union, the United Arab Republic and, strangely, Syria.

As the military crisis worsened, U.S. diplomatic machinery shifted into high gear. A Cyprus command post headed by Secretary Rusk was established in Ball's seventh-floor office on Saturday, August 8, and manned twenty-four hours a day. The Undersecretary himself spent the following three nights sleeping in his office. His key assistants were nearby. Each morning they woke him at seven o'clock. As he shaved in the adjoining bathroom, he was briefed on the preceding night's cables and events.

The briefings over, Ball and his staff moved into the conference room for breakfast and further Cyprus discussions.

"I insisted they have at least one full meal a day," one of Ball's aides later recalled. Everyone had lots of eggs, sausages and bacon-fried potatoes. There were hominy grits for the [Georgia-born] Secretary of State."

Late that Saturday night, Ball and his assistants were wrestling over the text of separate messages which they intended President Johnson to send to Inonu, Papandreou and Makarios. Around 10 P.M., Secretary Rusk walked in and suggested he might take a hand at drafting the presidential letters. Returning less than an hour later, Rusk brought a long yellow pad on which he had written the letter in longhand. "See what you fellows think of this," Rusk said and disappeared into his own office.

One of the Undersecretary's aides later described the draft as "the most effective bit of writing I have ever seen." After more consultation with Rusk, it was decided to send identical letters to all three capitals. The letters urged the "greatest possible restraint," adding that "no statesman would wish to bear the responsibility" for death and bloodshed, which were bound to accompany military operations.

In a companion message to the Greek premier, Secretary Rusk urged Papandreou to cooperate with General Grivas in handcuffing Makarios, who was threatening a "general massacre" on the island unless Turkish air raids were halted.

Cabling American Ambassador Henry Labouisse in Athens on August 9, Rusk insisted that Papandreou must be persuaded to prevent further attacks by Makarios against the island's Turks. The Greek prime minister must abandon "horse-trading or equivocation or passionate oratory" and act incisively to restore peace on Cyprus, Rusk declared. He told Labouisse the United States was urging the Turks to call off their air attacks and had warned Makarios he would be publicly branded as a murderer if his units went after the Cypriote Turks.

Rusk also advised Labouisse that the Makarios government had told the United States and Britain it was seeking military intervention from the Soviet Union. Rusk declared it was "utterly essential" to exclude Russian, U.A.R. or other foreign troops from Cyprus.

On the same day, August 9, the UN Security Council hastily and unanimously adopted a resolution (the Soviet Union and Czechoslovakia abstaining) calling on the Turks to stop their attacks, on the Cypriotes to halt firing, and on "all countries" to avoid any action that might expand the crisis. On the same day, Soviet Premier Khrushchev, abandoning his previous truculence, told Makarios he sympathized with him but believed a cease-fire would be an "important contribution" to peace. Khrushchev's Cyprus retreat recalled his Cuban missile crisis turn-around in 1962.

With Soviet support unavailable, Makarios accepted the UN's cease-fire call. Turkey promptly followed suit. Hostilities tapered off into an uneasy truce.

There was considerable hope the defusing of the crisis would prompt a political settlement at Geneva. But the talks there were getting nowhere, largely because of Greek obduracy. In an August 18 message to Ball, Acheson estimated the chances of obtaining a quick Greek-Turkish settlement on Cyprus were "about the same as the odds on Goldwater."

In seeming despair over his failure to work out a Greek-Turkish agreement, Acheson suggested the administration "liquidate" its Geneva effort and recall him to Washington. But he urged continued contact with Greece and Turkey to pre-

vent the transformation of Cyprus "into a Russian Mediterranean satellite."

Ball replied with a firm but friendly "no" to Acheson's
proposal for "liquidating" Geneva. Such a move, he said,
would embolden and delight Makarios, who might interpret
American withdrawal as evidence of United States indifference
and be prompted to plunge the island into another crisis.

Ball also told Acheson he was worried that the Turks
might resort to "recklessness" if the Geneva talks were ended.

Acheson's efforts at Geneva, Ball went on, already had
produced significant results. They had overcome Papandreou's
original refusal to negotiate with Turkey or accept a Turkish
base on Cyprus; they had won General Grivas' agreement to
consider such a base; they had eased some of Turkey's initial
demands.

Pressures, therefore, must be maintained both on the
Greeks and the Turks, Ball told Acheson. "*Aux armes, citoyens,*"
was Ball's appeal to the ex-Secretary.

And if the Geneva enterprise must die, Ball concluded, its
burial should not be conducted "by an orthodox archbishop,
but by the son of an Episcopal bishop"—which Acheson happens to be.

Acheson was not convinced by Ball's reply. In a return
message he said the United States should stop "irritating" the
Turks and Greeks by trying to pressure them into a Cyprus
agreement. If the United States walked away, the Greeks and
Turks would realize they alone were responsible for settling it.
And if an American retreat from Cyprus brought on a
showdown with Makarios, Acheson continued, "then let it
come."

The showdown, of course, did not develop. Deprived
of Soviet aid, pressured by the U.S. and the UN, Makarios
—with Grivas standing just off-stage—was not anxious
for a confrontation. In 1965, in fact, he embarked on an
unsuccessful "peace offensive" of his own to coax the
Turkish Cypriotes out of their island strongpoints. The Greek-
Turkish Cypriote fighting sputtered to an uneasy halt, super-
vised by the UN force which is still there.

A final solution of the Cyprus problem is still a long way off. A minor crisis reoccurs every three months, when additional funds are requested for the UN peacekeeping force. The Turks still snarl at joint Greek-Makarios statements demanding *enosis*. But a good deal of bitterness and fire has been drained from the issue. At least the Greeks and the Turks have agreed to talk and only the attitude of Archbishop Makarios remains the principal obstacle to a settlement.

Thus, on most counts, the 1964 U.S. venture into crisis diplomacy can be judged a success. It prevented the establishment of a Soviet satellite in the eastern Mediterranean. It staved off a Turkish invasion of Cyprus and, perhaps, a full-scale war between Greece and Turkey, two NATO allies. The U.S. managed to preserve its firm, if somewhat cooler, relations with both Greece and Turkey, in spite of the harsh words and pressures exerted in trying to prevent conflict. It also succeeded in avoiding increased tension with the Soviet Union.

And, more importantly, the entire enterprise was accomplished without commitment of American soldiers or equipment or the expenditure of American funds, except a pro rata share of UN peacekeeping costs. In this respect alone, the Cyprus incident is unique in the history of U.S. crisis diplomacy.

T·H·R·E·E

"Komer's war"

The Cyprus crisis was played almost entirely by ear. It was orchestrated in Washington by developments and events rather than plans, and conducted variously by an orthodox archbishop, an aging Turk and a temperamental Greek. The soloist was George Ball, who made up the score as the drama unfolded.

The crisis was keyed to one man's talents rather than to a policy. The uneasy armistice under which the island lives today was achieved with little foresight or planning. Though two years later Ball was to warn the United States against the dangers of pragmatism, he somehow managed to apply it in Cyprus without damage to American prestige or the risk of military commitments.

Some two years earlier, however, the United States had faced and handled another crisis in a different way. The Yemen episode, which began in the Kennedy administration and continued to plague Lyndon Johnson, was processed and filtered through the decision-making machinery of the United States government. And Yemen demonstrated graphically how even a meticulously studied and planned crisis policy may go awry in its long-term goals even though achieving some short-term objectives.

Nasser's entry into Yemen in the fall of 1962 was one

of the last crises handled through the National Security Council.

On September 19, 1962, Radio Sana'a announced that the Imam Ahmed had died and had been succeeded by Crown Prince Imam Mohamed al-Badr. Eight days later, Sana'a Radio asserted the new Imam had been slain in a palace coup. A "Free Yemen Republic" was proclaimed, headed by Colonel Abdullah al-Sallal, former commander of the Imam's personal bodyguard. Sallal's first official act was to execute ten of the late Imam's closest advisers and associates.

The United Arab Republic and most of the other Arab states (except royalist Saudi Arabia and Jordan) immediately recognized the new Yemen regime. So did the Soviet Union and Communist China. Britain withheld recognition, as did the U.S. Prince Hassan, the late Imam's brother and Yemen's delegate to the United Nations, flew hastily to Saudi Arabia and, with Saudi and Jordanian endorsement, called for the ouster of the rebels.

Fearing British or Saudi intervention to depose the Sallal regime which he had helped into power, Nasser immediately warned foreign countries to keep their hands off the "Free Yemen Republic." He began flying Russian-made planes with arms and military advisers to Yemen, plus scores of Yemen exiles and students whom he had been harboring in the U.A.R.

In mid-October, Nasser's "advisers" were replaced by regular Egyptian troops. Sallal, who had promoted himself to brigadier, obligingly declared he had asked Nasser for help to repel a "three-sided aggression" from British-ruled Aden, royalist Saudi Arabia and Jordan. On October 22, 1962, three Soviet-built bombers based in Yemen attacked a town in Aden.

To add to the confusion and sense of crisis, it developed that Imam al-Badr had not been killed after all. Heavily armed and snorting defiance at the rebels, the Imam met foreign correspondents in Yemen's northwest mountains, not far from the Saudi Arabian border, and promised he would lead his loyalist followers back into Sana'a in "a few weeks." Nasser promptly dispatched more troops to bolster the rebels.

By this time, concern was mounting rapidly in Washington. The National Security Council staff had been studying the crisis for months in an effort to fashion some sort of policy.

On October 17, 1962, Secretary of State Dean Rusk wrote President Kennedy that "we are hopeful we can recognize the Yemen Republic in a week or so."

Rusk's hope was based on recommendation by U.S. diplomats in the field. The U.S. chargé d'affaires in Taiz strongly urged immediate recognition in order to promote moderate policy on the part of the regime and to "prevent it from turning to the U.A.R. for support." However, U.A.R. troops and equipment were already being moved into Yemen. Britain was strongly opposed to recognition and begged the United States to delay it. In special messages to Washington, both Jordan and Saudi Arabia expressed fears that their integrity and independence would be gravely compromised by United States' approval of the revolutionary regime.

In reply, Secretary Rusk assured the two governments that, unlike Yemen, both had "powerful friends" gravely concerned and interested in their fate.

As usual, the administration was divided in its Middle Eastern loyalties. The State Department's Near Eastern Bureau, headed by Phillips Talbot, who genuinely but, as it turned out, mistakenly hoped that recognition by the United States would cause Nasser to limit his involvement in Yemen, favored immediate recognition. The Pentagon and others strongly urged against weakening the British position in Aden. The result was the usual compromise: a paper stating that "while there were overriding reasons against recognition" the State Department hoped to recognize the republic after obtaining Nasser's promise of a hands-off policy in Saudi Arabia. Recognition was to be coupled with U.S. reassurances to the kings of Jordan and Saudi Arabia.

In explaining his recommendation for recognition, Rusk insisted that under no circumstances should the United States try to weaken and defeat the United Arab Republic because the consequences could be disastrous. Having committed himself in Yemen, Rusk argued, Nasser could not afford a setback and might attack Saudi Arabia if he were pressed too hard. Moreover, withholding of U.S. recognition might cause the U.A.R. and the new Yemen republic to appeal for help to the Soviet Union and extend Moscow's foothold in the Middle East. Rusk's arguments were supported by intelligence reports predicting inevitable defeat for the Yemeni royalists. The royalists have continued their resistance to this day.

The Rusk rationale, following closely the reasoning of his Near Eastern Bureau, contained some obvious contradictions. Recognition of the Yemen republic could only provoke hostility from Saudi Arabia and Jordan for whose welfare the United States was professing solicitude. Moreover, recognition of a government spawned and completely controlled by Nasser would—and, indeed, did—give an added stimulus to his campaign to eliminate the Saudi and Jordanian monarchies standing in the way of his drive for leadership of the Arab world.

Rusk's opinions and his seemingly pro-Nasser memoranda in this period should be viewed against the background of the mood prevailing in Washington at the time. President Kennedy wanted to get American foreign policy "moving again" and nowhere was the need for new initiatives more obvious than in the Middle East.

Dulles' brusque rejection of Nasser's request for aid in building the Aswan Dam on July 19, 1956, coupled with the traditional U.S. commitment on the side of Israel, had brought U.S. policy in the Middle East to a complete standstill. Already, under the Eisenhower administration, policy planners were at pains to devise some means of getting out of the impasse, and the winter and spring of 1959 saw continuous intragovernmental discussions on the Middle East. It was at that time that a policy paper described Nasser as the "wave of the future" (see Chapter I) while Secretary of State Dulles, in the course of an eight-hour debate on the paper, branded him as "nothing but a tin-horn Hitler."

Kennedy's desire to be "moving again" in the Middle East

was never presented in a formal paper. All the policy makers had to go by was the President's obvious leaning toward more even-handedness in our dealings with Israel and Egypt. As evidence of a "new look" in the Middle East, John S. Badeau, a Middle Eastern expert, was appointed ambassador to Cairo with instructions to start an extensive dialogue with Nasser. Badeau's reports of the period made it plain that though Nasser was hostile to our interests he had a healthy respect for U.S. power and would shun direct confrontation if plainly and forcibly warned in advance.

Badeau's dialogues with Nasser produced the Egyptian dictator's categorical assurances that Yemen would not be used as a springboard for attacks on Saudi Arabia and that British possessions in Aden would not be molested. These assurances enabled Secretary Rusk on November 11, 1962, to urge the President once again to recognize the Yemen republic "in the next few days."

Rusk's recommendation reflected no illusion as to Nasser's trustworthiness. In the same message Rusk additionally recommended the dispatch of a combined destroyer and fighter task force into the area, as well as the publication of the President's letter of firm support to Prince Feisal, then acting as Viceroy in King Saud's absence.

After a great deal of soul-searching in the President's entourage, recognition was finally announced on December 19, 1962.

The announcement came with dramatic suddenness after the State Department had denied publicly and steadfastly that any such move was imminent. As explained later by Assistant Secretary of State (for Near Eastern Affairs) Phillips Talbot in a letter dated July 3, 1963, to Senator Bourke Hickenlooper of Iowa, recognition was based primarily on four conditions:

1. The rebel regime controlled the "apparatus of government" in Yemen.
2. The rebels had "apparent popular support" throughout the country.

3. They controlled "most of the country."

4. They were willing and capable of honoring Yemen's international obligations.

There is grave doubt that the first, third and fourth conditions obtained at the time of recognition. Without the continuing flow of Nasser's troops into Yemen, the rebel regime would have collapsed. Recognition, therefore, seemed more an endorsement of Nasser's involvement in Yemen than a certification of stability of the rebel government.

Talbot insisted, however, "that only by recognizing the regime could we play a useful role in preventing an escalation of the Yemen conflict, causing even more foreign interference and placing in serious jeopardy major U.S. economic and security interests in the Arabian peninsula."

Furthermore, Talbot went on, "the U.A.R. wants to withdraw its troops from Yemen. Its delay in doing so appears to result, therefore, not from any lack of desire." In spite of Nasser's alleged "desire" to withdraw, his troops remain in Yemen to this day.

American recognition of the rebel Yemen regime had several immediate effects, none of them beneficial to the United States. It delighted Nasser, and emboldened him in his campaign to seize the leadership of the Arab world. It infuriated the rulers of Saudi Arabia and Jordan, who saw in the American approval of an anti-royalist coup a threat to their own royal regimes. It miffed the British, on whose presence the United States depended to a great extent to preserve some kind of tenuous security in the strategically important Middle East. And it won little response from the pro-Nasser Arab states, paranoically persuaded that the United States, no matter what it does, is up to no good in the Middle East.

Flushed with victory, Nasser began a campaign of threats against Jordan and Saudi Arabia, warning their royal rulers that other Sallals would emerge in their own countries. Nasser's planes attacked a Saudi town on the Yemen border. In Sana'a, Sallal, echoing his master in Cairo, began proclaiming an imminent uprising in Saudi Arabia and offering "arms and men" to help depose the House of Saud. American hopes for "containment" of the Yemen conflict seemed doomed.

Simultaneously alarming reports began to reach Washington from Saudi Arabia and Jordan. Some Jordanian fliers defected and went over to the Yemeni rebels. The loyalty of the Saudi Arabian army, strained by the constant barrage of Nasser broadcasts, was also in doubt.

In an attempt to shore up the Feisal regime and, above all, to size up the situation there, the administration—in January, 1963—resorted to the traditional device of diplomacy— the undercover envoy. The secret emissary this time was an oil company executive, an intimate friend of Feisal, long familiar with the intricacies of the Saudi Arabian situation. The oilman's task was twofold: (1) to persuade Feisal to broaden the base of his regime and announce reforms modernizing the kingdom, and (2) to cause the cessation of Saudi military aid to the embattled Yemeni royalists. He failed in both missions and merely confirmed what Washington already knew from its embassy's reports—that Feisal's position was shaky.

Alarmed by the rapidly deteriorating situation, the administration swung into action. After long months of plodding study by the National Security Council, Kennedy demanded decisions. The result was the National Security Action Memorandum No. 227, dated February 27, 1963, which registered two presidential decisions: (1) to send a special presidential emissary (openly this time) to assure Prince Feisal of continued American support for his country, and (2) to dispatch—under certain conditions—a USAF squadron to protect Saudi Arabia from invading U.A.R. aircraft.

The price Feisal was to pay for the USAF umbrella was complete Saudi disengagement from the royalist cause on the ground that it would not be realistic to expect the United Arab Republic to withdraw its forces from Yemen without this gesture on the part of Saudi Arabia and Jordan.

The choice of the presidential emissary, charged with drumming up a compromise to keep the fighting from degenerating into direct Nasser assault against Feisal, was familiar— Ambassador Ellsworth Bunker, veteran of the West Irian settlement between Indonesia and the Netherlands. Bunker, who has since achieved the settlement in the Dominican Republic, is a lean, soft-spoken, tough-minded Vermonter, whose skills in the fine art of compromising the apparently irreconcilable provoked an admiring career aide to bestow the supreme foreign service accolade: "Now I have at last seen a true diplomat at work."

The original "rules of engagement" for the USAF air squadron, later code-named "Hard Surface," were tough. Hard Surface was to provide a deterrent to U.A.R. aggression. It was to intercept and identify all aircraft violating Saudi territory. If an intruding aircraft were to take evasive action and withdraw, it would be permitted to do so. But—upon interception and verification as unfriendly, U.A.R. aircraft would be treated as a "hostile intruder" and destroyed by the USAF. Though it seems almost unbelievable, under these rules of engagement the United States could have stumbled into a shooting war with Nasser for the sake of Yemen, a desolate, disease-ridden, primitive tribal enclave on the southwest tip of the steamy Arabian peninsula.

With this danger in mind, the White House itself took charge of the Yemen operation. Robert Komer, a former intelligence officer, a Middle Eastern expert and one of the ablest members of McGeorge Bundy's "little State Department," directed the political as well as the military aspects of the crisis. Komer's constant pleas to the Air Force, first to let him have and later to let him keep the "eight little planes" that were to deter Nasser from attacking Saudi Arabia, led President Kennedy to refer to the Yemen operation as "Komer's war."

Somewhere along the line President Kennedy appears to have had second thoughts about the rules of engagement in "Komer's war." Though hard facts are difficult to obtain, there is evidence that after Bunker had been sent on his mission, the rules were considerably watered down and called for shooting by U.S. aircraft in self-defense only. However, whether he knew about the change of instructions or not, in his talks with Feisal Bunker stuck to the original rules of engagement and was later privately criticized by some State Department associates for "exceeding his instructions."

From the outset, the Pentagon was opposed to sending actual military effectives into Yemen. There was no ground environment for Hard Surface and no radar. The squadron had no modern base from which to operate, the Dhahran base having been deactivated in April, 1962. When the military heard of the watered-down instructions which would, in their opinion, make U.S. planes sitting ducks for any sufficiently determined MIG pilot, they virtually rebelled. Air Force Chief of Staff General Curtis LeMay, protesting violently, agreed to dispatch the squadron only after he was satisfied that the new instructions had been written by the President himself and that it was absolutely essential in the national interest to save Feisal and the House of Saud from destruction by the U.A.R.

The U.S. national interest, as described to Ellsworth Bunker in State Department and White House briefings, rested on the need for containing Nasser's expansionism. It was argued in those briefings that:

A. The United Arab Republic was heavily committed in men, materiel and prestige in Yemen. Unable to afford a serious setback or disgrace after having made those commitments, Nasser would be forced to insure the survival of the Yemen regime, if necessary, by extending the war into Saudi Arabia.

B. The United Arab Republic and the new Yemen government might be willing to invite Soviet military assistance to help preserve the rebel government.

C. It would not be realistic to expect the United Arab Republic to withdraw its forces from Yemen before Saudi Arabia and Jordan had "disengaged" from the loyalist force and cause.

D. The United Arab Republic was under severe strain in Yemen, and in due time friction would develop between the U.A.R. and the Yemen rebels, and Nasser's influence would diminish.

And—Hard Surface notwithstanding—Secretary Rusk's parting words to Bunker as he left on his Yemen mission were: "Be sure to tell Feisal that we will not be dragged into his little war in the Yemen."

On March 6, 1963, special American presidential envoy Ellsworth Bunker arrived in Riyadh for talks with Prince Feisal.

Over small cups of Turkish coffee in the prince's air-conditioned office, Bunker proposed a cease-fire between Saudi Arabia and the United Arab Republic in their proxy war over Yemen. Simultaneously, Bunker suggested, the United Arab Republic would withdraw its troops while Saudi Arabia suspended aid to the Imam's loyalist forces. He told Feisal that Nasser had assured Kennedy he had no designs on Saudi Arabia.

Understandably, Feisal was skeptical. Kennedy should not put too much stock in Nasser's promises, he told Bunker. Feisal was interested in the proposal for a "simultaneous" halt in Saudi aid to the loyalists and a withdrawal of United Arab Republic troops from Yemen. But "what if they are not withdrawn?" he wanted to know. In that event, Bunker sternly replied, the prince would be freed from his no-aid commitment. And, added Bunker, the entire U.S. government, from the President down, would use its weight to get Nasser out of Yemen.

Bunker then proceeded to describe the President's views as follows:

> We have no policy to deal with Nasser as the chosen instrument of U.S. foreign policy. We don't think Nasser is the wave of the future.
>
> Americans appreciate Prince Feisal's friendship as an act of faith and haven't forgotten it. Our memory is long and does not change with administrations or individuals.
>
> The President, who is a very practical and pragmatic person with extraordinary grasp of detail, has taken a personal interest in this problem. He is aware of and intends to block Nasser's adventures toward weaker neighbors. The President recognizes Nasser has a predatory side to his nature and that prior to the crisis Nasser has shown little interest in Yemen, except when he could use it. When he could not, he worked against the previous government.

Feisal said he was pleased that the President recognized Nasser's predatory nature. "I," said Feisal, who at one time was Nasser's close friend, "knew that he had certain traits and distinctions which made him dangerous to neighbors. We propped him up and patched up his quarrels with Tunisia and Iraq. Yet Nasser has ungratefully turned against those who supported him."

Feisal then went on to say that in defense of its freedom, Saudi Arabia was prepared to fight to the last man. "What would happen as a result of our effort? We would die. Well, we are not afraid of death. At least we would die honorably, defending our people and our country."

Feisal had, he said, folded arms (he enacted the gesture) and refused to increase Yemeni aid as a result of U.S. demands. "Today I received the fifth telegram from the king asking me what I was doing and why was I not doing anything."

Bunker's reply was that the U.S. could not offer Saudi Arabia a protective shield while it was helping enemies of the U.A.R. with whom the U.S. had diplomatic relations. As for Feisal's willingness to die, Bunker commented, "While we appreciate the sentiment, we would hate to see it fulfilled."

On the following day, March 7, Bunker finally broke to Feisal the news of the President's offer to send a USAF squadron as long as Feisal stopped aiding the royalists.

Feisal reported that the "condition" attached to the U.S. offer was unacceptable. "In talks with the President in Washington, Mr. Kennedy did not give me the impression he was making help conditional. If U.S. government help and support is forthcoming only as a result of a condition imposed on me, then all I can say is we cannot have it that way," Feisal concluded indignantly.

At this point, at an approaching slamming of the door, everybody present, including the interpreter, started talking at once. Finally, the prince was told by Ambassador Parker T. Hart that the word "condition" in Arabic sounded much worse than in English. (Actually the interpreter had already tried to dilute the repulsive connotation of the word "shart" by using "basis" in its place. But for fear of diverging too much from the English, he made the sentence read, "We are fully prepared to carry out our commitment to protect Saudi Arabia against external threats, said commitment being based, conditioned if you will, on satisfactory progress in reform and development.")

Ambassador Hart then reiterated Kennedy's pledge as an act of personal faith in Feisal, whose liberal outlook promised progressive reforms for his country.

At this, Feisal rang the bell and ordered another round of Arabian coffee. The interpreter apologized for using the wrong word and hoped that the whole thing was merely "a storm in a coffee cup."

Bunker flew back to Washington and was ordered to confer with Secretary General U Thant in the hope that the United Nations could be persuaded to share the peacekeeping tasks in the Yemen.

Bunker told Thant of his talks with Feisal while UN Undersecretary Ralph Bunche described his visit to Sallal and Nasser. Bunche thought Sallal would be willing to promise nonintervention in Saudi Arabia, provided the latter would agree to terminate royalist infiltration into Yemen and banish the royal Yemen family to Europe. Nasser's terms were essentially the same except for his belief that expulsion of the royal family would be "a violation of Arab hospitality." Removing them from the border would be enough, Nasser thought.

Nasser said he needed no observers: the U.A.R. would know immediately if infiltration from Saudi Arabia had stopped. According to Sallal, the Yemen Arab Republic could dispense with U.A.R. help after Saudi aid to the royalists had ceased.

Throughout this and subsequent meetings at the UN, Bunker urged U Thant to send Bunche to Saudi Arabia as mediator, and the sooner the better. U Thant dragged his feet, partly because Feisal was chary of receiving Bunche who, during his visit to Yemen, had failed to look in on royalist-held territory, partly because he was doubtful about committing UN prestige to a likely failure. Instead, Thant was privately promoting a Nasser-Feisal-Sallal summit meeting in either Italy or Cyprus. This idea was opposed by the U.S. on the ground that it would undo Bunker's work and make Feisal harder to deal with.

Thus again, as in the Cyprus case, U.S. attempts to pass the buck to the UN had failed. Again, having once committed itself to a single-handed attempt at peacemaking, the U.S. had to continue alone, unable to persuade the UN or anyone else to share the burden and the risks.

Bunker was sent back to Saudi Arabia. Arriving in Riyadh on March 17, 1963, Bunker opened his talks with Feisal with a promise to send U.S. experts to study possibilities of a television network for Saudi Arabia. Feisal lost no time in seizing the offer. Then and there, his deputy foreign minister was ordered to discontinue negotiations with Italian television interests, and to make arrangements with the Americans.

But Bunker's diplomatic skill must have failed him momentarily when he mentioned to Feisal President Kennedy's belief that disengagement in Yemen would enable Feisal to attend to the unrest and rebellion which, according to U.S. intelligence sources, was rampant in the kingdom.

At this, Feisal blew up. He knew more about conditions in his own country, he said, than the President of the United States. "It pains me to say," he declared, "that every time we investigate rumors of revolutionary activity in this country, we trace them back to American sources.

"I also note," he continued, "that there is an attempt to intimidate us into agreeing to the proposals you have presented. This kind of attempt produces exactly the opposite reaction. We do not fear death, and once we feel our people do not want us we would be the last person to insist on staying in a seat of authority. I appeal to you to withdraw these notions from your mind."

With a wave of his hand, Feisal dismissed Bunker's assurances that the President had no desire to intimidate him.

"We have been subjected to attacks and attempts to crush us," he stormed. "All we receive from you is a stream of good wishes and noble sentiments. This is fine but it is not a deterrent. We suffered several attacks but we folded arms in deference to your advice. How far will you go in defending us?"

Bunker's response was to insist that once aid to the royalists was stopped, the U.S. would be in a position to apply pressure against Nasser and to defend Saudi Arabia with all its might. The U.S. government would stop, with force if need be, any aggression against Saudi Arabia by Nasser or anyone else.

This unconditional U.S. guarantee of Saudi Arabian security finally had its effect on Feisal. He agreed "in principle" to suspend aid to the royalists simultaneously with Nasser's withdrawal from Yemen. He also endorsed Bunker's plan for a trip to Cairo to win Nasser's approval of the plan.

Bunker arrived at Nasser's residence at Manchiet el-Bakri April 1, after waiting ten days in Beirut for an appointment.

Nasser was negative. Any statement that he was withdrawing his troops, he said, would only encourage the Imam's loyalists. Nasser agreed not to attack Saudi Arabia, but opposed simultaneous withdrawal of his troops with a cut-off of Saudi aid to the loyalists. The aid cut-off should come first, he said. He also objected to the assignment of neutral observers to Yemen. They could stay in Cairo and go to Yemen only as needed, he suggested. After much haggling, Nasser finally agreed to withdraw "one battalion" within fifteen days of the cessation of Saudi support for the Yemen loyalists.

Bunker then made a strong plea for the cessation of anti-Saudi propaganda. "All parties use propaganda," Nasser challenged. "But yours is more expertly done," Bunker retorted and Nasser laughingly accepted the compliment. Nasser made no commitment, merely observing that in 1958 King Saud "had paid two million dollars to have me assassinated."

After more exchanges of this kind, Bunker finally left with Nasser an eight-point proposal calling for suspension of Saudi aid to Yemeni royalists, cessation of U.A.R. attacks on Saudi territory, establishment of a 20-kilometer demilitarized zone on either side of the border, stationing of neutral observers on the border and the start of a phased U.A.R. withdrawal from Yemen within fifteen days of Saudi suspension of aid to the royalists.

Bunker returned to Saudi Arabia and reported to Feisal on his talks with Nasser. Feisal was skeptical. Bunker asked him if he still wanted the American air squadron "once disengagement was under way." Feisal said yes, "in principle."

Bunker went back to Cairo on April 9, thinking he had concluded an agreement.

Indeed, on April 30, 1963, Secretary General U Thant announced that the United Arab Republic and Saudi Arabia had agreed to "withdraw" from Yemen under UN observation auspices. Swedish General Carl van Horn and 200 Yugoslav soldiers and Canadian airmen were ordered to supervise the "disengagement."

The optimists were delighted by an emerging triumph of American crisis diplomacy. More hard-headed diplomats remained silent, stifling their "I told you so's" as the agreement began to crumble six weeks later, when Saudi Arabia claimed that eight Nasser planes had attacked a Saudi town.

Within a year of U Thant's proud announcement, the Saudi-U.A.R. agreement, as well as American forecasts of a prompt solution, had been torn to tatters.

General van Horn resigned amid rumors that U Thant was ignoring his reports. In January, 1964, the Secretary General dropped a hint on the possible content of those reports when he admitted there had been no actual "disengagement" between Saudi Arabia and the U.A.R. Two months later, he admitted that an additional 1,000–2,000 U.A.R. troops had moved into the rebel republic.

American hopes that U.S. recognition of the rebel Yemen republic might reduce Communist influence in the little Middle Eastern state went glimmering as Brigadier Sallal trooped off to Moscow and later to Peking. In Moscow, Sallal picked up a $73 million Soviet loan, and joined with then President Leonid Brezhnev in a testimonial of support for the "liberation" of British Aden. The number of Soviet military personnel in Yemen, described by Moscow as "technicians," jumped to 1,000. Yemen guerrillas, instructed by Soviet and Egyptian advisers, began attacking tribesmen in British-ruled Aden, prompting a Royal Air Force attack on Harib.

In essence, Saudi Arabia observed its part of "disengagement." Nasser flouted it contemptuously, both in its political and military aspects. Amid rumors of discontent, he flew to

Sana'a on April 24, 1964, ostensibly to inspect his forces and to proclaim under oath that Britain would be expelled from "all parts of the Arab world," including adjacent Aden. Four days later, following his discreet departure, a new constitution was proclaimed and a new and more popular pro-Nasser premier named.

On the military front, U Thant said on May 5, 1964, there had been a "small increase" in the United Arab Republic troop contingent, estimated by other observers to number 40,000 men at the time. Discouraged by his failure to effect the U.A.R.-Saudi "disengagement," U Thant announced on September 2, 1964, that the UN observation mission was being withdrawn. Impatiently, he called on Nasser and Feisal to end their "senseless dispute." Two months later, the U.A.R. and Saudi Arabia announced a cease-fire in Yemen, from which they had agreed some seventeen months earlier to "disengage." The subsequent formal armistice agreement was never observed. As of late fall, 1966, Nasser was estimated to have about 60,000 troops in Yemen which, he said, will remain there "as long as necessary."

If it was incomprehensible to the average American how his government could have risked war over remote Yemen, it must be equally puzzling why, in spite of the commitment, so little has been achieved.

To be sure, a wider war was prevented and American oil interests in Saudi Arabia were preserved. But they are just as precarious today as they were before the U.S. diplomatic offensive, supported by U.S. aircraft, began.

Though contrary to popular misconceptions, the moves taken by Washington policy makers were intended to be anti- rather than pro-Nasser, the reasons for recognizing Yemen were far off the mark. The suggestion that recognition might avert Yemen appeals to the Soviet Union was wrong. The Soviet Union is ensconced today in both Egypt and Yemen more firmly than it was in 1962. The predicted falling out between Yemen and Nasser has never materialized.

In June, 1966, Feisal, who had ascended the throne since

the Yemen crisis first broke out, came to Washington to plead again for more guarantees against a Nasser invasion. He left Washington with no firmer assurances than he had before. The assurances contained in President Kennedy's 1962 letter were reiterated but President Johnson stopped short of committing the USAF, which was more urgently needed in Vietnam.

The Yemen crisis proved that meticulous planning and careful staffing of a politico-military initiative do not guarantee its success. President Kennedy undertook to minimize his risks by narrowing his original commitment to use American aircraft against Nasser. But even this cautious application of military power carried a risk of direct confrontation which was potentially more dangerous than the intercession in Cyprus, where the outcome was more reassuring although there had been no planning at all.

The success of Dwight Eisenhower's full-scale landing at Lebanon in 1958 had encouraged a thesis that Washington could impose stability upon the Middle East with a mere show of its force. The failure to secure peace in Yemen raised the specter of future crises in a region where the United States has undertaken an essential role for which it has no enthusiasm and little experience.

F ⁕ O ⁕ U ⁕ R

Challenge on the doorstep

If Yemen was a test of American skill in coping with crisis conditions far removed from its borders, the Cuban missile confrontation of October, 1962, was a challenge on the doorstep, a test of nerve and determination under the dark uncertainty of a nuclear menace close to home.

Conventional guerrilla weapons made Cuba a Communist state but the nuclear umbrella of the Soviet Union served to maintain the island as a Communist satellite. President Kennedy was twice obliged, in the landing at the Bay of Pigs in 1961 and in the 1962 missile crisis, to defer his anxiety for a free Cuban government to the thin but awesome possibility that the Soviets would court holocaust to preserve their toehold in the Western Hemisphere.

In a thirteen-page critique of the 1962 confrontation written in February, 1963, the U.S. government's top planners, Walt Rostow and Paul Nitze, concluded that Kennedy and his advisers had erred in laying too much stress upon the danger of nuclear war. They argued that this exaggerated concern had prompted consideration of improvident actions (an air strike by American bombers to take out all the missile installations) and counseled hesitations where none were necessary. Since the United States could get its way without invoking nuclear weapons, the burden of choice rested entirely on the

54

Soviets. In the aftermath, it seemed clear to the planners that a Soviet nuclear initiative was a negligible prospect throughout the crisis because its consequences would have been suicidal to the Soviet Union.

Yet in the grim moments of decision as the adventure unfolded, Kennedy was inevitably prey to apprehensions that the Kremlin would fail to act rationally. As his picket ships waited for the Soviet freighters to draw near the blockade line and his advisers pondered Khrushchev's warning that he had ordered the captains to stay on their courses, the President had no clear expectation in his own mind as to how the Kremlin would respond to the sinking of a Russian ship.

As it was, some Soviet actions were responses to signals we did not intend to send. One example was the apparent interpretation by a Soviet ship captain of night photography with a flash cartridge as an attack on his ship, which fortunately was not taken too seriously in Moscow.

This uncertainty had been the controlling factor in Cuban policy since Fidel Castro linked his regime to the Communist system. Khrushchev banked heavily on it in planning the missile venture. He would not otherwise have risked a confrontation with American nuclear superiority in a place far removed from his sphere of influence. The Kremlin's bet was that if the missiles could be installed surreptitiously, the United States would accept a *fait accompli.*

The episode taught one key lesson, which Rostow and Nitze stressed in their post mortem. Advance and withdrawal are mutually consistent policies in the Kremlin. It is a mistake to assume, as some advisers did at the peak of the crisis, that one faction is in control when the Soviets advance and another when they withdraw. Kremlin politics did not impel the swift shift from advance to retreat; the reversal flowed from a recognition by the Russians that President Kennedy had the military power and the apparent determination to enforce his demand that the missiles be removed. They could see clearly, the Rostow-Nitze paper said, that Kennedy meant to do what he said he would do.

The Rostow-Nitze document also cited reasons for the

success of the action which may well serve as a prescription for handling similar crises in the future.

To begin with, the document explained, we had established definitely for ourselves and the world that Soviet action endangered our vital interests.

In Phase II we began an integrated and ascending program of political, economic, psychological and non-combatant military moves against a background of military preparations for combat.

The Russians could hardly mistake our readiness to move into Phase III, i.e., the application of non-nuclear combat force.

The timing of the Soviet withdrawal has also provided the planners with their most reliable clues to Moscow's behavior.

The withdrawal, the Rostow-Nitze paper stressed, did not come on the heels of the President's speech, with its mention of "full retaliatory response on the Soviet Union" and the immediate SAC alert that followed. It came only when non-shooting coercion had already been applied and when it became unmistakable that the U.S. was on the verge of using shooting force to enforce the guarantee and ready to destroy the Soviet missile systems in Cuba or invade the island.

Later information from Moscow indicated that the most impressive evidence from the Russian point of view was confirmation through their own intelligence channels that we had taken all measures consistent with serious military action.

But the affair nevertheless left the great puzzle of how the Soviets had been misled into believing they could carry off this bold venture with impunity. Kennedy especially was troubled by this "fantastic" misreading of the American character. "If they doubted our guts," he mused, "why didn't they take Berlin? Maybe I convinced Khrushchev on Berlin but not on Cuba."

The record of American policy toward the Castro regime certainly contained concrete evidences of the discrepancy between what the U.S. desired to do and what it dared to do in Cuba. The record was an accumulation of strong words unmatched by strong actions. President Eisenhower declared,

...unciated his support of the Castro regime,
...es would not permit "the establishment of
...ed by international Communism in the
...re." He hedged later, however, by adding
that ... ...ction must be drawn between Communism imposed from without and Communism chosen from within. He never specified the category in which he placed Cuba.

As a political candidate, John Kennedy spoke of his desire to find more ways to give support to the Cuban exiles and the anti-Castro underground. But the over-all tenor of his preelection utterances on Cuba was mild—he spoke of propaganda broadcasts, of defending the naval base at Guantanamo, and of resisting Communist penetrations into other Latin countries. Kennedy's campaign suggested that he might be content as President to contain Cuba.

Perhaps that is what Nikita Khrushchev had in mind in his enigmatic exchange with the poet Robert Frost in Moscow two months before the missile confrontation. He said Americans were "too generous to fight." Khrushchev clearly counted on Kennedy's absorption with the Congressional elections as a factor that would make him particularly unwilling to fight in Cuba. He had remarked wonderingly in 1960 upon the duration and intensity of the United States' presidential campaign. He obviously suspected that the 1962 campaign would induce a similar preoccupation.

Already in the early spring of 1962, the Soviets began to refer to the coming months as a period in which diplomatic dealings would be impossible because of the American elections. U.S. officials said this was ridiculous but the Russians persisted in talking of their anxiety to avoid difficulties for the President while the campaign was on. On October 16, as the missiles were being installed, Khrushchev summoned the U.S. ambassador in Moscow, Foy Kohler, and told him that he was angry at his own officials for announcing that they were constructing a new seaport in Cuba. The Western press had speculated that the Russians were building a haven for submarines but Khrushchev gave Kohler his most profound assurances that this was to be merely a fishing vil-

lage. He apologized profusely for the announcement an
that if he had been in Moscow, instead of on vacation, it wo
never have been made. "I am most anxious," he told Kohler,
"not to do anything that will embarrass the President during
the campaign." *

Ironically, Kennedy never considered the elections a factor
in his response to the discovery of the Soviet missiles.
He was aware that he would be charged by the Republicans
with timing the crisis to bolster his own party. But he was
so deeply aroused by the hazards of the confrontation and its
peace-or-war implications that even at close range he seemed
beyond concern for the elections as he pondered his strategy
for getting the missiles out of Cuba.

His private reaction was mildly derisive when Vice-President Johnson, rejoining the deliberations after a brief trip
away from the capital, began to discuss the alternative courses
of action in terms of their domestic political impact. The Executive Committee met nineteen times during the crisis and several participants recalled afterwards that, apart from this one
Johnson interjection, the subject of politics was never raised.

It is remarkable that Khrushchev could have so misjudged
the temper of President Kennedy and the United States. He
had travelled here in 1959, he read the American press closely
and he seemed to understand the chemistry of the nation. His
own contact with the personalities of the New Frontier had
been limited to the stiff meeting at Vienna with Kennedy and
to Pierre Salinger's visit to Moscow. But his son-in-law and con-
fidant, Alexei Adzhubei, had talked extensively with many of
the men around the President. One factor in the miscalculation
was undoubtedly the deep secrecy with which the Presidium
planned its Cuban adventure. The Foreign Ministry officials
who were the experts on the United States and had lived here

---

* On October 24, as the Kremlin weighed its response to Kennedy's
ultimatum, Khrushchev told William Knox, the president of Westinghouse
Electric Corporation who was visiting in Moscow, that he hoped Kennedy's strong action wasn't motivated by the coming election. He said
he had dealt many times with Eisenhower and was sure that if he were
President, the matter would have been handled in a more mature fashion.

as diplomats were apparently not consulted. The gambit was conceived and executed by tough old revolutionaries like Khrushchev and Anastas Mikoyan, who had seen Russia secure her greatest gains on the world stage in the post-war days when Joseph Stalin was bluffing and conniving.

In retrospect, the evidence suggests that Khrushchev took his big gamble almost completely in terms of his own pressing need to score a foreign policy success that would cancel out some of his misfires. Walt Rostow traced the extent of his dilemma in a speech delivered in Berlin three days after the missile sites were photographed but before Rostow himself had been apprised of their existence. He pointed out that Khrushchev had failed in agriculture, Russia was losing its hold on the world Communist movement, the underdeveloped countries were standing aloof from the Communists and the Soviet people's passionate desire for housing was being thwarted by the need to devote more resources to armaments. "Moscow must ask itself: where do we go from here? In the short run, the answer may well be Berlin," Rostow said. "It is possible that Mr. Khrushchev may miscalculate the will and the strength of the allies and attempt to precipitate another crisis in this city."

Rostow's precise analysis of the Soviet mood coincided with the thinking of the Central Intelligence Agency. But only one man came close to anticipating where this mood would lead the Russians to strike. All the signs of military activity in Cuba failed to stir Washington's apprehensions that a significant move against the United States was imminent. On the very day that U.S. reconnaissance aircraft were taking the first photographs of the medium-range missile sites, McGeorge Bundy, the President's national security adviser, declared publicly, "I know there is no present evidence and I think there is no present likelihood that the Cubans and the Cuban government and the Soviet government would, in combination, attempt to install a major offensive capability."

Next day, Edwin Martin, the Assistant Secretary of State for Latin American Affairs, was explaining to a Sigma Delta Chi audience in the National Press Club why the Russians would never undertake to put offensive missiles in Cuba. The Russians' main opportunities in South America lay in subversive channels, Martin argued. They would be unwise to risk the danger of military action which would wipe out Cuba as a base and make it more clearly identifiable as a satellite. As Martin finished his speech, he was notified that he was wanted at the White House. He learned in a few minutes how wrong he had been.

Almost everyone was wrong. Even Ambassador Llewellyn Thompson, who had acquired a sensitive understanding of Khrushchev and his policies during four years in Moscow. Even Ambassador Charles Bohlen, a pioneer Sovietologist with an extremely wary view of the Kremlin's capacity for mischief, did not believe that Khrushchev would make this brazen move. The experts all guessed wrong and in the aftermath they took some comfort in joking that they in fact were right and Khrushchev was wrong because the venture proved to be such a huge mistake.

If the Soviet experts erred in the degree of rationality which they ascribed to Moscow, the intelligence estimators were guilty of missing the logic of the Soviet ploy as it unfolded. They formally concluded on September 19, some nine days after the first missile-bearing ship arrived in Cuba, that while the military advantage of deploying missiles would be great, the risk would also be great and the United States would hold the advantage of a heavy balance of power if they were discovered. The estimators decided that while the deployment of missiles was a possibility, it would be such a rash gamble that the Soviets would be unlikely to risk it.

But John A. McCone, the director of the Central Intelligence Agency, had caught a train of logic which the estimators missed. In mid-August, before he left for a honeymoon in Cap Ferrat with his new bride, the former Mrs. Theiline Pigott, McCone told Kennedy that he suspected the Russians were engaged in emplacing missiles in Cuba. It was already clear that Russian crews were installing anti-aircraft missile systems (SAMs) around the island and McCone argued that this precaution could only be designed to ward off the air-surveillance flights which enabled the United States to learn what was going on within the island. The SAMs would be useless against a U.S. invasion because they could not destroy planes flying lower than 10,000 feet and could be quickly knocked out in an earnest aggression. What kind of installation except long-range missiles would inspire such precautions?

The President did not seem impressed by this logic. But the point weighed on McCone as he tried to enjoy the Riviera sunshine. The Russians had never given nuclear weapons to their satellites but Cuba was far enough away from the Soviet Union to make it the first satellite in which long-range missiles could be deployed without any danger that they might be turned on Moscow. McCone did not return home until September 23 and he urged his deputy, Lt. Gen. Marshall S. Carter, in several cables to press his thesis before the National Board of Intelligence Estimates. But his warnings were outweighed by the judgments of the men in Washington.

Senator Kenneth Keating, the New York Republican who was to be defeated in 1964 by Robert Kennedy, publicly announced on October 10 that six intermediate missile-launching sites were being constructed on the island. Keating had access to ground intelligence reports which were not being forwarded to the President. The disinclination of top intelligence officers (except McCone) to believe that the missiles would appear in Cuba deepened their skepticism of reports from the island, where native agents constantly tended to convey information that would sharpen the hostility between Washington and Havana. The CIA left no stone unturned to find evidence of offensive weapons. The agents in Cuba functioned with difficulty because of Castro's security measures, and three or four days were required to get their reports out. Nevertheless, the CIA received at least 1,500 reports of weapons at various stages of the military build-up. The offensive missiles were moved from the ports at night on cleared roads but by mid-September, agent and exile reports were asserting the presence of these missiles in terms which could not be discounted except by aerial photography.

None of these reports were sent to the President before

they were affirmed by photography on October 14. A President is not customarily briefed on material so raw and inconclusive and the CIA felt a particular obligation to be cautious in this instance because it was clear that discovery of the missiles would cause a major shift in tactics. The short-circuiting of these reports to Keating before they reached Kennedy was a phenomenon which reflected concern within the ranks of the military that the administration would not respond with sufficient force or alacrity to the peril of the build-up. The CIA was reacting, however, to the agents' reports. The San Cristobal area, where the first installation was later discovered, was marked suspicious on September 29 and certified for the highest priority for aerial photography on October 3. The persistent question about the missiles was: "Are you sure?" The CIA had to be absolutely certain, more certain than Keating, before it raised the alarm.

A combination of bad weather, bureaucratic wrangling and caution served at this point to impede the pace of the aerial surveillance. With the first signs of a possible build-up in July, the intelligence board ordered that Cuba be subjected to complete aerial photography surveys every two weeks. These overflights were inhibited during September by two mishaps. A U-2 operated under Nationalist Chinese auspices went down, apparently as a result of mechanical failure, in China in early September. A few days earlier, a U.S. surveillance aircraft had wandered for nine minutes over Siberia and drawn sharp protests from the Soviets. These circumstances, combined with the fact that the Russian crews had already installed anti-aircraft missile launchers on the western end of the island, had made the CIA wary. If a pilot were shot down, Castro might take the issue to the United Nations and provoke a debate which could block further surveillance.

So only four overflights took place between August 29 and October 14 and they did not reveal any installations which had not been seen before. There were no flights between October 7 and October 14, partly because of bad weather and partly because the CIA and the Air Force were disputing who should fly the planes. The CIA had developed the remarkable techniques and controlled the laboratories in which the long rolls of film are processed and examined. The system is so refined and the photographs usually so clear that CIA officials were unhappy later when several prints were published in London. They did not want the Russians to realize how proficient we had become at aerial photography. The controversy with the Air Force centered on the question of whether the pilot of a spy plane brought down in hostile territory is better off as an Air Force officer or as a civilian employed by the CIA. The dispute had raged for a long time but it was settled under the pressures of that week. On October 14, an Air Force officer flew the mission which produced proof that Russian skullduggery was afoot.

The spy plane caught the Russians as they were four days short of completing the emplacement of the first of the twenty-four medium-range missiles. The sixteen intermediate-range missiles, which required more elaborate launching sites, could not have been ready for a month. Earlier flights might have yielded an earlier warning but these bases developed quickly. At San Cristobal, for example, only tents and a motor pool were observed on October 14. Some twenty-four hours later, missile trucks were on the scene and the launcher, installed without concrete footings or severe scarring of the terrain, was ready to fire on October 18. When critics later charged the CIA with failing to secure the photographs at the earliest opportunity, the reply was that overflights a week earlier might well have discovered nothing and thus raised a false sense of security.

This was an intelligence crisis, one of the rare ones in history, and on balance the intelligence community had many reasons to take pride in its performance. The missiles were caught in time and the initial miscalculation of the Kremlin's intentions did not hinder the operational task of finding out what the Russians were up to. As the crisis unfolded, the Sovietologists and intelligence chiefs combined to give the President sound counsel on dealing with Khrushchev. They predicted that the Russian would not go for broke when his hand was called and, on this critical calculation, they were fortunately correct.

The Cuban missile crisis was secondarily significant as the reason for innovating the Executive Committee, a new type of top-level apparatus which Kennedy created on the day that he learned of the missiles. The Excom was really a compact version of the National Security Council. Its membership of sixteen or so excluded more than half of the assemblage entitled by law and custom to attend NSC meetings. This was its original virtue.

Tightly knit by the privilege of sitting as a council of war in a moment of national peril, and moved by the high drama to set aside the parochialisms which divide a bureaucracy, the sixteen men functioned with a secrecy and efficacy which delighted the President. Still smarting over the fact that it had taken the State Department six weeks to furnish him with a draft reply to the note which Khrushchev gave him at Vienna, Kennedy was particularly impressed by the swift dealings which the Excom inspired. He was pleased with the quality of judgment which most of his aides displayed in the deliberations and privately cited three—McNamara, Douglas Dillon and his brother Robert—as particularly impressive.

Kennedy could not have tackled the confrontation in league with his Cabinet. His respect for specialization made him reluctant to weigh foreign policy issues with men who were not devoting their full waking hours to foreign affairs. Some of the able and substantial Cabinet officers whose duties lay on the domestic side were frustrated by this discrimination. One of them, Secretary Abraham Ribicoff of Health, Education and Welfare, gave up his Cabinet post to run for the Senate in part because he felt he was being excluded from the most significant councils. When Kennedy was told of Ribicoff's complaint, he responded tersely: "Why would I want to listen to Abe Ribicoff on problems that have nothing to do with his department?"

Similarly, President Kennedy could not have confronted the missile threat in company with the National Security

Council because its size breeds formality and the young President did not characteristically derive inspiration from a formal atmosphere. During the Excom meetings, he maintained the guarded posture of the man who must make the ultimate decision. He did not show his hand or his preferences as the alternatives were discussed and only a few who knew him well could perceive the direction in which he was leaning. The Excom met eight times without him and the advantage of these sessions was that the committee members felt more freedom, particularly under prodding by Robert Kennedy, to speak their minds. The President wanted candid and personal exchanges. He wanted to study the men as they spoke and absorb the intangible factors which might help to refine his thinking. The intimacy of the Excom suited John Kennedy—he remembered vividly the failures in communications that contributed to his faulty plans for the Bay of Pigs.

The Excom operation met the needs of the Cuban missile crisis, which lasted only thirteen days, from Tuesday, October 16, when Kennedy was shown the photographs of the missile sites, until Sunday, October 28, when Khrushchev agreed to withdraw the weapons. Some like John McCone, who had served under Truman and Eisenhower and was more familiar with executive life than most of the New Frontier officials, maintained that Excom could not effectively have met the needs of a much longer crisis.

The "high-priced help," as McCone described Excom's collection of four Cabinet officers, and key men from State, Defense, CIA and the White House, was almost constantly absorbed by meetings during the confrontation. Their staff support was limited by the critical requirement for absolute secrecy. A few subcommittees were formed to provide back-up. But by and large, the full pressure fell on the men who sat at the long table with the President. For example, McNamara and his deputy, Roswell Gilpatric, had to struggle through the long deliberations and then return to the Pentagon to direct military preparations for eventualities ranging from the naval blockade to full-scale invasion. The key members of Excom were badly fatigued when the crisis concluded. Many of them could not have sustained the pace much longer. For this reason, the brilliant success of Kennedy's innovation failed to quash the criticisms that his national security operations could usefully have been buttressed with more elaborate staffing.

Dean Acheson and some others maintained after the crisis that Kennedy had been too anxious to make a deal with Khrushchev and that he would have been wise to keep tightening the screw to force a triumph of more decisive dimensions. The Kremlin suffered a very real setback in the intangible terms of prestige and world standing. The United States made real gains in the respect of allies whose security hinges on our readiness to stand up to the Soviets. But in the tangible terms of real estate and Communist control, the world changed very little between October 13 and November 13. In these terms, Khrushchev did not pay dearly for his errors and deceit.

Kennedy had the leverage to keep tightening the screw. His proclamation of an embargo against oil shipments to Cuba was already drafted when Khrushchev capitulated. An order to depth-charge Soviet submarines out of the water awaited his approval. McNamara's expansion of the nation's conventional forces enabled the President to contemplate an invasion of Cuba ten days after he announced the presence of the missiles. He had total dominance in the Caribbean and if he were willing to accept the casualties, estimated as high as 40,000 for a four-month operation, he could readily have used the missiles as an excuse to capture the island and expel the Communist government.

Khrushchev was correct in his apparent appraisal of Kennedy as a leader likely to shrink from a rash response to his duplicity. The President did not harken to the initial advice of a few, including McGeorge Bundy, that he make no response to the discovery of the Russian missile installations. Later he was surprised and displeased by Adlai Stevenson's proposal that the United States should negotiate its way out of the crisis by volunteering to give up Guantanamo Naval Base and the Jupiter MRBMs in Turkey. But as he contemplated the possible necessity of sinking the Soviet vessels approaching Cuba and studied his options of an air attack and an invasion of the island, the congenitally optimistic President recognized, with deep pessimism, that the consequences could be nuclear war.

As has been seen, the President seemed to some of his associates to have overstated the perils in his private and public statements. But the President did not have the comfortable vantage-point of this hindsight. Neither he nor any of his advisers could foresee how rationally the Soviet leaders would behave when faced with retreat. Llewellyn Thompson warned him, in opposing the option of a surprise air strike against the missile sites, that Khrushchev's reactions were apt to be particularly bad when he was faced with an ugly surprise. He should be given time, Thompson urged, to gather his poise and take a realistic view of the situation.

The danger that Khrushchev would react to our actions against the missiles with a move on Berlin was constantly before the President. Someone asked during an early Excom meeting, "Where will we be if Khrushchev knocks off Berlin?" Kennedy replied grimly, "In World War III."

It was at this time that United States policy makers were newly impressed with what a hostage Berlin was to their actions in the rest of the world. But the nuclear deterrent is particularly forceful in respect to this Achilles' heel. The Soviets know well that the American strategy for a defense of Berlin embraces a short-fused reliance on nuclear weapons. They would be the only meaningful answer to a sustained push by an overpowering force of Communist soldiers. "Knocking off" Berlin is not a step which rational Soviet leaders will take lightly. It is not a step they would have been likely to take in behalf of Cuba. But Kennedy and his counselors had to live through those thirteen days with a sense that Berlin was highly vulnerable to Soviet reprisals.

But Kennedy's reluctance to squeeze the last drop of advantage from his victory had a wider basis than his fear of the consequences to Berlin. In the first place, he was acutely sensitive to the attitudes and postures of his Russian counterpart. "If I were Khrushchev—" he would often begin, and then develop his thesis as to how the Soviet would react to a given set of circumstances. "Khrushchev would never stand for it!" he chided a White House secretary who brought him a typed paper containing errors. As an imaginative person, he undertook frequently, and particularly during the missile crisis, to place himself in the other fellow's shoes.

It was this consideration which prompted him to reject out-of-hand an informed suggestion in August that he give a public warning to Khrushchev to take all of his forces out of Cuba within sixty days. "There is one thing I have learned in this business," he said, "and that is not to issue ultimatums. You just can't put the other fellow in a position where he has no alternative except humiliation. This country cannot afford to be humiliated and neither can the Soviet Union. Like us, the Soviet Union has many countries which look to her for leadership and Khrushchev would be likely to do something desperate before he let himself be disgraced in their eyes."

This same concern caused Kennedy to defy the anger of spokesmen for the press and radio who pressed hard to have reporters and photographers assigned to the ships in the picket line around Cuba. "If I have to sink one of those Russian ships," the President explained, "I don't want pictures of drowning Russians on the front pages of every newspaper in the world. It will just make it harder to work things out."

As the affair ground to its climax and Khrushchev agreed to withdraw his offensive weapons, Kennedy's incentive to press for more was not sharpened by his decreased fear of nuclear war. Once he had the Russians on the run, the price of pressing on their heels would have been a diminution of his hopes for negotiating peace with Khrushchev. He could not mortify the man and hope to deal constructively with him later. The goals which he expressed in June, 1963, at American University—"a relaxation of tensions without relaxing our guard"—were in his mind from the day he entered the White House. "If we cannot end now our differences," he said, "at least we can help make the world safe for diversity." His experiences as President transformed the wistful aspiration to be a peacemaker into a hard-eyed and wary respect for the problems of doing business with the Russians.

But Kennedy was not a man to let go of his dreams lightly. The exhilaration of besting Khrushchev in a test of wills did not incline him to savor vengeance more than he savored his hopes of peace.

F ✩ I ✩ V ✩ E

Sonic booms over Hanoi

The irony of the epic struggle in Vietnam is the little-known fact that in 1954, when President Eisenhower was deciding whether to intervene with American military power to save the besieged French forces at Dienbienphu, the most vehement protest came from the Democratic Senate Majority Leader, Lyndon B. Johnson. One observer recalls that the Texan pounded on the President's desk to underline his refusal to support any move that might commit American troops to Asian jungles.

"Operation Vulture," the code name for the French proposal that the United States drop atom bombs on the Viet Minh surrounding the doomed garrison, was the last of a series of urgent requests from Paris for American help. Eisenhower's refusal to heed these pleas stemmed in large part from the Congressional opposition for which Johnson was the most emphatic spokesman. If President Eisenhower had intervened in 1954, President Johnson's role in 1964 might well have been an easier one.

Fate made Johnson a President with the gruelling task of holding the nation to its commitment in Southeast Asia despite his own intuitive instinct against involvement there. When President Kennedy urged him to go to Saigon in May, 1961, to reassure President Diem that the United States did not intend to pull out of Asia, he balked for almost two weeks. One day, as Kennedy was pressing hard, Johnson said, "Mr. President, I don't want to embarrass you by getting my head blown off in Saigon."

"That's all right, Lyndon," Kennedy replied. "If anything happens to you out there, Sam Rayburn and I will give you the biggest funeral in the history of Austin, Texas." Johnson finally agreed to go, on the condition that he could take Mrs. Stephen Smith, the President's youngest sister, and her husband along as a tender of Kennedy's concern for the region. He came back with the judgment that South Vietnam could be saved if swift moves were made against its hunger, ignorance, poverty and disease.

South Vietnam was the last of John Kennedy's legacies to Lyndon Johnson. Kennedy had found no answer to his dilemma there and in private he was as pessimistic as anyone in Washington on the prospects of establishing a viable government in Saigon. Shortly before he was assassinated, he had ordered a complete review of U.S. policy in Southeast Asia to confront the new set of conditions which developed with the overthrow of President Diem on November 1, 1963. No one can say with any certainty how Kennedy would have met the worsening problem if he had lived, but it is known that at least on one occasion he had warned McNamara against committing combat troops there.

The ouster of Diem and the escalation of America's combat role on February 7, 1965, were the two critical turning points in the long struggle. Each step marked a new phase of acknowledgment that the war against the Viet Cong had become the essential responsibility of the United States. Each step in its turn became the focus of the divisive domestic controversy which raged over the war. Each step was an awkward nettle for the President who grasped it, a reluctant recourse which strained and tested the process of decision-making within the government.

The pressures for escalation commenced almost as soon as Lyndon Johnson moved into the White House. The political disarray in Saigon under the insecure regime of Premier Nguyen Khanh and fear in Washington that the discouraged South Vietnamese might sue secretly for peace argued for an intensification of the military effort. Johnson sent McNamara and McCone on a joint survey mission in March, 1964, and found on their return that the CIA director held a much bleaker view of the situation than the Defense Secretary.

McCone recommended, in fact, that North Vietnam be bombed immediately and that the Nationalist Chinese Army be invited to enter the war. Johnson was perplexed by the disparity in the two men's views of the situation. "Am I to tell Congress that there is a division within the government?" he asked. "Work out your differences and come back here at 2:30." Arguing that the war must be won within South Vietnam itself, McNamara objected that in their opinions it would be impossible to bridge the gap. McCone, aware that his role as intelligence adviser did not entitle him to give policy advice to the President, said he would withdraw his recommendations. He added, however, that his report on the situation in Vietnam was an intelligence estimate and would have to stand unchanged.

Taunted by Khanh not to act like "a paper tiger," the United States approved in this period an expansion of the sabotage missions which South Vietnamese guerrillas had been carrying out in the north for the past three years. South Vietnamese pilots were being taken to the United States for training in large-scale bombing missions. Johnson himself, heavily preoccupied with the presidential election, talked ambiguously in a patent effort to hold loyalties on both sides of the Vietnam issue. Dean Rusk warned on May 22, 1964, that the war might be carried to North Vietnam if the Communists persisted in their aggression. On June 2, Johnson said he knew of "no plans" to carry the war north of the 17th parallel. But on June 28, in a speech in Minneapolis, the President declared that the United States was "prepared to risk war" to preserve the peace in Southeast Asia. In testimony before the Senate Foreign Relations Committee (released on July 9, 1964), McNamara revealed a "tit-for-tat" plan of military reprisals against North Vietnam for damage inflicted by guerrillas in the south. At this point, the American component in South Vietnam consisted of only 17,000 soldiers.

It was not publicly known at the time that, since March of 1964, the government had a plan for "measured pressure" against North Vietnam. The plan had been thrashed out by an inter-agency task force and was to become the blueprint for escalation. This was planning of a bold and thorough variety—the assumptions and anticipations which were an integral part of the thick loose-leaf volume prepared for the President have been proved by time to be valid. The planners recognized that little short of direct U.S. intervention would be likely to deter the Viet Cong more than momentarily and that the Viet Cong threat could not be dissipated even by subversion of the support coming from North Vietnam. They accepted the likelihood that Hanoi would respond to an American escalation by escalating its own role in the war, and warned that a major Communist escalation would be successfully met only by the introduction of "several U.S. divisions."

The objectives of the plan were modest in their balance. We should press for a complete end to the war in Vietnam, the planners said, but we should not, in the early stage, foreclose the possibility of settling for no more than a substantial easing of the Viet Cong pressure. They predicted that the destruction of North Vietnamese property and fear of rehabilitation might stir hostile sentiment in Saigon and that these attitudes would be fanned by France. The allies can be expected, they said, to charge that we are provoking war but they will swallow their charges if the U.S. initiative succeeds in bringing peace without a major war.

The planners advanced three main objectives for escalation: (1) to demonstrate to the world that the United States is prepared to use its power with restraint in defense of freedom, (2) to teach the Chinese Communists and the Soviets that the export of insurgency does not pay, and (3) to convince the people and government of South Vietnam that the United States is ready to help create conditions in which they can free their land from external interference.

The administration's plan contemplated a three-stage

escalation in which the pressures on North Vietnam would be steadily tightened. The initial scenario did not involve overt American participation in the actions which were to be low-impact aggressions tied to sabotage and psychological warfare. "Sanitized" aircraft without U.S. markings or U.S. crews were to dive at North Vietnamese targets, create sonic booms and streak off without dropping bombs. The United States would make contact with North Vietnam through its embassies or diplomatic missions and convey the connection between these covert intrusions and Hanoi's support for the insurgents in South Vietnam. The Communists were to be informed that the operations would cease if the support was cut off, but, in public, any hint of U.S. involvement was to be emphatically denied.

The planners specifically ruled out any effort to involve the Southeast Treaty Organization in the escalation on grounds that at least two SEATO members, France and Pakistan, would block any action by that alliance. The French would be useful only as "carrier pigeons" to and from Hanoi and only the British were to be fully informed of the new course of action. They would be urged to serve as a channel of communication with the Soviets. The plan held open the option of consulting with Australia and Canada.

The script for the second scenario was drawn to accelerate the aggressions with the American hand more plainly revealed. U.S. combat units would be used to secure Saigon and the U.S. Seventh Fleet would maneuver in the Gulf of Tonkin, just outside the territorial waters of North Vietnam. Sophisticated electronic equipment would be employed to disrupt North Vietnam's communications with the Viet Cong. But the planners recognized that even these steps would hurt the Viet Cong only momentarily. The plan was drafted with McNamara's emphasis that the only sure means of containing the Viet Cong would be an intense program of counter-insurgency in South Vietnam. The planners were not even certain that the Viet Cong threat could be disrupted by cutting off the support from North Vietnam.

The planners did not look much more hopefully upon an

international conference as a promising way to end the war. They agreed that this exit should be taken only if (1) the risk of the war to this country's national interests became disproportionately high, (2) the prospects seemed good for getting a formal Communist renunciation of the war in Vietnam, or (3) conditions in South Vietnam were stabilized to a degree that the conference would not heighten chances of a Communist takeover.

The planners' cardinal reliance, their ace in the hole, was scenario three—a direct U.S. attack on North Vietnam. Amphibious and airborne military units in battalion strength were slated for active roles in this script, which also contemplated a naval blockade and aerial bombardment. The objective of the scenario was not to destroy the military capability of the North Vietnamese—in fact, the planners specified that care must be taken not to inflict so much damage that North Vietnam would be deprived of material reasons to consider withdrawing support of the South Vietnamese insurgents. The scenario called for a limited aggression designed to raise fears in Hanoi of what might happen if support for the insurgents were continued.

This was the plan that was laid before Lyndon Johnson in March, 1964. It carried the endorsements of almost all the men upon whom Johnson leaned for foreign policy guidance. One exception was George Ball, whose talents as a lawyer and doubts about escalation led him to become a "devil's advocate" in policy deliberations, the man who asked questions like, "How can we be sure that Red China won't enter the war if we attack North Vietnam?"

But apart from Ball, the President was confronted by a government consensus which urged him to enlarge his commitment in Asia and let his combat men in South Vietnam put aside their flimsy cover as "advisers" to the native troops. Johnson characteristically ignored this consensus until the election was over and then entered a long, enigmatic phase in which no one knew exactly where he was headed in regard to South Vietnam. The questions that he asked gave no clue to his inclinations and doubts grew that he would buy the plan. These misgivings became particularly acute after he cancelled an air raid upon North Vietnam, laid on in reprisal for the bombing on Christmas Eve, 1964, of an American officers' billet in Saigon. Fears circulated within the government that Johnson lacked the courage to carry the war into a new phase.

In those days, Johnson apparently looked hard for an honorable way to slough off the war. The elections were behind him and his popularity was at a peak. The Great Society domestic programs were being cheerfully packaged for presentation to a Congress more heavily dominated by Democrats than any since 1936. The tax-cut legislation of 1964 had lofted the economy to new heights of performance, auguring still another year of healthy expansion. The President was privately planning an early trip to the Soviet Union, a first big step toward his ambition to make his name as a peacemaker. As 1965 began, the rosy view from the White House was marred only by the black cloud of South Vietnam, made to seem blacker than ever by the inability of the generals in Saigon to decide among themselves how the country should be governed. Most Asians, including many South Vietnamese, had believed that Johnson would find a way to cut loose from the mess after the election and the temptation at that point must have been strong.

But the same factors which made the war in South Vietnam such a disagreeable undertaking made it impossible for President Johnson to pull out. The disarray in the Saigon government, the lack of any sense of nationhood, the Viet Cong advances in the countryside and the ebb of confidence in American intentions had brought South Vietnam as close to Communist takeover as it had been since the partition by the Geneva conference in 1954. If Johnson withdrew, or even diminished his commitment, he would at that point have been leaving the country to the wolves and repudiating all the American avowals that these people had the right to choose their own form of government.

Johnson faced the options that were left to him in the withdrawn, agonizing and somewhat introspective manner which characterizes all of his major decision-making. This was an abrasive experience for his aides and associates within government. The President met his own doubts by trying constantly to shake their arguments with hostile questions and to catch their rationale off balance. He took immense pains to hide his own thoughts but he wrestled constantly with the problem and telephoned subordinates at all hours to seek answers to fresh misgivings. The intuitive radar which guides Lyndon Johnson demands more time, more questions and more worrying than the deliberating mechanism of the normal man. The process is protracted by his instinctive pursuit of consensus backing for his positions and by his anxiety to hear opinions from a range of individuals. Some argued later that Johnson lingered too long over this decision. They said that if he had acted when the plan was first laid before him, he could have inflicted more damage upon Communist morale with less escalation. But this was the Johnson style and few could argue seriously with it at a time when so much depended on the validity of his judgments.

The President delayed the launching of his attack on North Vietnam until February 7, 1965, after the guerrillas had supplied him with a provocation by attacking the U.S. base at Pleiku. As the Johnson escalation unfolded, the changes from the original plan showed the imprint of the President's character. Johnson distrusted covert operations and he dispensed with the unmarked planes and all the subtle intimidations which had been blueprinted in scenarios one and two.

A President in the nuclear age is inevitably more cautious than his advisers and Johnson stripped from the plan all ground incursions into North Vietnam, whether by South Vietnamese or American units. This was a form of deference to Red China, which warned on February 9 that it would "definitely not stand idly by" and was judged capable of intervening to resist an invasion of North Vietnam. Since similar warnings had preceded the Chinese response to the American crossing of the 38th parallel in Korea, Johnson was not disposed to take a light view of the possibility of intervention fifteen years later. The President's reluctance to court a confrontation was intensified by the fact that his military chiefs saw no alternative to reliance upon nuclear weapons if Chinese armies moved south. At Secretary Rusk's request, the Pentagon had already studied the strategy of taking out mainland air bases with atomic bombs if planes from those bases resisted the American bombers over North Vietnam. No one really thought the Chinese would intervene but no one could be certain.

President Johnson carefully followed the plan once he had embraced it. He was especially attentive to its recommendation that he give the Russians new reasons for not deteriorating their relations with the United States. The original plan called for engineering new discussions on trade and credits and Mr. Johnson faithfully launched his "bridge building" campaign aimed at stimulating trade with the Soviet bloc. This suited the Russian mood, although they were troubled by Peking's accusations of making secret deals with the United States.

The Communist Party Congress in Moscow in March–April, 1966, produced signs that Soviet influence with North Vietnam was on the rise and President Johnson yielded to the Kremlinologists who had urged him for some time to move to lower the tariff barriers on East-West trade. But the Communists noted the cautious fashion in which the proposal was submitted—it was transmitted to the Congress by the Secretary of State and not by the President, as is customary. This was a controversial bill, almost impossible to enact in the pre-election climate, and the President had been emphatically advised by Wilbur Mills, the chairman of the House Ways and Means Committee, not to push it. Johnson's compromise course reflected his need to balance domestic political pressures against his anxiety to enlist the Soviets as negotiating agents.

An even more difficult decision for Johnson arose from a hint by the Soviet Ambassador, Anatoly Dobrynin, in October, 1965, that a lull in the bombing of perhaps two weeks might produce an opportunity for negotiations. Johnson was wary— he foresaw that popular relief at having the bombing stop would make it difficult to resume. But his subordinates were enthusiastic. The escalation had been designed to dishearten the Hanoi Politburo and perhaps this was the moment to learn if the strategy had succeeded. Johnson, recuperating from his gall bladder operation in Texas, grappled verbally with his advisers. "Do you want to sell out?" he asked one of them grumpily one morning. No one was certain that he would approve the pause until he gave the signal in late December for the intensive peace drive which carried Vice-President Humphrey, Arthur Goldberg, Averell Harriman and McGeorge Bundy to capitals around the world. Some of them, like Harriman, did not even know whether they would be permitted to land in the country of their destination. Harriman received his Polish visa in mid-air after the Polish ambassador in Washington was roused from his bed by the State Department requesting immediate action on the visa. This airplane diplomacy was decried as "gimmickry" in many quarters but, like the escalation, it was an all-out, embellished Johnson response to an idea which he had tested rigorously and accepted.

The failure of any of these missions, including a visit by Alexander Shelepin of the Soviet Presidium to Hanoi, to find any chink in North Vietnam's will to continue the war cast a heavy pall upon the administration. The escalation had been keyed to hopes that success might come swiftly, and the President had to face up to a long, hard pull and to sterner measures that would enlarge the risk of Chinese intervention. He gathered all his principal advisers around the Cabinet table before he made the decision to resume bombing and heard from each of them in turn a judgment that a return to escalation was the best of the options that were available to them. These opinions were carefully recorded in longhand by Presidential Assistant Jack Valenti.

Johnson had learned a valuable lesson in the difficulties of holding a government together during a long and controversial crisis from John Kennedy's experience in the awkward period which preceded President Ngo Dinh Diem's ouster on November 1, 1963.

The coup against the Diem family arose from exasperation within their own country at the high-handedness and ruthlessness of mandarin rule. One of the most knowledgeable and respected observers of Vietnamese affairs, P. J. Honey of the University of London, holds that Diem had demonstrated by 1956, two years after he took charge of South Vietnam's new independent government, that he intended to establish an authoritarian regime which would tolerate no political dissent. Honey argues that the U.S. government should have used the leverage of its aid at that point to insist upon liberalizing policies and a genuine move toward democracy. But the State Department, and particularly Walter Robertson, then Assistant Secretary of State for Far Eastern Affairs, was deferring in those days to the wisdom of the mandarins who ruled Formosa and South Korea, as well as South Vietnam. Political expediency dictated a course of permitting Diem to follow his own thesis that democracy could not be imposed from the top upon his emerging nation. "Why try to humiliate and defame us," Diem asked his critics, "while we are fighting a terrible war for our survival and for the defense of a vital border of the free world?"

The weakness of the Diem thesis was revealed in May, 1963, by the prolonged and troublesome Buddhist reaction to a Diem government order barring the public display of religious flags. The protestors took to the streets and their demonstrations intensified the dispute that had already begun in Washington over Diem's political wisdom. The State Department was now in the hands of New Frontiersmen who maintained that the developing world must grow from the same foundations of personal freedom which sustain the developed world, at least in the West.

This State Department viewpoint was argued most vociferously by three officials: Averell Harriman, a flinty veteran of public life who then directed Far Eastern Affairs and whose capacity to listen when he seemed to be dozing had earned him the nickname of "the crocodile"; Roger Hilsman, a bluntly spoken graduate of West Point who had fought guerrillas in Burma, became an academic specialist on Asia and was director of the State Department's Bureau of Intelligence at the end of 1962; and Michael Forrestal, the brilliant son of the first

Secretary of Defense, who had left a New York law firm to join the White House staff as liaison between the President and Harriman, an old family friend. "You will be my ambassador to Averell," President Kennedy told Forrestal.

These three men, especially Hilsman, began in 1962 to press their fears that the apparent military progress in reclaiming South Vietnam from the insurgent Communist guerrillas was being undermined by the people's lack of sentiment for the Diem government. In mid-December, Hilsman's Bureau of Research and Intelligence forwarded a report to Harriman which said: "The South Vietnam government's failure to emphasize political, social and economic reform at the outset may deprive the entire effort of much of its impact. Much depends upon the ability of the government to show convincing evidence of its intent to improve the lot of the peasants. Instead, government efforts appear to be aimed at increasing government control over the peasants."

Such views brought Hilsman into an increasingly bitter conflict with the Pentagon, where officials, from Robert McNamara down, were impressed with the strategic hamlet program and gratified by the gradual reclamation of the rural areas from the Viet Cong. The Pentagon took the view that the nature of the struggle was essentially military and that the political aspects which Hilsman kept emphasizing were irrelevant to the immediate task of making the countryside secure from the night raids. These differences became personal and rather mean as time went on. At one briefing in the Cabinet room, Hilsman needled General Lemnitzer so hard that McNamara told him brusquely to give the chairman of the Joint Chiefs a chance to finish.

A breach grew between the Hilsman-Harriman duo and the U.S. Ambassador in Saigon, Frederick Nolting, who was far more tolerant of Diem. Nolting had been in Saigon since 1961 and he had worked hard at his initial instructions to secure the confidence of Diem and his regime. He had found the old president to be stubborn but not implacable in the face of reason, and their relationship had become a cordial one.

Nolting wrote Rusk in early 1963 that he would like to be

recalled at the end of his two-year tour in the following December. His children had reached boarding-school age and he wanted them to go away to school but not as far away as the distance between Saigon and New England.

The Hue riots of May 8, 1963, during which government troops were accused of shooting into the crowd and killing twelve persons, brought concessions from Diem, including an assurance that he would not countenance any discrimination against their religion. He was reported to have told the Buddhist leaders that they were "damn fools" to ask for religious freedom because they well knew that this was written into the Vietnamese Constitution. The Buddhists remained angry that the soldiers who fired the shots into the crowd had not been punished, but the scene was calm enough to permit Nolting to slip away on May 23 for a vacation cruise in the Aegean Sea.

President Kennedy was persuaded in this period that the time had come to send another ambassador to Saigon with instructions to deal more stringently with Diem. Henry Cabot Lodge had intimated that he would be interested in resuming his public service, and Kennedy, without much confidence that Lodge would be willing to go to Saigon, had his military aide, Major General Chester V. Clifton, sound him out. Lodge did agree and the succession was set when Nolting arrived in Washington from his Aegean cruise. He was about to be dumped as the first phase of a new policy toward Diem and no one knew exactly what to say to him. Hilsman, who had by now succeeded Harriman (who had in turn become Undersecretary of State), did not want Nolting to go back to Saigon and arranged for the President, then travelling in Ireland, to hasten the announcement of the Lodge appointment. It was made while Nolting was in Washington on June 27, a timing which did not accord with the most gracious diplomatic traditions. But Lodge could not leave immediately and Nolting argued that he should return to confront the worsening turbulence in Saigon. He left on July 5, despite his superiors' reluctance to let him go back.

The first of the bonze suicides which were to trigger a

world reaction against the Diem regime had taken place on June 11, 1963. The imperturbable Diem sensed the potential trouble in this human sacrifice and took the unusual step of making a broadcast in which he pledged: "I solemnly declare to you that behind the Buddhists in this country there is still the Constitution—that is I myself." A new attempt was made to strike an accord but five days later some 10,000 Buddhists staged the most virulent outburst against the government that Saigon had witnessed.

The Buddhists were responding to extremists and the dissents from this leadership by more stable figures were little noted in the rush of attention and headlines to the drama stirred by the activists. Later, as Americans came to know the characters in the Buddhist movement better, they recognized that the zealous monks were pursuing political power in a crafty, ruthless way. The truth was available at the time. The chief of the National Sanka Association, venerable Thich Thien Hoa, wrote Diem an open letter on August 22 in which he asserted that the government had constantly respected the principles of freedom of belief and religious equality. He said the pagodas had been improved and the number of Buddhists had increased steadily under Diem. Then he related that "politically minded people" had used Buddhist robes and pagodas to form clans and terrorize the "genuine religionists." He said they were "concerned only with attracting monks, nuns and Buddhists into the struggle for their political plots" and that "they incited Buddhists to riot and encourage immolations in complete variance with Buddhist law."

But Diem and his brother Nhu had given enough cause for grievance to allow these protests in the summer of 1963 to assume an air of legitimacy. They were avidly reported by a small group of young American newspapermen who had been totally disenchanted by the autocratic ways of the Diem regime. The publicity-minded Buddhists would notify these reporters to be in a certain place at a certain time and there another burning would occur to stir fresh indignation around the world. Nolting complained that the American reporters could serve their country well by letting him know when these events were scheduled so that the police could stop them. But the reporters were also disenchanted with Nolting for his closeness to Diem and a huge chasm grew between this crusading press corps and the government in the July–August period. The public impact in America of these press accounts was so powerful that Rusk said sadly one day, "I don't think we can take another burning." Even Kennedy was furious at the newspaper reports. "I'll be damned if I intend to let my foreign policy be run by a 27-year-old reporter," he said at one point, referring to David Halberstam, the dexterous Saigon correspondent for *The New York Times* who was later rewarded with a Pulitzer Prize for his part in the crusade against Diem.

Washington journalists also played a role in Diem's denouement because Hilsman was giving out background stories like one which appeared in *The New York Times* on August 7, 1963. It quoted administration sources as believing that Diem might be overthrown by his own bureaucracy if he did not settle the Buddhist crisis quickly. The same article reported that the Kennedy administration was veering away from its former belief that no alternative to the Diem regime would be capable of sustaining the anti-Communist effort. By this kind of leak, Hilsman gave enlarged significance to a viewpoint which was held at that point only by him and Harriman. Rusk, as usual, was non-committal on the developing issue and Kennedy had made no decision. Hilsman-inspired articles, emerging regularly from Washington, made relations between Diem and the Americans more complex and less cooperative.

In mid-August, Lodge flew out to Saigon, stopping in Honolulu for a weekend conference with Nolting, on his way home. The new ambassador indicated to his predecessor that he did not have many changes in mind. But it was clear to Nolting that Lodge had taken his briefing and his instructions from Harriman and Hilsman. Nolting related that Diem had never broken his word to him and that before he left Saigon he talked the old president into promising that he would not order his troops to raid the pagodas in which the militant monks had stored their arms and centered their conspiracy.

Such a raid occurred on August 21, while Nolting was still in Honolulu. He cabled Diem: "This is the first time you have ever broken a promise to me." Vietnamese friends told him later that when Diem read the cable, he shook his head sadly and said, "He just doesn't know how severe the provocations were."

The raids brought the emotionalism in Washington to a new peak. There were emergency meetings and the State Department issued a strong statement charging the South Vietnamese government with violating its own assurances that it was pursuing a policy of reconciliation with the Buddhists. The Nhus had clearly acted to present Lodge on his arrival with an accomplished suppression of the insurgent monks. The strategy was attributed to Diem's younger brother, Ngo Dinh Nhu, who had become embittered by the pressures from Washington. Some one hundred priests, students, and Boy Scouts were reported to have been killed in the attack and 1,000 Buddhists were said to be under arrest.

The U.S. government's outlook was glum on Saturday morning, August 24, 1963, when Harriman, Hilsman and Forrestal sat down to draft a fresh cable of instructions to Ambassador Lodge. He had requested orders on how to respond to some high Vietnamese generals who sought out Americans after the raids to say they were not responsible and to warn that Nhu was plotting to kill them all and to make a deal with the Communists. They seemed to want to know how Washington would react to a coup—similar plots in the past had been flatly discouraged by American officials. But the long and disturbing sequence of events had drained the last of Harriman's and Hilsman's patience. On that day, August 24, they sent Lodge an historic cable with the instructions: "Do not abort."

This meant that Lodge would flash a green light to the plotting generals. It was a bold step and the objective toward which Harriman and Hilsman had been driving for months. It was also a remarkably crucial decision for a Saturday meeting unattended by any officials of Cabinet rank. The President, McNamara, McCone and Rusk were all out of town for the weekend. Forrestal merely telephoned Kennedy in Hyannisport and read the cable to him. Kennedy may have misunderstood the purport of the cable but offered no objections.

With Kennedy's endorsement, Hilsman did not have to seek further consent as he conveyed the contents of the cable to the other departments by telephone. He reached the number two man at Defense, Roswell Gilpatric, and the number three man (later the director) at CIA, Richard Helms. Neither actually saw the text of the cable until the following morning, and neither was in a position to question its contents because Hilsman stressed that the instructions had been approved by the President. General Maxwell Taylor learned about the development as he sat at dinner in a New York restaurant Saturday night.

A storm gathered on Sunday, August 25, 1963, however, as the extent of Hilsman's activities on the previous day became evident. He had summoned the UPI's State Department correspondent Stewart Hensley, and put out a sharp background statement blaming the pagoda raids squarely upon Nhu's secret police and warning that the United States might sharply reduce its aid unless President Diem discharged the men responsible for the attacks. The Voice of America, at Hilsman's urging, picked up the Hensley story and relayed it, in Vietnamese, to the Far East on Sunday. Lodge saw the transcript only a few hours before he was scheduled to present his credentials as ambassador at the palace and he was angered that he had not been consulted. "Jack Kennedy wouldn't approve of doing things this way," he told his USIA aide, John Mecklin. "This certainly isn't his way of running a government."

Hilsman had gone even further to make his point. On Monday, August 26, 1963, *The New York Times* carried authoritative speculation from Washington that the emerging U.S. policy would "encourage army commanders to intervene in Vietnamese politics." The Hilsman-inspired article emphasized the hopes in Washington that the military leaders would force a change in the regime.

By Monday, John Kennedy's administration had, as he phrased it, "fallen apart" over the cable. It had ignited the simmering split in the government—McNamara, McCone and Taylor were furious. Kennedy quickly summoned a meeting of his key advisers. Nolting, who had weekended in Virginia after his return from Honolulu, was on hand and he bluntly denounced the Harriman-Hilsman-Forrestal cable as an improvident act. Harriman yelled at him to shut up. Kennedy sternly interjected that he wanted to hear what the ambassador had to say. The agitation at the meeting was compounded with surprise that nothing had happened in Saigon. The fuse had been lit—why hadn't the bomb exploded? The fact was that Lodge, having received his instructions, asked aides to take soundings among seven Vietnamese generals who had exhibited enthusiasm for a coup. The reports came back that the generals were wary and reluctant to move. They had been discouraged for so long from taking any step that might disrupt the conduct of the war against the Viet Cong that they found it hard now to believe that the Americans were willing to approve a coup d'etat. The generals' mood, conveyed to Washington by Lodge in a cable which arrived on Wednesday (August 28), stimulated proposals to reverse the instructions of August 24. He said, "It's not too late—we can still back out." Kennedy was plainly tempted. But he recognized that if he withdrew his readiness to accept a coup, he would lose his credibility to the generals, who might yet prove to be a last resort against Diem's obduracy.

The tense meetings in Washington dragged on through the week without any further decision by the President. He went away on Friday to Hyannisport and at a Saturday meeting Secretary Rusk, who had so far taken no strong position on the issue, called with a slight flourish for an opinion from Vice-President Johnson, who had been quietly encouraging Nolting although no one had previously asked him to state his views. "I don't believe in this cloak and dagger stuff," the Vice-President drawled. "I think we should try to live with what we've got. I've never been happy that Otto Passman [the Louisiana congressman who was chairman of the Foreign Operations subcommittee of the House Appropriations Committee] has complete control of our foreign-aid appropriations.

But since he has this control, we try to get along with him as best we can. We don't try to overthrow him. I think we ought to keep trying to do the best we can with Diem."

To Johnson's credit, he never brought up this judgment publicly in complaint against the mess which fell upon him after both Diem and Kennedy had been killed. Harriman, Hilsman and Forrestal lost their influence when Johnson became President, but he did not continue to argue the moot point as to who was right at this crucial turning-point. (Harriman later regained his status. By the end of 1966, Johnson was saying that if Harriman were ten years younger he would make him Secretary of State.)

Lodge's first meeting with Diem had not raised any hopes for closer collaboration. The old man stared at the ceiling while Lodge preached the need for liberalization and the ambassador went away determined not to visit the palace again. It had been an unpleasant and long exchange, more than four hours—Lodge noted in his cable that Diem never seemed to need to go to the bathroom. Lodge took the position that he had said all he could say. He had laid out his government's position that if Diem wanted to save himself and his regime, he would have to get rid of the hated Nhus. Even Honey, the London professor who was an old friend of Diem, had told him that they would all be killed if his brother didn't leave the country. Lodge argued that the next move was up to Diem and that it would be a gesture of surrender if he sought another appointment at the palace. For the next crucial three weeks there was no direct communication between the two men.

The gap was widened by a series of incidents. Under orders from Washington, Lodge consented to give sanctuary in the embassy to the most militant Buddhist leader, Thich Tri Quang. This was an affront to the government and collaterally an antecedent to the new Buddhist troubles which erupted in 1966. In late August, 1963, the Saigon government had been suddenly informed that aid to the Diem government was being suspended. This took everyone by surprise because the President had not decided upon this ultimate step. An investigation disclosed that the announcement was perpetrated by a minor official in the AID agency whose indignation at Diem swelled way beyond his official responsibilities. Relations between the White House and the palace were strained further when Kennedy, in a television interview on September 1, said that Diem's government had fallen out of touch with the people over the past two months and that Diem could only hope to win back popular support "with changes in policy and perhaps in personnel." When Kennedy saw Nolting the next day, he asked, "Do you think I went too far?" The ambassador replied that he thought Diem would understand it in the context of the whole broadcast.

To assist his view of the situation, Kennedy dispatched several observers to Vietnam. Marine General Victor H. Krulak, of the counter-insurgency task force, Rufus Phillips, an experienced AID man, and John A. Mendenhall, an old Vietnam hand, went out together. Krulak returned to report at a small NSC meeting in the Cabinet room that the military effort was proceeding splendidly with no damage from the demonstrations. Phillips and Mendenhall reported that the political dissent threatened to unravel the whole effort against the Communists. "Have you three been to the same place?" Kennedy asked incredulously. On September 24, he sent Robert McNamara to learn what was going on. When the Secretary reappeared in the Cabinet room on October 2, he had completely reversed his espousal of the Pentagon position. He said he found that there were serious political problems and that the war against the Communists could not succeed unless they were resolved. Kennedy said, "I take it that what you mean is that we must disassociate from Diem, no matter what the consequences." McNamara doubted that Diem could last, no matter what concessions he made. He asked the President to approve the release of a statement which had been prepared before the meeting. It was a sop to the pride of the military officials whose stubborn position McNamara had come to doubt. The release said that "the military program has made progress" and "Secretary McNamara and General Taylor reported their judgment that the major part of the U.S. military task can be completed by the end of 1965." This prediction, at the moment a simple tactic to ease the unhappiness of General Paul Harkins and his officer colleagues, was utilized by critics many times after the war dragged on past 1965 to challenge the validity of McNamara's judgments.

The denouement was inevitable from that point. Lodge took no pains to hide his distaste for the Diem family, aid to Nhu's CIA-trained special forces was cut on October 19, and Kennedy instructed Lodge to control the situation as long as he could but not to block the coup when it developed. Diem was frozen into a rigid posture and he made no conciliatory moves until he met with Lodge on November 1. The embassy had been notified by the conspirators on the previous day that they were ready to move and Lodge had cabled Washington that the coup would take place at any moment. The ambassador went to the palace with Admiral Harry Felt, the Pacific Fleet commander who had been in Saigon on a visit. Felt was an old friend of Diem and wanted to say goodbye. As their visit ended, Diem asked Lodge to stay behind for a talk. The ambassador demurred, pointing out that he must see the admiral off at the airport. Diem said he would have an equerry perform that courtesy and the two hostile men sat down. "Tell me what you want me to do and I will do it," Diem said. "If you don't know what you want me to do, cable Washington for instructions and then tell me. I will do whatever you want me to do."

The proud old man's capitulation had come too late and there was little that Lodge could say. Within twenty-four hours the palace fell to the generals and Diem and his brother had been slain.

The wisdom of deserting Diem was laid open to question by the ensuing eighteen months of political chaos which settled upon South Vietnam. Even the fabric of constitutional government that Diem had maintained was lost in a succession of military dictatorships. Nhu's security forces served as a bulwark of morale in many villages and, as they disintegrated, the Viet Cong easily regained their dominance in some 70 per cent of the country. The Buddhist militants proved to be self-seeking opportunists and the fragility of their hold upon their people was demonstrated by the collapse of their pretensions after Premier Nguyen Ky's crackdown in the spring of 1966. If Diem had been permitted to carry out a similar repression in 1963, the consequences of the Buddhist insurgency would almost certainly have been less far-reaching. It must be remembered that before the religious revolt began in 1963, the Viet Cong were being contained by the South Vietnamese army plus 15,000 American military observers. In the fall of 1966, the same task was challenging the South Vietnamese army and over 400,000 American military personnel.

On the other hand, it is doubtful that Diem, denied by heritage the capacity to function as a persuasive politician and suspicious by instinct of popular gestures, could have been induced to launch the revolution of expectations that has proved to be crucial in drawing the allegiance of the peasants toward the central government. It is doubtful that President Diem and his brother could have brought themselves to look with favor upon the PATs (Political Action Teams) which work as democratic agents to raise the morale, the living standards and the sense of nationhood among the peasants. Even in the days of 1962 and 1963, when the military seemed to be winning its struggle against the Communist guerrillas, Kennedy's political antenna had told him that something was not right, that the United States was not backing a winning cause.

From Harry Truman through Lyndon Johnson, no American President has been permitted to confront Vietnam as a problem in isolation. Truman was required to assist the receding cause of the French in Indochina because they were allies. Eisenhower injected American influence because the French defeat at Dienbienphu left a vacuum which the Communists would certainly fill if the United States did not. Kennedy deepened the commitment because he had surrendered the West's toehold in Laos in preference to waging a war there and did not wish to preside over a total disintegration of non-Communist influence in that corner of Asia. Johnson carried out the pledges made by his predecessors because he was unable to discover any alternatives which held promise for American foreign policy objectives.

Opponents of the war in Vietnam see it as a useless dissipation of resources and a brazen reflection of an exaggerated concept of this country's role in the world. Those who endorse the war believe that it will eventually become an enduring evidence of American determination to resist Communist encroachments and thus avert the necessity to wage similar struggles in other nations closer to home.

Only time can return a just verdict on this debate and on the wisdom of the decisions which the gruelling crisis elicited from Kennedy and Johnson.

S ☆ I ☆ X

Self-made crises

Some of the crises involving the United States have resulted from actions of other governments over which the administration in Washington has had no control. But quite a few have also been created by the rigidity of American foreign policy and by the apparent inability of its makers to adjust it promptly enough to constantly changing conditions.

To a large extent, this weakness has been due to the intimate involvement of most foreign problems with considerations of domestic policy. "Anti-Communism," in whatever form, has become a firm and permanent plank in any political platform. The U.S. attitude toward the Middle East has necessarily been conditioned by the passionately pro-Israel sentiment of its big cities. Non-recognition of China has been part of the anti-Communist stance and, whatever the arguments for a change, the U.S. government has never been able to move against its own assessment of the state of public opinion. This has produced anomalies at home and bewilderment abroad.

The 1962 crisis over the application of UN Charter Article 19 sanctions against the Russians for their refusal to pay the special UN-Congo peacekeeping assessments is a case in point. The U.S. insistence on abrogating the Soviet Union's right to vote for non-payment of dues was based in part on the

Kennedy administration's desire to please Congress, which was
then being asked to appropriate funds for the purchase of UN
bonds. It also rested on several misconceptions.

A proposal to purchase UN bonds had been sent to
Congress without prior consultation with the Republican leadership. When it was discovered their votes were needed to put
the plan across, President Kennedy took the matter out of the
State Department and ordered his own White House staff to
handle it on the Hill.

The Republicans, notably Senators Aiken of Vermont and
Hickenlooper of Iowa, peeved at not being consulted, were reluctant to promise support. As a special inducement, the senators were then given a solemn promise that the administration
would make "everybody" pay up their delinquent dues as the
price of the U.S. contribution to the UN bond purchase. Thus,
without considering the diplomatic implications of the deal, a
U.S. commitment, which could have wrecked the United Nations, was made simply because two key senators had been
mishandled.

The policy of the Kennedy administration, adopted in
due course by President Johnson, also rested on the mistaken
belief that the Soviets would give in under pressure of world
opinion. Soviet experts had not even been asked for their
views. Had they been, they would have warned that the
Russians were most unlikely to pay for an operation they
considered deliberately contrived to thwart their interests. On
several occasions, the late Ambassador Stevenson pointedly advised both Presidents against insisting on the literal application of Article 19, but his warnings were ignored.

Without going into details of the Congo peacekeeping
operation, it is enough to recall that it was originally sponsored
by the U.S. Indeed, at the end, after the overthrow of
Lumumba by President Kasavubu, the operation was directed
against the deposed Premier and his partisans, who were
strongly supported by the Soviet Union. Hammarskjold's so-
called Congo Club by that time consisted of three Americans,
an Indian, a Britisher and a Canadian, but no Russians. Because of their involvement, the Soviets were not allowed to see

confidential papers coming in from the field. They had sabotaged the UN peacekeeping activities and were trying to restore Lumumba to the Premiership.

In securing the exclusion of the Soviet Union from the
Congo, U.S. diplomacy had won a significant diplomatic victory. But it managed to forfeit success when it also insisted
the Russians must pay the cost of their defeat. To strengthen
its claim under Article 19 of the UN Charter, the administration turned to the law. In a brilliantly prepared brief submitted to the International Court of Justice at the Hague,
the legal case against the Russians was firmly established. As
expected, the court split on East-West lines, the majority
favoring the U.S.

For three years, right up to December, 1965, the administration insisted on the legality of its case and tried to ram it
through the UN General Assembly. It all but wrecked the UN
in the process.

There was no question that the administration was right in
principle. It had all the legal and moral arguments behind it.
The only thing it lacked was good sense. And the application
of simple common sense would have told the Washington
leadership that—whatever the rights and wrongs—no power of
the size and importance of the Soviet Union could be compelled to take action which it considered inimical to its own
interests. The United States would be unlikely to make a
contribution to the welfare of Castro's Cuba, however
just and legal the cause. And the Soviet Union should not have
been publicly pushed to the brink for not contributing to an
action designed to thwart its interests in Africa.

As a propaganda exercise, the campaign had considerable
validity but only up to the point when it became obvious the
General Assembly would have to suspend operations if the
U.S. persisted in its demands.

Moreover, while insisting on teaching the Russians a lesson by an "irrevocable commitment" to Article 19, President
Johnson was not at all averse to discussing with the Russians
the strengthening of the Security Council's role in *future*
peacekeeping operations. The Russians had always pressed this

point because Security Council decisions require unanimity of its permanent members, i.e., are subject to the veto of any of the Big Five powers. In an exchange of letters with Chairman Khrushchev, President Johnson was ready to concede the Russians' claim, provided they paid up the arrears.

The administration's private fear was, of course, that Congress would revolt if the administration yielded. This was another misconception. Senator Aiken, the original proponent of the plan, was the first to warn President Johnson that the campaign had reached a point where it was damaging U.S. interests. He disputed the idea that sentiment in Congress could not be changed.

It is only very rarely that Congress has failed to respond to the Executive's determined foreign policy plea. Actually, when Ambassador Goldberg finally announced the retreat, only Representative Gross of Iowa and a few diehards registered objections.

In too many cases, recent administrations have shown timidity and exaggerated concern as to what others may say. In contrast, former Secretary of State Dean Acheson, describing President Truman's attitude to decision-making, has stressed that "he did not care a hoot what Congress, Schlesinger or any other historian would say. The question he would ask was: 'Is this the right thing to do?' Convinced that it was, he made the decision, however unpopular it may have seemed."

The unwillingness to change before a change has been forced by others is a frequent cause of crises which could have been avoided. The desire to cling to remedies that have served in the past has become an obsession under the Johnson-Rusk administration of foreign policy. And in no instance was this better demonstrated than in the handling of the 1966 crisis which engulfed the NATO alliance and U.S. relations with General de Gaulle.

The NATO alliance was conceived in 1949—at the height of the cold war. It followed the Communist coup in Czechoslovakia and the ever-increasing evidence that Soviet expansionism was on the march. Europe was prostrate and only beginning to recover from the devastation of World War II. Barring an all-out U.S. commitment to defend the continent, there was nothing to prevent the Russians from marching across Europe to the Atlantic. At the time the alliance was conceived, it was hailed as an act of unprecedented courage and vision. Its architects, President Truman and Secretary of State Dean Acheson, were showered with deserved praise for their efforts in welding the alliance together.

No one thought of the NATO alliance as a permanent feature in U.S. relations with Europe. As far as its military arrangements went, they were designed to meet the actual and growing Soviet threat. Its more permanent character stemmed from Article II of the treaty, which called for economic and cultural cooperation among its members. John McCone recalls that when he visited General Eisenhower in his SHAPE headquarters in 1950 and wondered about SHAPE's temporary housing, the general breezily observed that "we don't expect to be here five years from now." Several of the U.S. generals assigned to the original NATO never expected their assignment to last over a year or so.

In Europe, the example of the NATO alliance started a new trend: integration. The Schuman Plan of May, 1950, placing French and German coal and steel production under a common high authority was a revolutionary move for its time. Schuman's statement in launching the High Authority proclaimed that it was intended "not merely to make war between France and Germany unthinkable but also to provide the first step in the federation of Europe."

Instrumental in the formulation of the Schuman Plan was an extraordinary Frenchman, Jean Monnet, who has had more influence on U.S. foreign policy than any foreigner ever had or could hope to have. The 79-year-old economist was John Foster Dulles' favorite foreign visitor, second only to Chancellor Adenauer. Similarly, Monnet impressed and influenced such diverse personalities as Dean Acheson, General Marshall, Adlai Stevenson and former Undersecretary George Ball, as well as scores of foreign policy planners, publishers and journalists.

Monnet's success among Americans is attributed by his detractors to the fact that he is one of the few top-level Frenchmen who speak English fluently, know the United States and even the American idiom intimately. Monnet has always maintained excellent connections in Wall Street that date back to his partnership in a New York investment firm. He spent the war years in Washington as a member of the British Supply Council.

Monnet's imaginative thinking at the time when Europe drifted rudderless and weak under the unrelenting Soviet threat brought him all kinds of recognition from the U.S. and England but few from his native France. His *Who's Who* entry lists honorary degrees from Columbia, Princeton, Yale and the Universities of Oxford and Glasgow but none from a French or continental institution of learning. The entry lists his decorations as Freedom Award (U.S.A.), 1963, the U.S. Presidential Medal of Freedom and an honorary British GBE, but is silent on the subject of French decorations.

To the hearty applause of the United States, Jean Monnet opened new vistas for Europe in the early '50s. The exciting developments which he had set in motion were interrupted by the Korean War. The North Korean foray beyond the 38th parallel on June 25, 1950, was the first overt aggression of a Communist state. Intelligence reports showed that it had been approved and planned by Moscow.

During the summer and fall of 1950, the NATO Council, recognizing the shortages of its means in relation to its tasks, began to consider the possibility of German rearmament. To make this event as palatable as possible, the U.S. proposed an integrated force under centralized command and offered to provide an American commander plus additional U.S. ground forces.

American pressures were constantly applied to foster German rehabilitation, European unity and integration. The prompt acceptance of federal institutions by the six western European nations concealed the frictions which the pace of developments under the pressures of the cold war had generated. Fears and emotions stirred by the prospect of a remilitarized Germany gained ground, even though John Foster Dulles threatened an "agonizing reappraisal" and withdrawal of newly made U.S. commitments unless the European Defense Community and the political integration that was to accompany it were accepted.

Meanwhile, the tensions of the cold war had eased. The Korean truce had been in effect for over a year. Stalin had died and Soviet policy seemed to take a more moderate line. The ignominious defeat of the once proud French army in World War II, the costly war in Indochina and the prospects of its merger into a European army combined to awaken a latent nationalism in France. The effect of it was that on August 30, 1954, the French Assembly declined to ratify the European Defense Community by a majority of fifty-five votes. De Gaulle's MRP voted solidly against the proposal.*

Within NATO, the newly formed alliance chafed under U.S. leadership and demanded a finger on the trigger of the U.S. nuclear arsenal. In the dying days of the Eisenhower administration, Secretary Herter put forward the first concept of a multilateral MRBM force with the offer of five U.S. Polaris submarines. The "assignment" of the five nuclear submarines to NATO sounded like a generous gesture. But in effect, the submarines remained under the command of an American commander of the Atlantic fleet to whom they were transferred in his capacity as SACLANT.

The resultant publicity over the multilateral nuclear force, which received its final accolade in the Kennedy-Macmillan Nassau agreement of December, 1962, created confusion as to what U.S. policy really was. Some of the enthusiasts who saw in MLF the answer to all their idealistic dreams were accused of arm-twisting by the reluctant Europeans and, no doubt, were guilty of the charge. The United States kept on saying that the whole project had been conceived entirely for Europe's benefit to provide the extra finger on the trigger which the Europeans allegedly wanted.

Thus, while there was doubt as to what U.S.-NATO policy

NATO In Transition by Timothy W. Stanley, Praeger, 1965.

was, there was never any doubt as to where General Charles de Gaulle stood. Even before World War II, while a junior officer, De Gaulle wrote that "to be great, one must conduct a great quarrel." He has been working at his maxim ever since.

Step by step, De Gaulle began to sever his ties with NATO. He first withdrew his contingent from the Mediterranean and later from the Atlantic fleets. He failed to return the several divisions "borrowed" from the war in Algeria. He obstructed measures to integrate air defenses, sabotaged NATO strategy projects and at first ignored and later challenged the concept of an integrated nuclear force. He has managed to sabotage every step proposed to implement the alliance. "Integration" along with "les Anglo-Saxons" became dirty words in the general's vocabulary.

The defeat of the European Defense Community in 1954 should have given U.S. policy makers a pause in their headlong rush toward integration. It should have caused them to question the glib assertions of Monnet and his U.S. supporters that France and the continent were ready to embrace military integration. Actually, apart from the United States and Monnet, only the Germans saw in integration a solution to their problems. Integration in a European military club would do much to restore German respectability and to appease fears of German remilitarization.

Throughout the eight years of De Gaulle's anti-NATO offensive, the U.S. has never seriously considered the validity of his claims. Only President Eisenhower, receiving in 1958 a De Gaulle proposal for the establishment of a U.S.-British-French "governing board" within NATO, played briefly with the idea of accepting the proposal "under the table." But De Gaulle wanted full publicity and Eisenhower could not agree for fear of offending the rest of the alliance.

The De Gaulle proposal was sent to President Eisenhower on September 17, 1958. It consisted of a four-point memorandum and a covering letter assuring the President of De Gaulle's "sincere and trusting friendship, loyal sentiments and highest consideration."

The memorandum asserted that the Atlantic alliance was

functioning in a way that no longer corresponded to political and strategic realities. "One cannot consider," the memo said, "an organization like NATO as if what's happening in the Middle East or Africa did not immediately and directly concern Europe. The range of present missiles and aircraft makes this concept outdated."

According to De Gaulle, it appeared necessary that "on the level of world policy and strategy there be set up an organization composed of the U.S., Great Britain and France to make decisions on political questions affecting world security and to put into effect strategic plans of action with regard to nuclear weapons."

Stressing that France considered such an organization indispensable and that negotiations on this subject should start as soon as possible in Washington through the embassies or the Permanent Group, the memorandum served notice that, "should this appear necessary," France was ready to invoke Article XII of the NATO treaty providing procedure for revision after the treaty had been in existence for ten years, i.e., by 1959.

President Eisenhower replied by letter on October 20, 1958.

Dear General de Gaulle,

I have given considerable thought to the views expressed in your letter of September 17.

We are, I believe, in full agreement that the threat we face is global and our policies have to an extent already been adopted to this end.

In recognition of this threat the U.S. has joined with its allies in establishing elements of strength throughout the world. The U.S. and France are closely associated in certain world groupings such as NATO and SEATO.

As for the Atlantic alliance I believe there has been a significant evolution of NATO over the past 12 years. Consultation in NATO has been in fact extended well beyond the confines of the European area. We, for example, have sought to use the NATO Council to inform or consult with our allies on the threat facing the Free World in the Far East and Middle East.

We have also used the Council to develop common policies toward the Soviet bloc. We feel this "habit of consultation" among NATO nations must be further broadened but cannot be forced. I do not believe that we can afford to lose any of this developing intimacy among all the NATO members and the closer bonds it forges.

As for means for dealing with this problem which you propose our present procedures for organizing the defense of the free world clearly require the willing cooperation of many other nations both within and outside NATO.

We cannot afford to adopt any system which would give to our other allies or other free world countries the impression that basic decisions affecting their own vital interests are being made without their participation.

As regards NATO I must in all frankness say that I see very serious problems both within and outside NATO in any effort to extend its coverage beyond areas presently covered.

All this having been said, I must add that a community association to live must constantly evolve and find means to make itself more useful in the face of changing conditions. I am quite prepared to explore this aspect of the matter in appropriate ways.

With best personal regards,

Dwight D. Eisenhower

The Eisenhower letter, which had been drafted by State Department professionals, displayed a grievous lapse of diplomatic finesse. Its wooden phrases failed to take into account the exaggerated pride and striving for recognition of General de Gaulle. It was an obvious brushoff while the delay in answering and the grudging concessions in the last paragraph were scarcely calculated to appease the general's vanity.

In retrospect, seasoned diplomatic observers have expressed the view that the reply would have been much more effective had the President accepted the proposal on condition that General de Gaulle obtain authority from the other NATO members for delegating their powers to the U.S.-British-French triumvirate. This would have put the ball in De Gaulle's court and forced him to seek approval from the rest of the alliance, or admit what he had consistently denied, that his "organization" was tantamount to a three-power dictatorship.

As it was, the State Department went through the motions of calling in the ambassadors of Britain and France for "consultations," but the meetings were allowed to lapse when it was discovered that French Ambassador Hervé Alphand's instructions were merely to listen and to say nothing.

Spokesmen for succeeding administrations have asserted that the United States had wanted to introduce NATO reforms of their own but found De Gaulle uninterested and unwilling. No one can be sure what may have been a proposal or a mere "private talk" among representatives of fourteen nations meeting regularly twice a year. But no formal American proposals or substantive replies to De Gaulle's demands for treaty revision have ever been made. The U.S. continued to temporize in the hope that something might turn up: De Gaulle might die, he could be overthrown by the electorate, rebuffed by the Assembly or condemned by the other thirteen NATO members.*

Nothing of the kind happened. De Gaulle has always had a strong popular following within France and since his election in 1965 and his June, 1966, visit to the Soviet Union, where he handled himself with great skill, his views have been gaining under-the-counter popularity throughout Europe, which pays lip service to Washington's integration refrain but secretly seeks re-insurance with De Gaulle and his attempts at an East-West détente.

It was not until De Gaulle's demands for the withdrawal of U.S. forces from France were publicly announced on March 29, 1966, that the administration decided to take serious action. Though it has never been admitted, an all-out offensive (conducted in secret through diplomatic channels as well as through all available news media) was launched to thwart General de Gaulle.

As is his custom in crisis situations, President Johnson summoned from retirement the "big names" associated with NATO, France and Germany. Former Secretary of State, 73-year-old Dean Acheson, architect of the NATO alliance, was installed in a seventh-floor State Department office as the

* See Appendix, pp. 222–24.

"President's adviser on NATO affairs." Seventy-one-year-old John J. McCloy, a former U.S. high commissioner in occupied Germany, was sent to Bonn, and diplomats in all allied capitals were instructed to rally the governments involved around the U.S. position.

The purpose of the offensive was twofold. On the diplomatic front, the U.S. wanted in effect to establish something it had been denying De Gaulle since 1958—a three-power directorate for NATO affairs, with Germany replacing France. In the public sector, it appealed, through newspaper interviews, to dissident French deputies, the military and French public opinion in an attempt to slow down the relentless general by an adverse vote either in the Assembly or in the parliamentary elections of 1967.

While McCloy conducted the NATO operation in the field, Dean Acheson acted as the chief of staff on the home front.

Elegant in his English tweeds, with white mustache bristling, Acheson cheerfully admitted his disdain for the general and all his works. He told visitors that the Frenchman who has no place in the twentieth century cannot be permitted to turn the clock back. Acheson saw in De Gaulle's demand for the ouster of U.S. troops from France an act of revenge for the "capture" of Germany by the United States at the time when De Gaulle himself had nursed ambitious plans for dominating Europe through his alliance with Germany.

Acheson was the chief drafter of notes and speeches that spearheaded the administration's extensive publicity campaign.

President Johnson's opening statement, delivered on March 23, 1966, before a hastily convoked forum of the Foreign Service Institute, was originally drafted by Acheson. Acheson's draft named names and castigated De Gaulle. But by the time the speech was delivered, there was no similarity between the draft and the speech, except—in the words of one official—"that both were written in English." All Acheson's anti-French and anti-De Gaulle sallies had been blue-pencilled by the President.

The President himself had adopted a do-nothing approach to De Gaulle.

Speaking privately to a group of French correspondents in June, 1966, President Johnson described his own attitude toward the French president.

"I keep mum," he said. "If you hear something nasty about De Gaulle, it has not come from me or from anybody in the White House. I told everybody in the government to be polite to President de Gaulle. Just tip your hat and say, 'thank you, General.'"

Outwardly, at least, this homey presidential advice has been observed and public altercations avoided. But in private, U.S. officials never sought to conceal their anger and their attitude hardened during the General's Moscow trip in June, 1966.

With Vietnam occupying most of President Johnson's attention, the "tip your hat to General de Gaulle" attitude has been adopted as the most effective way of keeping the lid on "the other crisis." Secretary Rusk has seen his role in Europe as that of a professional negotiator and has delegated responsibility for French affairs to George Ball and others. Rusk can be counted upon to say the right things and make the right motions at NATO meetings but he has seldom expressed firm opinions on how to deal with De Gaulle.

Thus, by default, the conduct of U.S.-French policy was left to Undersecretary George Ball. One of the most brilliant and articulate members of the Johnson administration, Ball fervently preached that Gaullism was evil, that it was a destructive force keeping Germany off balance, preventing Britain from playing its rightful role in Europe and ultimately leading Germany back into militarism and Europe to disaster. He was firmly supported in this view by former Deputy European Chief, Robert Schaetzel, and Policy Planning Chief Henry Owen, the co-author of the abortive MLF scheme.

Defense Secretary McNamara tried to find acceptable compromise military solutions, while his own International Security Affairs Chief, John McNaughton, favored accommodation with De Gaulle.

Ambassador Charles E. ("Chip") Bohlen treated De Gaulle with aloofness and resignation. Early in his ambassadorship, Bohlen decided that "you cannot do business" with De Gaulle and he has maintained that posture throughout. "Mr. Bohlen," one of his ambassadorial colleagues remarked, "not only does not know what De Gaulle thinks but is not even interested."

By June, 1966, direct relations between the two countries had virtually broken down. In Paris, Ambassador Bohlen kept in the background and improved his golf score. French Foreign Minister Couve de Murville was his occasional, but uncommunicative, partner.

In Washington, French Ambassador Lucet, a brilliant diplomatist, is treated by the State Department as a "cultural attaché" and spends most of his time promoting cultural exchanges and celebrating French-American anniversaries, unable to contribute anything to the NATO debate because he is kept completely in the dark by his chief.

Meetings on the foreign minister level have been rare. One in April, 1966, between Ball and Couve de Murville, was a disaster. According to reports of those present, it ran roughly as follows:

Ball: "I should like to give you a preview of the Vietnam presentation I will make before the NATO Council tomorrow."

Couve shrugged his shoulders, listened to the presentation and said nothing.

Ball, pulling out a copy of *France-Soir* with a preview of France's demands on the U.S. to withdraw its troops: "Is this statement accurate?"

Couve: "It is not inaccurate."

Ball, complaining that government-owned French TV refused to give him time unless he agreed to have the tape edited by the station: "But when you were in New York you had thirty uncensored minutes on *Meet the Press*."

Couve, with a thin smile: "I am not in the TV business."

On this note the interview ended.

The low in U.S.-French relations was reached in the first days of De Gaulle's visit to Moscow. On June 22, 1966, after De Gaulle had been in Moscow for only two days, Ambassador

Bohlen reported to the White House and State Department from Paris that the general in Moscow had read the United States out of the European picture and allegedly implied that close and immediate cooperation with the Soviets was desirable forthwith "in all fields." "If this was not a reversal of alliances," Bohlen added acidly, "it was at least a neutralist position," closer to the U.S.S.R. than to the United States. Even De Gaulle's approving remarks of the role the United States has played in the reconstruction of post-war Europe were bluntly dismissed with the parenthetical admonition to "note the past tense!"

Even the most anti-Gaullist officials in the State Department conceded that Bohlen "had gone too far," especially since the long "Moscow Declaration" issued at the end of the Soviet visit contained nothing to which the United States could rightfully object and, indeed, showed no signs of yielding to the Soviet positions on Germany, disarmament or anything else.

Moreover, Gebhardt von Walther, German ambassador in the Soviet capital, reported to his government, at the time Bohlen was reporting to Washington, that De Gaulle staunchly maintained the West German position on all problems discussed and that Bonn should regard the visit as a great success for the Western cause. Herr von Walther, who was singled out by De Gaulle for special briefings, was told the Russians tried to get the French leader to agree that the Bonn government was nothing but a bunch of revanchists who had to be watched. De Gaulle, who in the past had privately expressed somewhat similar sentiments, reported that he had this time indignantly denied Soviet charges and in turn described Eastern Germany as "an anomalous creation." "When you say you have talked to the East Germans," De Gaulle chided the Russians, "you really mean you have talked to yourselves."

Immediately after the Soviet visit, Bohlen and Harlan Cleveland, the U.S. ambassador to NATO, were summoned to Washington for consultations. With Ball's and Schaetzel's departure from the State Department, the entire problem of U.S. relations with France and General de Gaulle was scheduled for relentless review.

Washington's dismay with De Gaulle has been due to a

large extent to the incredibly bad manners the general has employed in dealing with his allies. Though icily polite in private talks, since the 1958 exchange with Eisenhower the general has been unyielding and uncommunicative and has treated the United States to a series of public threats, ultimatums and demands.

There is little consolation in the fact that the French president has treated his own officials, notably his ambassador in Washington, with the same disdain and that he has made a mockery of the "politesse" for which the French are allegedly famous. The general's bad manners have had the effect of obscuring the essential realities of his policies.

Had the general covered his intentions with the normal niceties of diplomatic practice, there would have been less incredulous indignation at the fact that what De Gaulle was doing was merely exercising the "tyranny of small powers," taking advantage of his unique geographic position and practicing a brand of elegant blackmail which has always been the chief ingredient of diplomacy.

The general gains additional advantages from the fact that he has been the advocate of change against a status quo power, that he has used nationalism as a means of blunting U.S. influence in Europe and that he has been taking advantage of the sterility of U.S. policy planners, who have had no new European idea since the Marshall Plan and the NATO alliance came into being some twenty years ago.

But none of this has meant that the general could, as George Ball has suggested, eliminate U.S. influence from Europe, for the simple reason that no super-power with the military and economic power of the United States can have its influence eliminated by a secondary power like France. Also, it has been conveniently forgotten that De Gaulle gave unqualified support to Kennedy during the Cuban missile crisis and has consistently sided with the United States in the series of Berlin crises. He has probably disliked this role, but he has never lost sight of the fact that his own security depends on the United States' nuclear umbrella.

Moreover, a cool analysis of De Gaulle's position, viewed

completely apart from the manner of its presentation, must disclose a certain logic to his claim that U.S. commitment to defend *any* member of the NATO alliance against Soviet aggression under *any* circumstances has doubtful validity.

De Gaulle is fond of recalling that at the height of the Cyprus crisis President Johnson's personal letter to Turkish Prime Minister Inonu, dated June 5, 1964 (see page 23f.), warned the Turks by innuendo that the United States might conceivably stand aside if, as a result of their Cyprus adventure, the Turks became victims of a Soviet aggression. There is no convincing answer to the argument that what has been done to Turkey could also be done to France, or to De Gaulle's demand for an alliance only against "unprovoked" aggression. This differs little from the administration's thinking as it surfaced at the time of the Cyprus crisis.

The administration has been marshalling legal arguments to bolster its case and at one time prepared a formidable brief showing De Gaulle's violations of legally binding treaties. The intention of the brief was to reach the conscience of the legalistic French but it misfired completely. The French could not have cared less.

The brief was to be followed by an insistence on specific performance to be underscored by a citation before the International Court of Justice. But wiser counsel prevailed and the project was abandoned. As other U.S. ventures into the legal field (such as the Article 19 crisis) have shown, no means exist to force any sizable power to adhere to agreements which it believes to be inimical to its interests. The U.S. demonstrated this to the Turks during the Cyprus affair, the Russians made the point in connection with Article 19 and De Gaulle has been bolstered by the same principle in his dealings with NATO.

The administration's bitter anti-De Gaulle policy has been eased somewhat with Undersecretary Ball's departure from the State Department. The anti-Gaullist forces have been left leaderless and President Johnson, ever the consensus seeker, has indicated readiness to try something new.

To replace Ball's pre-eminence in French affairs, Mr.

Johnson has appointed Professor Eugene Rostow, a former dean of the Yale Law School, to be Undersecretary of State for Political Affairs with prime responsibility for the conduct of our relations with the French.

On being appointed to the job, Dean Rostow told the President that he had been considered a "Gaullist" and that this may embarrass the administration. "Well," the President remarked, "the other policy failed, didn't it?"

Only President Johnson knows whether this remark meant a radical change in U.S. policy toward De Gaulle. But the French have been encouraged: their Foreign Minister, Couve de Murville, came to see the President in October, 1966, and spent an hour discussing the wedding of the President's daughter, the joys of grandfatherhood and the glories of Texas. Whatever the significance of this encounter, it was a far cry from the frosty Couve-Ball dialogue six months earlier. It has definitely improved the Washington-Paris atmosphere.

But atmospheric gestures are not enough. Imponderables of geography, tradition and self-interest—rather than treaties—govern the relations between nations. And the one imponderable of the U.S.-French relationship is that De Gaulle needs the United States for survival. The general's antics have obscured the fact that the slightest threat by the Russians in Berlin will cause him and his adherents to run for the cover of the American nuclear umbrella. American diplomats may find it more useful in the long run to seek ways of exacting a price for this cover than to wring their hands over De Gaulle's obstructionism.

In nations, as well as in individuals, there is always a great reluctance to let go of a "good thing." To the United States, NATO, as conceived in 1949, has been a "good thing." It has given the United States a firm alliance against an outbreak of conventional warfare and an advance base on the continent. It has provided integration of NATO allies without imposing any serious limits on the sovereign power of the United States. The Supreme Commander has always been an American and so has the Naval Commander in Norfolk. When the U.S. command transfers Army, Air Force or naval units to NATO,

American generals and admirals continue to command them. They simply put on NATO hats. There has been no "integration" in SAC, the ultimate arm of NATO defense against the Soviet, which continues to operate under purely American command at Omaha, Nebraska.

It is perfectly legitimate for the United States to try to maintain the status quo as long as possible. It is equally legitimate for France, or any member of the alliance, to try to obtain as much sovereignty and independence in the alliance as possible. But it is the art of diplomacy to avoid crises and head-on collisions. It has been perfectly obvious for the last decade, and certainly since De Gaulle's return to power in 1958, that NATO could not be preserved in its original form and that some form of accommodation with De Gaulle's views would have to be found. The successive Washington administrations did nothing to find such accommodation.

It is easy enough to condemn De Gaulle's nationalism as a means of weakening U.S. influence in Europe. But the United States has been trying to do exactly the same to Soviet influence in Eastern Europe. In fact, the policy of loosening Eastern Europe's dependence on the Soviets through "building bridges" has been one of the few worthwhile diplomatic initiatives of the Johnson administration. Both the United States and the Soviets had a "good thing" in their alliances. Neither can hang onto it forever. The United States could have shown wisdom and skill in practical diplomacy by meeting De Gaulle part of the way before he himself decided to go all the way.

Diplomat in Chief

The oval office of the President of the United States is an agreeable room with windows and french doors that look out on green lawns and magnolia-shaded gardens. On sunny, calm days it radiates a cheerful, unpretentious air which belies the burdens of its occupant.

But when the clouds gather and the lightning of crisis strikes, the office is transformed. It is possible to envy the President on the sunny days when he has the ease to relish his pinnacle of power. But a President confronted by serious crises in the nuclear age is a man beset by awesome uncertainties. The nation looks to him for reassurance and the huge government looks to him for direction.

A crisis is the President's show—he can seek advice in many quarters but he alone makes the decisions. He must find the wisdom to do the right thing and then summon the leadership and persuasiveness to carry the government, his people and the allies along the course he has chosen.

In the crucial hours in which a response to the crisis must be fashioned, a President instinctively turns to the people whose judgment has served him best in the past, whose opinions are likely to be most informed and whose loyalties are unquestioned. Each of the last three Presidents had his own style of working with them. Truman, with limited background in

112

foreign affairs, leaned heavily upon his subordinates. He asserted that only the President can make policy, but he responded quickly to counsel from trusted advisers like George Marshall, Dean Acheson and Robert Lovett. The historic Truman Doctrine, his 1947 commitment to support Greece and Turkey in their struggles against Communist infiltration, was formulated within the State Department by Loy Henderson, a veteran career officer, less than forty-eight hours after the British served notice that they could no longer furnish the necessary financial assistance to those troubled countries. Secretary of State George Marshall took the proposal to a Cabinet luncheon on the third day and Truman directed him to coordinate it with the other departments. On the morning of Thursday, February 27, 1947, only a few days after receiving the British note, Truman told Congressional leaders that he had decided to extend aid to Greece and Turkey.

Although he himself had played a leadership role in world affairs before he reached the White House, Eisenhower tended similarly to defer to the wisdom and experience of his Secretary of State, John Foster Dulles. "Whatever you do is O.K. with me, Foster," Eisenhower used to tell his Secretary of State.

In spite of this intimacy, however, there were many decisions which could not be made crisply between the President and Dulles because they raised issues which spilled over into other departments and stirred controversies within the government. In confronting these, Eisenhower insisted upon the careful processing which marks good practice in a military staff and which soon became the prime function of his National Security Council. This meant long coordinating sessions at lower levels of the bureaucracy and a patient effort to harmonize the divergencies, even of phraseology, in a projected policy paper. If the differences persisted, they were laid before the President at the NSC table with painstaking clarity. The differing views were spelled out in tidy papers from which Eisenhower guided the meeting, and they were argued out under prodding by his special assistant for National Security Affairs. All the men who held this post under Eisenhower—

Robert Cutler, Dillon Anderson, William Jackson and Gordon Gray—clung to a rigid neutrality on every issue in order to work impartially at insuring that the President was exposed to all sides of the question before he came to his decision.

Informality in handling national security affairs was the keynote of the Kennedy administration. Presidential Assistant McGeorge Bundy signalled the new approach on his first day of work. He asked Bromley Smith, an astute specialist in security affairs, whose White House career had bracketed most of the life of the NSC, to recommend how a certain problem should be handled. Smith was stopped short by the question —the cardinal tenet of the NSC staff under Eisenhower had been to swallow one's personal opinions. The theory was that any advocacy by a member of the President's personal staff would inhibit the readiness of departmental officials to speak their minds. But in the charged, informal atmosphere of the New Frontier, the readiness to speak one's mind became a virtual test of manliness.

John Kennedy brought a personal interest to his foreign policy responsibilities and a natural feel for diplomacy. Intellectual curiosity also was one of Kennedy's strongest attributes, and he had almost perfected his talent for eliciting information. He preferred to talk to the people most deeply versed in the subject on his mind, and this led him to call meetings and make telephone calls without respecting bureaucratic custom.

Often these sessions would begin as an innocent quest for information. "I merely want to be filled in on the situation," the President would say to the specialist, who might be only a desk officer at the State Department. Later, as their conversation wound into the details of the matter, the President would interject, "Now I think we should do this—" and at that point he was making policy, an exercise usually performed in the presence of the Secretary of State. The drawback in this short circuit was that it exposed the bureaucrat to the possible resentment of his superiors and created a danger that the President would not secure a full reflection of official thought. The advantage was that it stimulated the bureaucracy and ex-

pedited the transaction of business. The President was enabled
to play an early hand in the formulation of policy proposals
and to accumulate insights which could serve him well in the
later stages of a crisis, when the big decisions had to be made.

Kennedy had been stimulated before he entered the
White House by Woodrow Wilson's observation that "the President is at liberty, both in law and conscience, to be as big a
man as he can—his office is anything he has the sagacity and
force to make it—his capacity will set the limit." The young
President's first day in office appeared to be his happiest—he
radiated then his sense of the opportunities that lay within
reach, seemingly limitless opportunities to exert his capacities
in every direction, to achieve noble innovations and reforms
and, above all, to take meaningful steps toward world order.
Experience inevitably taught him that his opportunities were
bounded by the strict limitations of political circumstance.
Reforms and innovations proved difficult to wring from a
balky Congress. Khrushchev, it turned out, was more interested in testing him than in treating with him. The pressures of
crisis—foreign, domestic and administrative—bore in on him
so relentlessly that the presidency seemed at times like a sustained exercise in firefighting—with scant time to rest and
recoup between fires. "No man should really want to take more
than eight years of this," he once observed in discussing the
two-term limit upon presidential tenure.

Lyndon Johnson came to the White House conditioned to
crisis, like a seasoned fire-horse. A legislative leader is selected
by his colleagues to preside over a constant succession of
crises—legislative leadership is the art of exerting foresight and
persuasion to ward off eruptions of partisan folly. The direction and philosophy of a political course are far less important
to such a leader than the task of managing dissent so that the
majority will move in the chosen direction at maximum speed.
The telephone and the lapel are the instruments of this
leadership—the lapel is tugged and the telephone is worked;
the wayward fall in line; another crisis of dissent is averted.
Leadership in the legislative arena is not a creative role or a
reflective one. It is rather an action role requiring shrewdness

and resourcefulness, an instinct to respond promptly and an indefatigable doggedness. This strenuous environment gave Lyndon Johnson his heart attack in 1955, but it also gave him excellent training for crisis management under White House pressures.

Johnson's first foreign affairs experience as President was to receive the leaders who came to the Kennedy funeral. He sensed the grief and anger felt around the world at Kennedy's loss and the uncertainty of foreign capitals in regard to the intentions of his successor. He assured the visitors that he intended to continue Kennedy's policies and especially his efforts to improve East-West relations. He told Mikoyan he wanted to keep up the private correspondence that Kennedy had initiated with Nikita Khrushchev and later asked McGeorge Bundy to prepare some suggestions for his first letter to the Soviet Premier.

But these letters proved to be less of a symbol of Johnson's foreign policy interests than the two news ticker machines which he soon installed in his office. The correspondence with the Russians lapsed in 1964. It was Johnson's turn to reply to one of Khrushchev's letters when Brezhnev and Kosygin took over in Moscow. Johnson later explained to the Russians that he did not know which of the two leaders to address and decided to do nothing until he discovered which one was in charge of foreign affairs.

But the teletype machines, their staccato noise somewhat cushioned by soundproof cabinets, rumbled on month after month, year after year, less than fifteen feet from the President's desk. Eisenhower had often admonished his aides that they had been derelict in their duties when one of the government's problems reached the news tickers; he told his aides over and over that he expected them to solve these problems before the tickers made them public.

If knowledge is power, up-to-the-minute knowledge yields special power to a crisis operator like Lyndon Johnson. The ticker machines give him a sense of immediate touch with events developing outside his door. The noise does not distract him as it would most men—the President likes to hear some kind of background cacophony, especially taped music, when he is alone. To the contrary, the persisting metallic rumble is a hum of reassurance that the planet is still in orbit, a calming force to a restless spirit, and a guarantee against conspiracies at lower echelons to keep him from a full knowledge of events.

Indeed, Johnson uses the ticker as a running check on his subordinates. Key officials, none of them working with the President's physical proximity to the tickers, became slowly accustomed to sudden phone calls that began with the question: "Have you seen UPI item number 89?" Once, during the crisis in the Dominican Republic, the UPI reported that 12,000 rebels were poised to overwhelm the first contingent of American troops then being landed by helicopter on the island. Tearing the item from his ticker, Johnson placed an urgent call to McNamara, who happened to be testifying before a Congressional committee. McNamara had not heard of this menacing rebel force but he called General Earle Wheeler, chairman of the Joint Chiefs of Staff. One of Wheeler's subordinates, a colonel, was directed to call General Bruce Palmer, the commander on the scene, to learn what the report was all about. Not aware that the President had initiated the inquiry, the colonel balked, saying it was ridiculous to clutter up the communications channel with such garbage. By the time the query reached Palmer, the President had already telephoned him directly and been advised that the report was totally untrue.

Johnson's strenuous response to disturbing news bulletins added to the burdens in Saigon during low moments in the struggle against the Viet Cong. When reports of a misjudgment on the part of Americans there—a civilian slain or a friendly village bombed by mistake—emerged on the wires in Washington, the President would habitually bombard his officials in the field with cables of criticism and fresh instructions. Sometimes, as one of the top Americans in Vietnam put it, Saigon was discomposed more by the President's cables than by the enemies' blows. As the war dragged on, Johnson became less and less prone to these personal interventions. They were largely a reflection of the legislative leader's instinct to apply his hand to the trouble spot.

Although he admitted to Eisenhower he was unfamiliar

with foreign affairs, Johnson chafed during his first year in office at the repeated press comment that he was closely attuned to domestic concerns and relished his tug-of-war with Congress but had little appetite for the more subtle problems of foreign policy. He argued in protest, "People have been coming to me for thirty years to ask for post office jobs, flood control projects and places on committees, and I can't say that I still get a great thrill out of dealing with these requests. It's part of my job and I'm going to keep doing it but the press is wrong to say that I find it more interesting than dealing with Mike Pearson or Ayub or all the other problems that mean life or death for the country."

Much later, one perceptive aide was to say that Johnson liked to let foreign affairs wash over him like a wave. But during his first year in the White House, his pragmatic sense of priorities dictated a rigid concentration upon domestic politics. All that really mattered was to get elected in his own name and he pushed aside the postponable duties and issues that did not relate directly to the November election. This was a reasonable precaution on Johnson's part—he could not be sure until July that he would have the good fortune to be opposed by Senator Barry Goldwater and he could not know until November that his grizzled Western personality would prove palatable to the voters.

This was good politics but poor diplomacy. One incident which characterized the President's preoccupation involved the Prime Minister of Iceland, Bjarni Benediktsson, who flew to Washington four weeks before the election to see the President. He earnestly wanted to discuss one or two problems. The prime minister was escorted into the oval office, where Johnson greeted him warmly and suggested that aides bring in the press so they could have their picture taken. The reporters came in with the photographers and Johnson proposed that they all take a constitutional walk around the White House drive. With the visitor from Iceland at his side, Johnson led the way around and around the drive, sparring with the press all the way about the progress of the election campaign. Finally he signalled a halt and suggested to the prime minister that they return to his office. Miss May Craig, who had achieved almost institutional stature as correspondent for the *Portland* (Maine) *Press Herald,* suddenly announced that she had obtained some fresh political-opinion samplings from Maine. "Come with us, Miss May," said Johnson, and they talked for the next fifteen minutes in his office of nothing but Maine politics. Then he suddenly turned to his visitor from Iceland and said, "Mr. Prime Minister, it's been very good to see you and I'll look forward to seeing you soon again." A stunned look spread across the Icelander's face and his State Department escort, Assistant Secretary of State William Tyler, moved quickly to ease the situation by saying, "Mr. Prime Minister, you have just had a wonderful opportunity to see the dynamics of the American political system in action." Johnson beamed delightedly in agreement and the meeting was over.

Similarly, Prince Bernhard of the Netherlands, normally a relaxed and amiable visitor, was miffed when, instead of the scheduled private talk with the President, he found himself being photographed with a dozen or so bystanders selected at random by the President with the invitation: "Come on, have your picture taken with a *real* prince." And the prime minister of Trinidad was not amused at all when, after waiting for more than an hour past his appointment time, he was greeted with a hearty handshake and a "howdy, *Mr. Ambassador*" but not asked to sit down.

Because Mr. Johnson felt uncomfortable with foreigners, the State Department tried to reduce these visits to a minimum. However, some visitors simply have to be accommodated and in such cases the department insisted they refrain from business discussions and limit their calls to strictly courtesy exchanges.

One such visitor was Spanish Foreign Minister Fernando Maria Castiella, who stopped over in Washington in the spring of 1965. Faithful to the State Department's injunction, the Spaniard struggled manfully through a strictly nonbusiness monologue. He told the President about his mother's Texas relatives and about a Spanish invitation for Lynda Bird Johnson to visit the Feria at Seville.

Much to Señor Castiella's surprise, the President suddenly interrupted the social chit-chat and demanded to know why Spain continued to trade with Cuba. To Castiella's further discomfiture, Mr. Johnson ordered his assistant, McGeorge Bundy, to tell the visitor what the administration thought of such trade at a time when the United States imposed sanctions on dealings with the Castro regime.

The presidential assistant minced no words in castigating the Spaniards for signing a trade agreement with Cuba. Castiella entered a spirited defense and found himself arguing with the presidential assistant instead of the President himself, a change which, to the protocol-conscience Spaniards, "lowered the level" of the discussion, as well as the status of the foreign minister.

To top off the exchange in a lighter vein, the President offered the comment that "Old Pat McCarran would turn in his grave if he knew what you were doing." * The Spanish ambassador, who had been interpreting, thought it wiser to leave this remark untranslated, but the foreign minister understood enough of it to leave the White House sizzling.

McGeorge Bundy dutifully informed the State Department of the incident, and explained that a few minutes before the Spaniard's arrival he was told by the President to "give Spain the works" for trading with Cuba.

Departmental officials, who proceeded to soothe Spain's bruised feelings, admitted that Bundy could do no more than follow presidential instructions but they felt he would have served the cause of orderly foreign policy better had he attempted to persuade the President that a "courtesy visit" should not have been turned into a slugging session.

This period was equally difficult for foreign ambassadors permanently assigned to Washington. Kennedy had had a rough encounter with German Ambassador Wilhelm Grewe, who virtually accused the President of bad faith over the re-

---

* The late Senator McCarran was a staunch admirer of General Franco and once tacked a rider on the Appropriation Bill which would have effectively stopped the functioning of the U.S. government until the Truman administration withdrew its opposition to a Spanish loan.

turn of German assets confiscated during World War II. But by and large, the late President made a great effort to maintain good relations in diplomacy. He was invariably polite and interested in his dealings with both friend and foe.

The late Polish Ambassador, Edward Drozniak, recalled that when he arrived to present his credentials to President Kennedy, two minutes past the appointed hour, Mrs. Evelyn Lincoln, his secretary, came out and apologized that the President might be late. She came back again a couple of minutes later with another apology. Immediately afterwards the President came out, and, as they walked through the outer office, he introduced a girl of Polish origin, saying: "I have another Polish ambassador right here in my office."

Kennedy wanted to know [the ambassador recalled later] why I, an economist, changed my profession to that of diplomatist. I replied that a few years ago I was offered the embassy in either London or Washington but turned it down. However, the appeal of the new administration was so profound that I could not resist the latest offer. The President looked at me and said: "I see you have learned your new profession pretty well."

He told me he was most anxious to help my country because he had tremendous sympathy for Poland and her people, and also he was the godfather of a Polish nephew.

He urged me to get in touch with Walt Rostow if I had any problems, and I have every evidence that whatever was said to Mr. Rostow promptly reached the President. When I saw the President several weeks later, he came right to me and said: "I haven't heard from you for a long time. Have you no troubles?" I said life would be dull without problems but that since Mr. Rostow left the White House I had lost my liaison.

The next morning at 9:00 o'clock, the telephone rang at my private house. It was presidential assistant Ralph Dungan who, on instructions from the President, wanted me to know he was entirely at my service if and when I required it.

By contrast, under Johnson, foreign ambassadors initially found themselves ignored by the White House and handled in a highly informal fashion on unavoidable occasions like their presentation of credentials. Diplomatic custom, including the rules for the reception and treatment of ambassadors, has continued almost unchanged since the so-called *Règlement de Vienne* was adopted by the Congress of Vienna in 1815. An Act of March 1, 1893, incorporated the Vienna regulation into the law of the United States.

Broadly speaking, the *Règlement de Vienne,* expanded over the years by subsequent agreements, established strict rules of precedence and treatment of ambassadors by the government to which they are accredited. The rules, which, by tradition, include the right of each new ambassador to have a private talk with the Chief of State, are followed by conservative and Communist governments alike. The protocol governing the reception of ambassadors to the Vatican covers six printed pages. But, equally, the Soviet Union observes elaborate formalities in accrediting ambassadors.

This is not a practical tradition, particularly in an era when there are 111 embassies in Washington. Custom has it that in the course of the new ambassador's first meeting with the Chief of State, no business is discussed. This is an anachronistic injunction in today's busy world, and Eisenhower found that new ambassadors would sometimes launch into controversial matters and refuse to be interrupted. His protocol chief, Wiley Buchanan, recalls one occasion on which an ambassador kept pressing a point after the President had twice suggested that the matter be taken up with the State Department—"I practically had to drag him away, still babbling," Buchanan relates, "while over my shoulder I could see the President shaking his head with a look of patient resignation." *

This kind of thing was not for Johnson. He kept the ambassadors of several major powers waiting for weeks before he would give them an opportunity to present their credentials. Since they could not consider themselves in residence in their new post until this formality was completed, they were obliged to decline speaking and dinner invitations and to exist in a sort of purdah until the White House gates opened for them. When that day came, they were brought to the White House

* *Red Carpet at the White House* by Wiley T. Buchanan and Arthur Gordon, E. P. Dutton & Co., 1964.

in a group, herded before the press photographers and hastily sent back to their embassies.

It took a great deal of effort on the part of Secretary Rusk and Angier Biddle Duke, then the Protocol Chief, to persuade the President to see the ambassadors at all. "Who are these birds?" he would fume. "Have Rusk see them; they are his clients, not mine." At first, the President would not receive them even if they carried messages from the chiefs of their governments. Rusk's job was to pick up the pieces and smooth the ruffled diplomatic feathers. Ambassadors who insisted they must hand their messages to the President had to be told in Rusk's best diplomatic manner that "you must either deliver the message to me or not have it delivered at all." Ambassadors for whom White House appointments were reluctantly made sometimes were kept waiting for an hour or so in the reception room. One African ambassador refused to wait any longer and left the White House muttering under his breath, "I see I am not wanted."

American ambassadors returning from their posts abroad fared no better than their foreign colleagues. Mr. Johnson had been receiving them in groups. On one such occasion, the President suddenly turned to Ambassador John M. Cabot and asked for his views on the administration's policies in Vietnam. Cabot mumbled he had been in Poland for the last three years and had not followed Vietnam too closely. Mr. Johnson then treated the ambassador to a spirited presentation on Vietnam. It may have been a coincidence but shortly thereafter Cabot was recalled from Poland and replaced by the then Postmaster General, John Gronouski.

Accumulating resentments at the Johnson treatment almost precipitated an ambassadorial revolt. The grumbling mounted to a level at which it began to depress American influence abroad. The coldness to the ambassadors became part of the Johnson administration's international image, which had assumed an aspect of insensitivity in foreign dealings. Mr. Johnson is known as a stubborn man, but his stubbornness does not extend to the rejection of criticism which he senses to be valid. In 1965, with the election behind him, he decided to revise his behavior. "I am going to meet with all the ambassadors," he told a visitor, "maybe take them down to the ranch, or go for a boat ride. I think that's more than any other President has done."

He went at this reform with characteristic thoroughness. By the end of 1965 he was able to boast that he had had 357 private conversations with ambassadors, more than four times the number he permitted in 1964. All the ambassadors were invited to go boating with the President on one of a series of dinner cruises down the Potomac. Some of them acquired as many as five photographs taken on these occasions and personally inscribed with warm phrases by Johnson. Above all, the dignity of the accreditation ceremony was restored. White-gloved troops now lined the driveway and presented arms when each new ambassador drove up. The credentials were exchanged in the oval reception room on the second floor of the White House and the President and the new ambassador were secluded for a "private talk" in the adjoining Treaty Room.

The President warmed to his task of dealing with these diplomats and in March, 1966, when James Symington replaced Lloyd Hand as the Protocol Chief, Johnson told him, "These ambassadors are our constituency. We have to work closely with them and give them a feeling of access to the President."

Perhaps the most significant innovation was the custom of small White House lunches hosted by a member of the staff—Jack Valenti until he returned to private life—and designed to give the diplomats a chance to meet the President and get their problems off their chests.

The State Department, normally the sole agency to deal with ambassadors of foreign powers, was seldom consulted on the guest lists or on the subjects to be discussed, although department officials have occasionally been invited. State Department officials requesting memoranda of these conversations were usually told they were "lost." However, Mrs. Lois Williams, a veteran protocol officer, since retired, has been invariably consulted on what foods should be served, so that Indians can be kept away from scale fish and Israelis from ham, and Catholics need not eat meat on Fridays. Apart from that, Valenti or the other members of the White House staff have been the sole arbiters of the guest list and of the subjects discussed during the meal.

The high point of each of these lunches was the appearance, at cocktail or dessert time, of Johnson, who would discourse in his informal, effective style on his view of the world. These occasions supplied the ambassadors with something that improved their peace of mind, an opportunity to impress their home governments with the recital of a close encounter with the President. Diplomats like German Ambassador Herr Heinrich Knappstein, whom Johnson once handed a leash holding the late beagle "Him," have been particularly warmed by Johnson's informality. Others have raised their eyebrows at "Texas-style diplomacy."

One element of this style has been occasional bluntness. Presenting their credentials on April 13, 1965, the new British, Chilean and Danish ambassadors were exposed to a storm of wrath at their governments' indifference to the American role in Vietnam. "I just don't know what's wrong," Johnson exploded in a voice that carried outside his office. "Here are innocent American civilians killed by Viet Cong bombs and you complain that we bomb bridges in the north. Bridges don't bleed. Americans do."

The Johnson temper has interfered occasionally with his diplomacy. Once when a group of ambassadors who had been invited to lunch were slightly late, he began shouting at his aides that he wasn't going to be kept waiting by these foreigners and that the staff had better produce them immediately. Unfortunately, the ambassadors were waiting on the other side of the door and heard the President's words.

These flare-ups spring from Johnson's complicated chemistry and they erupt and subside like geysers. One day in his first year in office, he lashed out bitterly at everyone around him. The victims of his spleen were startled to see Bill Moyers suddenly take the President of the United States by the arm and lead him out of the room with these words: "We've had enough of this. You're wasting all of our time." Later when someone asked Moyers how he had the nerve to do this, he replied, "It's easy—I'd rather be in the Peace Corps." When the storm passes, Johnson is invariably penitent and conveys his remorse in the indirect fashion of a proud man. He gave one official whom he had upbraided remorselessly an expensive cowboy suit when they met again.

These outbursts have had occasional diplomatic consequences. Relations between Washington and Ottawa became frosty when Prime Minister Mike Pearson questioned the President's bombing of North Vietnam in a speech in Philadelphia on April 2, 1965. Johnson was indignant and let his reaction be known. The chill persisted in the President's mind and several months later he needled the ambassador from Canada, Charles Ritchie, by saying, "Don't let your man come down here again to make speeches." White House aides, looking for a turn in the President's mood, began keeping a "Mike Pearson massage file" to hold friendly communications which had been sent to Ottawa over the President's name without being seen by him.

Johnson's determination to avert similar criticisms from visiting heads of state led him to the abrupt cancellation of the planned visits to Washington by President Ayub of Pakistan and the late Indian Prime Minister Shastri. The brusqueness of his gesture was damaging to his stature as a statesman. Ayub had already mailed out invitations to a dinner that was to be held at his embassy in Washington for Johnson. The State Department particularly resisted the affront to Shastri; U.S. planners had recently approved a policy paper which stressed the political vulnerability of the post-Nehru leadership in India and urged that the United States take every reasonable step to enhance Shastri's prestige and self-assurance. His state visit had been regarded as a means of demonstrating the respect in which the diminutive Indian politician was held by Johnson.

The White House rebuff was expanded into a cancellation of the consortium negotiations for new aid grants to Pakistan. This stern treatment stirred frustrations in Pakistan which played a large part in prompting the attack on Kashmir in August. After this short but frightening war ended in a way which settled little, the Soviet Union was enabled to heighten its prestige in the subcontinent by arranging truce negotiations at Tashkent. Johnson, out of favor in Karachi as well as in New Delhi, had no option except to support Premier Kosygin's peacemaking initiative.

The fortunate and significant irony is that Johnson's display of indignation toward these two impoverished nations created a fluid climate in which it was ultimately possible to work out sounder diplomatic ties than had existed before. The Indians and the Pakistanis met Johnson's complaint that they had begun to take this country's enormous donations of aid for granted. Ayub and Shastri's successor, Mrs. Indira Gandhi, came to Washington in the following December and January and were warmly, almost effusively, welcomed by the President. He gave them no cowboy suits but he promised to resume aid and support their expansion plans. Ayub later demonstrated that he had learned his lesson by discharging the foreign minister, Z. A. Bhutto, who had agitated his government's differences with Washington. Mrs. Gandhi, risking charges at home that she had capitulated to Washington, commenced a policy of responsiveness to the economic guidance of the World Bank, whose experts had long felt that Indian development was being badly hampered by the bureaucrats' commitment to Fabian socialism. Johnson had run grave risks in offending the pride of these sensitive young nations, but he could point after eighteen months to some benefits which had flowed from his rough gambit.

Britain's Prime Minister, Harold Wilson, also tasted Johnson's anger. Troubled in the winter of 1964 by opposition in the left wing of his party to American policy in Vietnam, Wilson announced in the House of Commons that he was leaving for Washington to consult with President Johnson. He telephoned the British ambassador in Washington, Lord Harlech, to secure an appointment at the White House. Harlech was turned down by McGeorge Bundy but Wilson declined to take "no" for an answer. At his request, a three-way telephone circuit was set up to tie in Johnson, Wilson and Harlech. The President blasted the prime minister in no uncertain terms. "I won't have you electioneering on my doorstep," he stormed. "Every time you get in trouble in Parliament you run over here with your shirt-tail hanging out. I'm not going to allow it this time."

Wilson was left to face the embarrassment of announcing that he would not go to Washington after all, but ultimately he also derived more than a cowboy suit from his dealings with Johnson. The administration backed the Wilson government closely through all of its hairline maneuvers to protect the pound but not until the prime minister had paid lip service to the American effort in Vietnam. Mr. Johnson belatedly realized that he could ill afford to alienate the leader of an important NATO ally and the only socialist government expressing any kind of support for U. S. policy in Vietnam. Wilson and Johnson, it was later reported by White House sources, became so intimate via the direct telephone link between their offices that the President's intimate, William S. White, wrote in a column that no warmer trans-Atlantic relationship had existed since the Roosevelt-Churchill era. Privately, the British have chuckled over this assessment.

Subtlety is not the essence of Johnson's nature, but he is fully capable of dealing much less brusquely than he did with Pearson, Ayub, Shastri and Wilson. He is almost more fearsome to foreign statesmen when he employs the honeyed words of a Texas horse-trader.

In the spring of 1964, the newly established Malaysian Federation found itself in the throes of a guerrilla war waged by Indonesian forces which had infiltrated into the Malaysian states of Sarawak and Sabah. On April 23, 1964, the Malaysian government issued a White Paper charging Indonesia with plotting the assassination of Tunku Abdul Rahman, the prime minister, and other high-ranking Malaysian officials. Shortly thereafter, the British, responsible for the defense of Malaysia, but chronically short of troops and funds, asked the United States for help. The U. S. had already lent its diplomatic support to the Malaysian cause. On May 5, William P. Bundy, Assistant Secretary for Far Eastern Affairs, declared that unless Indonesia abandoned its North Borneo campaign, it would be judged guilty of aggression and its flow of aid from the United States would be cancelled. In that same month, British Ambassador Lord Harlech secured an appointment with the President to ask that additional units of the Seventh Fleet be assigned to show the flag in the Indian Ocean and demonstrate U.S. military backing for the Malaysian and British cause. The President, advised by State to turn down the British request, told Harlech that he had always hated Sukarno. "He is an SOB," Mr. Johnson explained. "If I had to choose between the British and Sukarno, of course I would choose the British. I love Sir Winston Churchill," the President continued with genuine tears glistening in his eyes, "but right now I cannot do much to help you."

Similar treatment was accorded West German Chancellor Ludwig Erhard. When he first arrived at the LBJ ranch on December 28, 1963, Erhard was overwhelmed with presidential hospitality. To this day, the Germans describe that particular reception as *fantastisch*. But by June, 1964, when Erhard came again, the barbecues and the ten-gallon hats were forgotten. Instead, LBJ had managed to wring from a reluctant chancellor a secret commitment to ship U.S.-made tanks and submarines to Israel. The agreement specified that some $80 million worth of equipment would be delivered to Israel over a period of sixteen months, beginning in October, 1964. The rationale behind this pressure was the administration's belief that Soviet arms shipments to the United Arab Republic had upset the delicate military balance between Israel and the Arab states. Inevitably, the story broke. In March, 1965, the Arab states threatened to break relations with the Federal Republic if West Germany continued the arms deliveries, and they soon made good on their threat.

This reaction caused Chancellor Erhard to have second thoughts. He was determined to reopen the question and seek a better deal for Germany on his 1965 trip to Washington. But the President was ready for him—as soon as the chancellor raised the matter, Johnson stopped him. "You and I are good friends," Johnson said softly, squeezing the chancellor's arm. "I have been praying for you every day. My heart is with you and I trust you will succeed in whatever you do." The chancellor knew he was beaten.

The volatile nature of the President's temperament gives

cause for some fears that he is capable of responding angrily
with military muscle to a provocation from abroad. He controls great power and if he were to succumb to one of his brief
but encompassing rages at a tense point in an international crisis, he possesses the capacity to unleash forces which could not
be recaptured by subsequent remorse. Responsible men who
have worked alongside Johnson over the long pull and have
themselves felt the sting of his anger argue strongly that this is
not a danger to be taken seriously. They maintain that the
President's anger is invariably touched off by small frustrations—a badly prepared paper or a tardy visitor—and they insist that Johnson is rigidly disciplined when he sits in the eye
of a crisis. At these moments, they maintain, he becomes a
steely, deliberate figure beyond the reach of provocation and
beyond being diverted by happenstance from closely calculated objectives.

Support for this thesis can be derived from a study of
Johnson's experiences in the vice-presidency. This was a painful period in which he was deeply frustrated by the impotence
of his position and by the disposition of some in the Kennedy
camp to treat him with disdain. His last foreign travel as Vice-
President was a trip to Scandinavia in September, 1963. His
morale was low and he wanted the boost that an informal
send-off by President Kennedy would afford his mission. He
asked Kenneth O'Donnell, the tight-lipped appointments secretary, if his plane could stop by Hyannisport so that he might
meet briefly with Kennedy before he flew across the Atlantic.
O'Donnell brushed him off without even consulting the President. Kennedy's military aide, Major General Chester Clifton,
interceded to arrange the appointment because he perceived
that Johnson had been stung and knew that Kennedy would
react sympathetically. The Vice-President talked with the President for half an hour in the latter's summer cottage at Cape
Cod. He sat, as one witness to this meeting recalls, almost
like a schoolboy as Kennedy read over the speeches he was
taking with him and suggested some changes. Clifton escorted
the Vice-President to the helicopter waiting a hundred yards
away to carry him back to his airplane at Otis Air Force Base.

Over the roar of the engine, Johnson shouted, "You tell the President he did a very gracious thing today. I won't forget it and I'm going to do my damndest for him in Europe."

This was not an easy role for a proud, critical, egocentric man—the important point is that he swallowed his pride and played the role without any recorded whimper, public or private, for thirty-four months. No complaint, no whisper against Kennedy or even his aides, no criticism of the administration's mistakes, no hint of even a momentary defection on Johnson's part was ever reported, as far as is known, to Kennedy. Johnson's intimates relate that while he was unhappy much of this time, even they never heard him give vent to his grievances. Through it all, he clung tightly to his self-imposed rule that he would never offer advice unless it was sought from him. All in all, this was a remarkable exercise in personal discipline.

Johnson's performance under crisis conditions lends credence to the claim that these pressures have the effect of causing him to become more cautious and deliberate. He has not shot from the hip at any crucial point. When the Panamanians rioted outside the Canal Zone and severed diplomatic relations after Johnson had been in the White House for fifty days, he personally telephoned President Roberto Chiari to arrange for immediate negotiations. The haste in dispatching troops to Santo Domingo on April 28, 1965, was precipitated by the advice of Ambassador W. Tapley Bennett, Jr. that American lives were in danger and that all the key officials in the embassy agreed that the time had come to land troops. Johnson's haste was also encouraged by mistaken advice from his Special Assistant on Latin Affairs, Thomas Mann, that the rebels would stop fighting as soon as the first contingent of American soldiers appeared on the scene. Johnson has been justly criticized for his failure to consult with the OAS ambassadors before he acted and for ascribing a Communist menace to the situation that exaggerated his solid evidence, but the timing and necessity of his intervention have been increasingly difficult for his critics to dispute, particularly after the beleaguered nation moved toward the re-establishment of democratic government. Some of the sharpest critics of the intervention were ready to concede fourteen months later that Johnson had done the only thing he could do.

In his Vietnam decisions, Johnson consistently lagged behind the aggressive mood of his associates in the bureaucracy. His military response to the naval attacks in Tonkin Bay flowed from a previously adopted policy to impose tit-for-tat reprisals for aggressions against American personnel. As we have seen earlier, he moved slowly into all the phases of escalation, so slowly that some experts complained that the impact of the moves was diminished by the delay in carrying them out. He held off the bombing of the oil refineries near Haiphong and Hanoi for more than a year after the military commanders had proposed them.

Impetuosity has proved to be much less of a weakness in Lyndon Johnson's conduct of foreign affairs than other personal traits. His preoccupations as a crisis manager have inclined his leadership to stifle the development of new policies and new thinking in regard to non-crisis areas. The bureaucracy's interests inevitably reflect the President's. When he picks up an issue, the bureaucrats pick it up, and when he lets it go, they do the same. The stimulation which arose within the government in Kennedy's time withered under Johnson. The brilliant young men most apt to come up with good ideas sensed that this was a time to lie low. Many left the government or sought transfer out of Washington. Johnson had convinced them that he was an operating man who did not want intellectual ferment and who would not reward them for pushing their thoughts forward.

This was an imprecise reading because Johnson sensed his problem in himself and was straining, in an executive way, to encourage new ideas. He had barely emerged from the ether after his operation in October, 1965, when he began to berate two staff members in his hospital room. "I never get any ideas from my staff or from the departments," he complained. "When I was secretary to Congressman Kleberg I kept the office open around the clock and gave him at least fifty memoranda with new ideas every day. Why can't I get any new ideas now?"

Johnson's selection of Walt Rostow, undoubtedly the most fertile and irrepressible innovator in the government, to succeed Bundy as his National Security Council assistant reflected this frustration. He gave full rein to Rostow, expounding one of his new ideas to a foreign visitor before the State Department had even heard of it. Johnson wanted desperately to bring the intellectual side of his foreign policy operation to life.

This craving for new ideas without too much thought of implementing the old ones has produced bafflement and skepticism among foreign diplomats at home and abroad. Within a few weeks of Rostow's appearance at the White House as the chief assistant for National Security Affairs, the President launched half a dozen new initiatives in the foreign field. Expanding trade "bridges" with Eastern Europe, a new deal for Africa and a new policy for Asia followed each other in rapid succession. But when foreign governments started making anxious inquiries as to details, they could get none.

The Rumanian diplomats kept referring to the President's speeches and reminding the State Department that out of some hundred items on a trade list submitted some two years ago, not one transaction has yet been consummated. The Africans, who were treated to an elegant East Room reception for the President's announcement of a new aid policy for their continent, were at a loss to discover details. Ambassador Edward Korry, who headed the African task force, had submitted a voluminous report calling for *more* foreign aid, to be distributed through the World Bank, at a time when Congress was dead set against *any* foreign aid.

The "new ideas" followed such Johnsonian initiatives as the peace offensive in the winter of 1966 which sent Vice-President Humphrey and Ambassadors Harriman and Goldberg to the four corners of the earth with U.S. "peace proposals," which were nothing but the fourteen points announced publicly by Secretary Rusk several months before.

"What does Mr. Johnson take us for?" one ambassador complained. "To be named ambassador to Washington you have to be a pretty sophisticated fellow," he continued, "and Mr. Johnson treats us like morons."

To the foreign diplomats, at least, Mr. Johnson's "initiatives" were mere attention-getters, unworthy of serious consideration by the governments concerned. The Russians particularly resented what they considered "being used" by Mr. Johnson for propaganda purposes. When in June, 1966, the President wanted to send Averell Harriman to Moscow for a general review of the situation, the Russians refused a visa, although up to that time the ex-governor of New York and lend-lease expediter of World War II fame had always been a most welcome visitor.

Part of Mr. Johnson's problem lay in his methods of doing business and in the mistrustfulness that is part of his nature. Johnson is happiest when his key advisers come to him with a unanimous recommendation. He then pounds them with questions which obscure his own view of the proposal but probe at the weak points. When McNamara, Rusk, Bundy and Moyers were urging a halt to the bombing of North Vietnam in early December, 1965, they met with Johnson at his ranch. He asked 176 questions by one count, and when the long meeting was over Bundy said to Moyers, "I'll bet you five dollars that he'll never go for it." No one could be certain that he would agree to the pause until three more weeks had passed.

Johnson takes ideas submitted by his staff and works them over privately with friends like Abe Fortas or Clark Clifford. A former Johnson aide maintains that Fortas accepted the appointment to the Supreme Court chiefly to escape Johnson's constant calls for advice. He is anxious to keep the hot breath of his aides off his back while he is mulling an important decision and he pulls back from candid exchanges within the government. This instinct, combined with his hatred of leaks, leads him to avoid large meetings at crucial junctures—in the 1965–1966 phase of the Vietnamese war over one year elapsed between meetings of the National Security Council. The President's transformation of the decision-making process into highly personal, informal and frequently secretive procedures has in practice narrowed the circle of men whose opinions have an impact on decisions and downgraded the role of presidential adviser. Creative minds thrive best in an atmosphere in which they are privileged to participate in a free-and-easy interchange of thoughts. He urges his subordinates, "Don't be afraid to push your ideas," but his strong, brooding personality has created a climate in which reticence has become the rule. "No one ever laughs in the White House," an ex-aide commented.

After it grew apparent in late 1964 that Johnson would have to turn his hand to foreign policy, his aides became anxious to insure that he met regularly with Secretaries Rusk, McNamara and the White House advisers for National Security Affairs. They conceived the famous "Tuesday lunches" as a focal point for these deliberations and labored to establish the regularity of these meetings and their acceptance by the President. Word was quietly passed to the press that great decisions flowed from these gatherings, and the interest of the press served to crystalize the interest of the President. Actually, the lunches developed slowly as a forum for serious palaver. Johnson at first used to bring Mrs. Johnson and an occasional outside visitor to the meetings. The President tended to focus his attention on whatever had been in the headlines that day. Newspaper stories trigger his interest in foreign issues far more than government reports. When unpublicized problems like Yemen or the Congo were mentioned, the President tended to pass quickly over them, sometimes with a yawn. He often interlarded the discussion with Texas folklore, reminiscences from his Senate days and recent public-opinion polls.

The only subject on which Johnson's interest has never flickered is Vietnam. A jest circulated in the State Department that the Tuesday lunches began with a prayer and concluded with the selection of bombing targets in North Vietnam. A typical agenda was the one for September 28, 1965. The Vietnam items were: (1) Force levels and whether new authority was needed to supply them, and (2) the possibility of meeting Hanoi representatives at a Red Cross meeting in Vienna, scheduled for the following week (the Hanoi representatives never showed up). The issues outside Vietnam were: (1) Which chiefs of state or foreign ministers arriving for the UN General Assembly should be received or visited by the President, and (2) the forthcoming Pope's visit to New York. The final item on that particular agenda was Fidel Castro's speech, which had opened the way to Operation Exodus—a vast program of repatriation for Cuban refugees.

The most serious drawback to the Tuesday lunches is the absence of any machinery to record the discussions and, more important, the decisions taken at the meetings. One aide suggested that a tape recorder be placed at the luncheon table, but the President violently objected. Another suggestion was to have Rusk dictate his account of the meeting on the drive back to the State Department. This proved impracticable because the ride from the White House takes only five minutes. Rusk's Executive Assistant, Benjamin Read, often tried to piece together the fruits of the meeting by debriefing the Secretary and conferring with colleagues on the White House staff. But almost no reflection of the President's mood or inclinations filters down through the government because Rusk and the rest are unwilling to risk becoming the source of leaks that may infuriate Johnson.

The President is well briefed for the Tuesday meetings. Each night he receives in his "evening meal reading" file a résumé of State and Pentagon activities. A typical mid-November, 1965, report for the President's bedside dealt with measures to tighten up safety at sea in the wake of the *Yarmouth Castle* disaster; discussions with Maritime Union leaders on the fifty-fifty proviso for the use of U.S. ships to carry foreign aid; talks with Senator Fulbright and Representative Morgan, who demanded and were given a firm commitment that no new aid to Nasser would be forthcoming without consultation with the Congressional leadership; and, finally, a résumé of the anti-U.S. diatribes published in a book on neo-colonialism by ex-Ghana President Nkrumah.

At the President's insistence, the night reading reports are concise and usually written on one page. He will, aides say, read longer memos only if they are "fact-packed." The President does much reading at night and there is every evidence that he peruses these reports when they are brief and well written. They almost always bear his pencilled notations when an aide brings them back to the office next morning.

But the variety and terseness of these memoranda prevent them from being much more than short looks at immediate problems. The President is too practical and busy to spend his time on speculative treatises which probe the future and grapple with remote contingencies. His dilemma has been summed up by Rusk: "This is a time for thinking and it is hard to get time to think."

Johnson wants to be everything that his critics say he is not, and he would clearly like to become the instigator of a grand new foreign policy design. The rather wistful way in which he himself inserted at the last minute a promise to travel to the Soviet Union in his 1965 State-of-the-Union message signalled his anxiety to be associated with an historic move toward peace.

But, deep down in his heart, an aide has reported, the President is somewhat of an isolationist, who does not relish dealing with foreign affairs. "He would chop off the rest of the world if he could," another former White House associate commented.

Despite his ambition to achieve peace with the Soviet Union, Mr. Johnson sometimes talks about the Communist conspiracy in terms reminiscent of the late Senator McCarthy. He was expounding such views one day on an airplane when an aide, Eric Goldman (who now teaches history at Princeton) interjected, "Mr. President, you know this isn't true." Mr. Johnson replied by shrugging his shoulders. Next day, a White House secretary told Goldman she had heard from the President that he was "very interesting" on the plane.

The records of Presidents are shaped by the circumstances which confront them and the human qualities which they bring to bear on their problems. Johnson's triumphs as a politician depend heavily upon his remarkable store of doggedness, his skill as a negotiator and his talent for twisting arms. If he achieves any successes in foreign policy, they are more likely to stem from these same powerful attributes than from any deep-rooted instinct for diplomacy.

E·I·G·H·T

—But not the Secretary of State

Any Secretary of State is in a theoretical sense only the mouthpiece of the President. The Constitution places sole responsibility for the conduct of foreign affairs upon the President. The only check on this power is the Senate's authority to advise and consent. That, at least, is the theory.

In practice it doesn't work out quite as the drafters of the Constitution intended. Foreign affairs in these times are too far-flung and complex to be managed by a President heavily burdened with other duties. He must delegate to his Secretary of State the responsibility for day-to-day operations. He must also rely upon his subordinates for ideas and guidance in matters of high policy.

It is even possible for the mouthpiece to overshadow its principal. This is what happened in the Eisenhower administration, when John Foster Dulles ran foreign affairs with rare interference from the President. It also happened in the Truman administration when foreign policy became the exclusive province of Dean Acheson. Both Eisenhower and Truman had enough confidence in their Secretaries of State to reserve only a passive role for themselves in foreign policy making.

138

In a June 1, 1953, statement, President Eisenhower said he regarded the Secretary of State "as the Cabinet officer responsible for advising and assisting me in the formulation and control of foreign policy." In essence, however, John Foster Dulles did more than advising and assisting. He was the key man on most of the foreign policy issues which arose during the Eisenhower administration.

When he was named Secretary, Dulles did not even want to work in the State Department. He wanted an office in the White House and indicated he would have nothing to do with the administration of his department. He viewed his job as an assignment to think—"and I never have any chance to think at all," he once complained to a Senate committee—and a mandate to originate foreign policy ideas. "The State Department can't keep control of foreign policy simply because it is known as the Department of State," he once told an aide. "We'll only keep control as long as we have the ideas."

Dulles never hesitated to suggest ideas and take firm stands on foreign policy issues in the Eisenhower administration's policy debates. He often worried that State was not turning out enough foreign policy ideas. He once complained that the only State-originated idea he could recollect was the "open skies" concept, which actually originated in the Pentagon.

Dulles deferred to Eisenhower's constitutional prerogatives in foreign affairs, but he was abrupt and lordly about foreign policy suggestions from anyone else, including White House staff members. He once scuttled a presidential staff foreign policy proposal submitted to him through a State Department official who acknowledged he had put forth the suggestion only because "the White House wanted it."

"Don't ever use that as a justification for anything," Dulles scolded. "There is only one man over there who can give orders. Listen to the others and be polite."

Although history will credit him with several major foreign policy programs, Harry Truman—somewhat like Eisenhower—was not and did not want to be his own Secretary of State.

Even if Truman had wanted it, Dean Acheson would not

have let him. Acheson's philosophy was simple. He once told President Truman, "you should listen to everybody who has anything to say on foreign affairs. That's what the National Security Council is for. You must hear all the rows. But when it comes to final advice, it must come from your Secretary of State."

The two big-war Presidents, Woodrow Wilson and Franklin Roosevelt, were plunged into world affairs willy-nilly. They had no alternative. As it happened, both were predisposed to act as their own Secretaries of State and might have done so in any case. Events gave them no choice.

President Kennedy was different. More than any of his predecessors, he possessed an intense curiosity about the world beyond the boundaries of the United States. Curiosity powered a demand for new initiatives, new men and new programs. Kennedy was ambitious to make America's and his own influence felt in world affairs.

Restless and dissatisfied with the State Department, anxious to use it to better advantage, Kennedy kept trying doggedly to understand and prod that cumbersome agency into action, into closer kinship and harmony with his ambition to get this country "moving again." He never did fathom it, in spite of frequent telephone calls to astonished State Department desk officers. In despair, he once asked veteran career officer Charles E. (Chip) Bohlen, "What's wrong with the State Department?" "You are, Mr. President," Bohlen shot back, explaining that the President's preoccupation with the State Department was upsetting the normal performance of its tasks. Kennedy was not amused.

On August 16, 1961, some seven months after his inauguration, Kennedy sent a plaintive memorandum to his Secretary of State, asking for a definition of "the present assignment of responsibility within the Department of State. . . .

"I think, if we could get it down on paper," the memorandum continued, "all concerned on the White House staff, as well as the State Department, could have a better idea of how they should conduct their responsibilities." *

* See Appendix, p 224.

The President never received the written reply he had requested. Instead, the State Department's files disclose a notation by the then Undersecretary Chester Bowles, saying that Mr. Rusk saw the President and answered the memorandum orally. But the answer could not have been very helpful. Most of the Secretary's top assistants had been given their assignments before Rusk received his. And Rusk, a retiring man, aloof from the internecine strife within his own department and unsure of the limits of his own responsibility, could hardly be expected to define it for others who were better known in the political world where Rusk was unknown.

Some of Kennedy's bewilderment and anger with the State Department stemmed from the man he selected to head it, Dean Rusk.

During his electoral campaign, Kennedy, after much discussion with his advisers, drafted seven qualifications for his ideal Secretary of State:

First, he must be a man whose views on American foreign policy broadly accord with my own. This requirement is not a matter of personal arrogance. There is no more dangerous situation for the nation on the world scene than one in which the President and the Secretary of State do not see eye to eye and cannot communicate in full sympathy. Such situations have arisen in the past; and they have always been costly to the national interest.

Second, he must understand the deep historic interest and instincts which determine American objectives on the world scene. He must feel in his bones that Americans are not merely concerned to protect our frontiers but that our history and our destiny permit us to struggle for the cause of human freedom wherever it is engaged.

Third, he must understand the multiple nature of the Communist threat. He must understand and respect its military dimensions; but he must equally understand that military strength and military pacts are not enough to stop Communism. He must understand that the Communist leadership seeks its objective by military pressure, subversion, economic penetration, diplomacy and ideological attraction. He must have the vision and operational skill to orchestrate all the instruments of American policy necessary to deal with the non-military aspects of the Communist threat.

Fourth, he must understand what it is like to live in a system where the average income is $50 per head a year; that is, he must have human sympathy for the problems and aspirations of the men and women who live in Asia, the Middle East, Africa and Latin America. It is in these areas of the free world—containing more than 1,300,000,000 human beings—the most challenging problem of the 1960s will lie.

Fifth, he must know Europe and Japan well. He must understand the great changes that have come about in those regions since the days of the Marshall Plan. He must be prepared to deal with our allies as strong, dignified and assertive partners, not as weak and weary states needing emergency aid in order to survive. But he must understand equally that despite all the changes of the 1950s the Free World Alliance cannot work in the 1960s unless the United States leads the way.

Sixth, he must be prepared to deal with the Congress and the American people on the basis of candor. He must know from the beginning the job of Secretary of State is hard. The Secretary of State has no constituency at home to support him: neither farm, nor labor, nor business interests. Nonetheless, he must come to the Congress and to the American people knowing in his heart that Americans want the truth and that they will do the things that need to be done if they get the truth.

Seventh, and above all, the Secretary of State must understand that his job in the 1960s will be not to counterpunch against Communist initiatives but to launch American initiatives. His mission will be not to react to history but to make history.

It may be argued that some of these qualifications were tailored to the needs of the political campaign and intended to be indirectly critical of Eisenhower's Secretary of State. But there can be little argument that Rusk has been found grievously wanting on the seventh count, by Kennedy as well as by Johnson. Rusk has launched no initiatives nor made history under either President.

Rusk's inactivity is all the more striking when his immediate predecessors are measured against the standards of initiative and history. General George Marshall was the author of the plan bearing his name which saved Europe from economic chaos; Dean Acheson fashioned the Truman Doctrine and the

NATO alliance; John Foster Dulles hammered out the CENTO and SEATO pacts. The value of these agreements is debatable, but they were Dulles-inspired. And, ironically, the Johnson administration has been citing the SEATO pact as the legal basis for the American involvement in Vietnam, although Dulles had specifically barred an automatic U.S. involvement under the treaty.

Dean Rusk's first intimation that he was being considered for Secretary of State came on the afternoon of December 9, 1960. A message from Fred Holborn, a Kennedy aide, asked Rusk to remain home that evening because the President-elect might telephone him. Rusk had promised to take his wife out to dinner, but said he would gladly remain home if Kennedy wished.

Actually, the call did not come until the following morning, although Kennedy had settled on Rusk the previous day. The two men met for the first time on December 8, but during the meeting the President never stated the purpose of the interview. In fact, it had been Rusk's impression he was being considered for the job of Undersecretary, which he intended to turn down.

However, Rusk had been in contact with the President-elect two weeks earlier, but not on the subject of his appointment. In a long letter to Kennedy dated November 22, 1960* —which may have been an attention-getting device—Rusk had suggested a presidential response to "the pressures arising from the threat of certain delegations to disregard the popular votes in their states in casting their ballots in the electoral college in December."

Addressing the President-elect as a "Georgia-born citizen who believes that the Supreme Court decision on integration was long overdue," Rusk advised him not to dicker with the Southern electors who threatened to throw their votes to Nixon.

If you challenge these Southern delegations on the issues of Civil Rights [Rusk wrote], the inflamed tempers in the South

* See Appendix, pp. 224–26.

(freshly stimulated by New Orleans) could lead a number of them into an irrational action which could inflict wounds on our American democracy which would require decades to heal. On the other hand, if you offer these groups the kinds of assurance which would quiet them, a large majority of your own supporters in other parts of the country would be deeply offended and your administration would take office under a cloud of cynicism which would hamper you at every turn.

If it becomes necessary for you to make a public statement before the electoral college meets, it might be worth considering a statement which rests upon the long-range historical and constitutional traditions of the country rather than upon the immediate issues now involved.

He then went into brief reviews of the constitutional system and electoral college traditions, and wound up his two-page, single-spaced epistle with this sentence:

I hope this letter will be useless by the time it reaches you.

Rusk was never Kennedy's first choice for Secretary of State. The late President's friends insist that Senator J. William Fulbright was the preferred candidate. Coincidentally, Fulbright was also the then Vice-President Johnson's favorite for the job. But the senator from Arkansas knew his Civil Rights stand would make him a liability to the Kennedy administration.

In a move to let the President-elect off the hook, Fulbright asked his Democratic colleague from Georgia, Senator Richard Russell, to tell Kennedy he was ideologically and temperamentally unsuited for the Secretary's job and would not accept it if it were offered to him. Initially, Russell refused to transmit the Fulbright message, but finally agreed to do so "against my better judgment."

At any rate, Kennedy did not need Russell's persuasion to pass over Fulbright for the Secretary's post. The President-elect was well aware of Fulbright's political liabilities. Further, Robert Kennedy, one-time aide to a Fulbright arch-foe, Senator John McClellan, also opposed the Fulbright appointment. Fulbright effected his withdrawal in good spirits and, though deeply disappointed, never bore a grudge.

Kennedy had several other candidates in mind for the Secretary's post in addition to Rusk. They included David Bruce, Adlai Stevenson, Chester Bowles. But none of them stood much chance.

Stevenson was never seriously considered. After Kennedy's primary victory over Hubert Humphrey in West Virginia, the Senator visited Stevenson in Chicago, expecting support for the presidential nomination now that Humphrey was out of the way. Stevenson demurred, saying he wanted to remain "neutral" so he could act as a middleman between Kennedy and Johnson when the new administration took office. That embittered Kennedy. "I am being turned down right and left," he told a friend, adding, "I don't mind. But how could I make Stevenson Secretary of State after this absurd performance? How could he serve as a go-between when Johnson has no use for him and regards him as a weakling?"

Nor was Bowles strongly in the running. He was on the list of possible Secretaries of State, having been added to that catalogue by Kennedy the same day he named Johnson as his running mate. However, Bowles and Stevenson were soon scratched from the list and named "foreign policy advisers" instead. That happy compromise was suggested by Arthur Goldberg, now ambassador to the United Nations, on the evening that Johnson was nominated to be vice-president. Goldberg proposed the announcement of Stevenson and Bowles as advisers in order to placate the liberals who were in revolt over Kennedy's choice of Johnson.

David Bruce was on Kennedy's final list of candidates for Secretary, largely because of powerful backing in the Democratic party hierarchy. But Kennedy had his misgivings. A member of the President's family reported that Bruce and his wife, Evangeline, staunch Stevenson fans, had broken into tears when Kennedy was nominated and later elected. Kennedy removed Bruce from his list, and named him ambassador to London. He sometimes observed privately that Bruce, an experienced diplomat whose talents he appreciated, had obtained a free ride from his administration.

Rusk's name as a potential Secretary was broached to Kennedy by Robert Lovett and Dean Acheson, and his candidacy for the post was endorsed by Professor William Y. Elliott of Harvard, a former adviser to Richard Nixon. On November 22, 1960, the same day Rusk wrote Kennedy on the electoral-college issue, Professor Elliott said in a letter to Fred Holborn, for transmission to Kennedy:

A man who combines both negotiating skill, a cool head and a proper understanding of the Secretary's role with his President and his colleagues in the Cabinet and with Congress is hard to come by. I am sure the President-elect understands these aspects of the matter about as well as anyone would be likely to. But I hope he will not neglect the possibility that Dean Rusk could be attracted from his important duties as president of the Rockefeller Foundation to the post that may be most critical for the success not only of the next President but of the American nation in confronting the world we presently live in. . . . Dean combines a thorough knowledge of not only military but of political strategy and of the realities of economics that escape too often both our bankers and theoreticians.

Although he did not know Rusk personally, the President-elect had been impressed with Rusk's writings. What impressed him even more was Rusk's handling of his own meeting with UN Secretary General Dag Hammarskjold after the American presidential ballots had been counted.

Almost immediately after the election, Rusk had tried to sharpen Kennedy's image as a champion of the UN.

"The wholly new situation at the UN," Rusk said in a telephoned message to Senator Kennedy,* "calls for a re-casting of the United States delegation to provide dramatic evidence and effective implementation of the interest of all the American people and the leadership of both political parties in the future of the UN."

It is suggested that Senator Kennedy present the foregoing view to the President [Eisenhower] and suggest that perhaps the two career people on the delegation and perhaps at least two of the alternate delegates who are not known public figures withdraw and be replaced by such outstanding public figures as Governor Nelson

* See Appendix, pp. 226–27.

Rockefeller, John J. McCloy and Thomas E. Dewey from the Republican Party, and Adlai Stevenson, Mrs. Eleanor Roosevelt and Chester Bowles from the Democratic Party.

The suggestion should be made privately and in all sincerity. If the President should act upon it, the national interest would be served and the political laurels would be at least equally spread, as Senator Kennedy's initiative would inevitably become known and the performance of the foregoing Democrats would certainly reflect credit on the party and on Senator Kennedy's leadership in selecting them.

Should the President reject the suggestion, Senator Kennedy is provided with an excellent opportunity to reveal to the American people the kind of administrative leadership he would assert in foreign policy if he were President.

Kennedy apparently liked the Rusk suggestion and its implications, but failed to act on it. A few weeks later, however, he took a closer look at the UN, and what he saw upset him.

Soviet Premier Nikita S. Khrushchev had just used the General Assembly as the launching pad for a major diplomatic offensive to reshape the world organization more to Moscow's liking. His attacks on Hammarskjold had created a threat to the life of the UN. All this was occurring before an unprecedented number of Chiefs of State and foreign ministers attending the General Assembly session. Further, Henry Cabot Lodge, titular chief of the American delegation, had just been defeated as a vice-presidential candidate. And the world was waiting for Kennedy to take over as President, and watching expectantly for his first UN move.

Kennedy decided to start with a gesture toward Hammarskjold. Rusk was approached and asked to act as the President-elect's go-between with Hammarskjold. Rusk consented at once. In a memorandum dated November 30, 1960,* and addressed to Kennedy via Paul Nitze, head of Kennedy's task force on National Security Affairs, Rusk described his meeting with the UN Secretary General:

The conversation proceeded upon these assumptions: (1) that the Senator [Kennedy] would not wish to be in a situation where

* See Appendix, pp. 227–30.

he would either have to meet a large number of Delegates to the UN or to make arbitrary choices in singling out a few; (2) that the Senator would not wish to be drawn prematurely into any of the issues now before the General Assembly; (3) that the Senator would not wish a meeting with the Secretary General to be elaborately "staged"; (4) that it would, however, be important that the fact of such a meeting be publicly known as an indication of the Senator's interest in the United Nations, and (5) that it would be helpful if the two could have some opportunity for an unofficial but frank talk about the UN before the new administration assumes responsibility.

Hammarskjold apparently did not object to any of Rusk's conditions for a meeting with Kennedy, which was held on December 7, 1960, over a breakfast table at the Carlyle Hotel in New York.

The Rusk arrangements for that meeting and his endorsements clinched Kennedy's decision to name him Secretary of State. Previously, Kennedy and his aides had carefully scrutinized all Rusk's writings and found nothing likely to cause trouble. On December 9, Philip Graham, late publisher of the *Washington Post,* suggested another man for the Secretary's job.

"Too late," Kennedy replied. "I have decided to appoint Rusk." The Rusk appointment was announced on December 12.

Before Rusk's appointment was made official, Kennedy had already filled several key posts at State. Chester Bowles was named Undersecretary, Averell Harriman was designated ambassador-at-large, ex-Michigan Governor G. Mennen (Soapy) Williams was appointed Assistant Secretary for African Affairs and Adlai Stevenson was posted as ambassador to the UN.

This rash of appointments coincided with a curious error on the President-elect's part, which triggered some hasty reshuffling. Kennedy apparently believed there were three Undersecretary posts (there were only two) at State, and had chosen nominees for them. He wanted one for Bowles, a second for McGeorge Bundy and a third either for William Foster or Livingston Merchant. His appointment program was complicated further when Senator Fulbright urged him to name George Ball instead of Foster to one of the openings.

When it was discovered there was no Undersecretaryship for Bundy, the President-elect wanted to name him chief of the Disarmament Agency—a post which eventually went to Foster. Since Bundy showed no enthusiasm for the disarmament job, Kennedy eventually moved him into the White House.

After he was named Secretary, Rusk seemed concerned only about two men: George McGhee, a former Rusk colleague in the State Department, and Walt Rostow. Rusk wanted McGhee to head State's policy-planning staff, a job Kennedy had promised to Rostow. The latter's record of tilts with former Undersecretary Herbert Hoover, Jr. on Eisenhower's "open skies" plan had earned Rostow the reputation of being "difficult."

With that evaluation blocking Rostow's appointment as Policy Planning Chief, Rusk succeeded in securing the post for McGhee. Rusk balked at Kennedy's proposal to name Rostow as McGhee's deputy. The President-elect had no choice but to bring Rostow into the White House. Ironically, after McGhee was named ambassador to West Germany, Kennedy ordered Rostow to State to take the policy-planning post—which Rusk had earlier denied him. Rusk evinced no emotion, but subsequently paid little attention to Rostow. Ironically, again, after Bundy departed for the Ford Foundation early in 1966, Johnson summoned Rostow back to the White House as the final act of dismantling the Kennedy apparatus.

After his administration took over, Kennedy displayed great respect for Rusk, and consistently silenced criticisms of the Secretary which began leaking almost immediately from Cabinet sources. The criticisms focused almost entirely on Rusk's unwillingness to take a forceful stand on any issue. For example, Rusk opposed Kennedy's unsuccessful Bay of Pigs venture, but never in strong or convincing terms. The day after the Cuban fiasco, the President commented to a friend, "I'll bet Dean Rusk wishes he had spoken up in a louder voice."

But even a "whisper" from Rusk has been a rarity. A former administration official who sat with Rusk regularly in Cabinet and other policy sessions insisted that in four years of attendance at such meetings he never heard the Secretary voice a firm opinion on any subject. And another sub-Cabinet colleague who took part with Rusk in key strategy sessions at Honolulu and in Washington has quoted the Secretary as boasting after such meetings, "I hope you notice I haven't expressed an opinion."

This astonishing record has apparently stemmed from Rusk's concept of his role as Secretary of State. He has been consistent in his belief that his duty is to communicate his views only to the President and not to air or debate them with the Cabinet or the White House staff. During the 1962 Cuban missile crisis, Rusk thus refused to act as "just another member" of the President's policy-shaping executive committee, on the ground it was his responsibility to convey his opinions privately to the President.

This concept of his role has produced some startling developments, such as having Undersecretary George Ball outline his "private" opinions to the executive committee working out the plan for countering Khrushchev's installation of missiles in Cuba, an "opinion" which might have brought on a nuclear war with the Soviet Union.

"We cannot have an institutional view," Rusk is said to have told Ball. "It will be best if we present our views as individuals." But, given the absence of the Secretary's views at policy-making meetings, and the expressions of his ranking lieutenant's opinions only as "private" remarks, there has always been grave doubt as to who spoke for the State Department and outlined its policy recommendations.

Rusk's admirers have insisted that his demands on subordinates to assert their "views as individuals" have produced a great deal of initiative and imaginative thinking. They have quoted him as urging his assistant secretaries to "reach for the horizon," and assuring them that "I'll always back you up and none of you need ever fear exceeding his powers."

But critics within the State Department have coun-

tered that Rusk's refusal to state his opinions or to make decisions within his own agency have caused precisely the opposite
effect.

"In a quarter of a century in the department," one old-
timer complained sadly, "I have never seen such a communications blockage between the seventh floor [Rusk's office] and
the rest of the place. Oh, sure, routine traffic of memos goes
on, and briefings and meetings are held, but how are we going
to deal with the tough ones if we don't know what the Secretary is thinking?"

"When you go into a meeting with Rusk," said another department official, "you come out with exactly what you took in.
He does not contribute ideas. He asks a lot of questions
and you try to figure out if they are meaningful—or merely
rhetorical—and you never know."

As for the horizon-reaching, some assistant secretaries
have remarked, in effect, "How can we do anything on the
Congo, for example, if the assistant secretaries for Africa and
Europe are at loggerheads and Rusk will not listen to their
differences and decide what is to be done?"

Some of Rusk's key subordinates have been known to circle him, and take their problems to the Undersecretary. Others have devised a different method. "Unless you disagree, Mr.
Secretary," they have told Rusk, "I propose to do such and
such." Since the Secretary seldom disagrees, his decisions thus
have often been made by default.

As time went on, Kennedy became increasingly frustrated
with the State Department, and some of its top officials. Chester Bowles irked the President at one of their first meetings in
the new administration by talking in generalities as Kennedy,
Rusk and Bowles undertook to select a slate of new ambassadors. Bowles persisted in expounding upon the qualities required for each post as Kennedy, who did not like abstrac-
tions, twinged with impatience. (See Appendix, p. 230f.)

Bowles' demotion was delayed temporarily by a newspaper
report hinting that he was becoming a liability and was on the
way out. But the shift finally materialized in the so-called
"Thanksgiving Day massacre" in November, 1961, in which

Ball was named Undersecretary, Bowles an ambassador-at-large, Harriman the Assistant Secretary for the Far East and McGhee the Deputy Undersecretary for Political Affairs.

When told that he was to be shifted from the presidential adviser's post to the job of ambassador-at-large, Bowles asked one anxious question: Would he rate a chauffeured limousine? "Everyone in Washington knows that if you arrive at the White House gate in a taxi, you have had it," he explained.

But Bowles was not Kennedy's only frustration at the State Department. The President was irritated with its smugness and bureaucracy and his own inability to prod it into action. In the spring of 1963, a Soviet diplomat visited President Monroe's birthplace at Montpelier, Virginia, and punctuated his visit with an offhand declaration that "the Monroe Doctrine is dead."

Kennedy, concerned by the propaganda implications of this statement, asked the State Department to draft a revision of the Monroe Doctrine which might serve as a more current expression of the United States' policy toward the Western Hemisphere. State reported back to the White House that it was opposed to any changes in the Monroe Doctrine. Kennedy handed the task to McGeorge Bundy, whose White House staff quickly assembled some ideas for revising the doctrine. Kennedy cited the incident as an example of the lamentable lack of responsiveness in the State Department.

Kennedy felt a deep loyalty toward the people who worked with him and he rarely permitted himself to express any criticisms. But in the last months of his life, thoroughly vexed by Rusk's failure to function as a coordinating force, he talked enthusiastically of a change that he intended to make after the 1964 election. Adlai Stevenson, fatigued by the UN, had requested a transfer to the embassy in London. Kennedy contemplated offering the UN post to Rusk and State to Robert McNamara, who lacked diplomatic experience but had thoroughly sold the President on the soundness of his judgment and his administrative genius. "Maybe he can bring that place to life," Kennedy said. He did not discuss this plan with

McNamara before he died but he did discuss it with most of his intimate aides and friends.

Kennedy's disappointment with State seemed to hinge on two factors: the failure of the Secretary and his department to initiate or produce foreign policy ideas, and the lethargy with which the Secretary and the department moved when policies finally were defined and adopted.

The President's anger with State stemmed also from his own role in foreign affairs and his dominance of his own administration. Unlike Truman and Eisenhower, Kennedy wanted to be his own Secretary of State. It is conjectural, therefore, if his attitudes toward the State Department and foreign policy would have been altered significantly if he had ousted Dean Rusk and replaced him with someone else. For Kennedy was unlikely to defer to any Secretary of State, even if that Secretary rained proposals and suggestions on him.

After the tragedy in Dallas, Lyndon Johnson, at first striving to retain as many Kennedy-appointed officials as possible to create an impression of continuity, kept Rusk at State. The Secretary accepted the change in Presidents with the bland imperturbability which has earned him the nickname of "Buddha," and maintained toward Johnson the same *sotto voce* attitude and concept of his job which he had displayed toward Kennedy.

But there is little doubt that Rusk established a better relationship with Johnson than he ever had with Kennedy. Both are "poor boys" who made good and both are Southerners. There have been many times when the two have abandoned discussions of weighty international affairs in favor of an earthy exchange on Southern politics.

Another reason for Rusk's success with Johnson has been his ability as a Congressional witness. Rusk has been a resounding success in his appearances on the Hill. He was the first Secretary since Cordell Hull who was Southern enough and plain-spoken enough to enlist the respect and attention of skeptical lawmakers. After Rusk's testimony on the Civil Rights Bill and its effect on foreign relations, Johnson told him, "You would make a great attorney-general."

Rusk has treated each Congressional appearance with utmost concern, despite the fact he has spent more than one-fifth of his time before Capitol Hill committees. Before each appearance, a mock hearing was held in Rusk's office, with associates masquerading as Congressmen and firing questions at the Secretary. The results of his homework were always impressive. Even such implacable opponents of State Department spending as Congressmen John Rooney and Otto Passman have softened visibly after Rusk's appearances.

The President was so convinced of Rusk's prestige on Capitol Hill that he used to prod him constantly to "go and see Bill Fulbright and have breakfast with him." In a show of spirit one day, Rusk countered the presidential urgings by producing his diary which listed the number of meetings and telephone conversations he had held with Fulbright. "Go and see him some more," the President urged.

The presidential pressure on Rusk to see more of Fulbright has proved embarrassing to both men, increasingly so as the senator has become more critical of the administration's Vietnam and China policies and its intervention in the Dominican Republic. Both have observed the traditional courtesies of Congressional hearings, but Rusk seemed perilously close to exploding at Fulbright during questioning at the latter's China policy sessions in early 1966. Further, Fulbright has never found Rusk's company stimulating. And, in addition, the senator likes to have breakfast with Mrs. Fulbright.

Rusk's popularity on Capitol Hill has been marred by senatorial complaints that he has never been known to say what was on his mind. If a senator raised an objection to a Rusk point, he would get a courteous response—often to the effect that "we can also do it the way you suggest, and will consider it." And there have been relatively few instances in which Rusk insisted on any particular course of action while meeting with Congressmen, another reflection of his theory that the Secretary of State should expound his foreign policy views only to the President.

As Rusk's refusal to take stands on foreign policy issues irritated Kennedy, so has it vexed Johnson. After one White House meeting at which Undersecretary Ball represented the

State Department, Johnson told a friend, "I wish Dean Rusk would come over here and pound the table once in a while the way George Ball does." And in spite of wholesome praise in public, Mr. Johnson has been known to make highly uncomplimentary remarks about Rusk in private.

In a seeming effort to goad Rusk and State into more activity on foreign affairs, Johnson, early in 1966, endowed the Secretary and his department with increased authority and responsibility.

A White House announcement on March 4, 1966, said the President had "directed the Secretary of State, as his agent, to assume responsibility to the full extent permitted by law for over-all direction, coordination and supervision of interdepartmental activities of the United States government overseas (less exempted military activities)."

Heretofore, the announcement continued, the Secretary of State "had performed a coordinating function in interdepartmental matters abroad, but now he has received formal and specific over-all directive authority from the President."

Commentators made much of Rusk's new "directive authority," as contrasted with his previous "coordinating" responsibility in foreign policy. That newly conferred authority, however, would be meaningless unless exercised. Rusk has not been a power-wielder. As for Rusk's previous coordinating responsibility, most of the foreign policy coordinating since he took office has been done in the White House, first by McGeorge Bundy and later by Rostow.

Rusk evinced no elation over his new stature or the upgrading of his department. Nor did he display any new forcefulness. In a memorandum to his departmental colleagues explaining State's new responsibilities, he called on them for "an overview of wisdom and judgment that focuses on the needs and purposes of the United States government as a whole in its relationships with other nations." Then, typically, he cautioned them against indulging in any "parochial viewpoints or petty bureaucratic 'infighting' under State's new mandate, even though that mandate seems certain to generate some lively intra-mural battles."

The world called for American foreign policy initiatives as

Rusk's primacy in the administration's foreign policy councils was proclaimed. But Vietnam had long ago ceased to be a foreign policy problem and, in spite of Mr. Rusk's newly acquired ascendancy, the conduct of the political and military aspects of the war was heavily dominated by the White House and the Pentagon. There were suggestions across the United States for a new policy on Communist China—even though Peking was rejecting every American overture. But these were not matched by new policies. Restlessness, uncertainty and unease were rustling across Asia, but there was no visible long-range American foreign policy for that vital region, except to settle the war in Vietnam.

It was much the same in Europe. Most of the NATO nations were wavering in their loyalty to the alliance, which General de Gaulle was trying to dismantle. The United States seemed to have no ideas for a long-overdue recasting of NATO, and its only policy response to De Gaulle was to berate or ignore him. Soviet influence was declining visibly in Eastern Europe, but the United States was making no great effort to take advantage of it. Germany was still divided, and West German nationalists becoming more powerful, but the United States seemed to have no fresh ideas on how to end the division of Germany or handle the West Germans. Cyprus was unsettled, and the Greeks and Turks disgruntled with American policy—or the lack of it—for that troubled island.

Both north and south of the American border, in Canada and Latin America, there was continuous grumbling about United States policy. Africa was writhing with coups d'etat and economic distress, and headed for more of both.

Curiously, despite periodic and largely conventional blasts at one another, the United States and the Soviet Union were getting along almost comfortably. The world's two greatest powers obviously had measured each other well, concluded their mutual arsenals were too terrible to unleash against each other and decided to observe a truce.

Rusk's "don't rock the boat" attitude on foreign affairs, his seeming failure to look ahead to spot incipient troubles abroad, has been one reason why American diplomacy appeared to

be on a crisis-to-crisis course. For instance, Rusk has shown only
the mildest interest in Atlantic affairs, despite the fact that the
Atlantic area provided the most promising fields for U.S. diplomacy. Atlantic affairs have been left almost entirely to
former Undersecretary Ball and his associates. Since Ball's
departure they have been transferred to Undersecretary
Rostow. The file on the Cyprus crisis, which enmeshed Britain,
France, Greece, Turkey and NATO, contained very few significant documents drafted by Rusk.

Rusk has been inclined to be petulant about Europeans, as
evidenced by his reactions to De Gaulle. Like Johnson, Rusk
has felt the Europeans were lax in not providing "more flags,"
more material support for South Vietnam. Egged on by the
President, forever seeking the outward symbols of "popularity," Rusk has regarded aid to Vietnam, however insig-
nificant, as one of the prime criteria of allied loyalty. He has
seemed oblivious to the popular indifference about Vietnam
in most European nations, to the difficulties which some of
their governments would encounter if they even paid greater
lip service to the United States' cause in Southeast Asia.

Curiously, Rusk has occasionally taken a strong position
on odd issues, like the resumption of American aid to the
United Arab Republic. He has also developed sudden and un-
explained interests in obscure disarmament projects or scien-
tific programs, but has often dropped them in mid-stream.
"I think I have his support on one of those projects," a key
aide complained mournfully, "so I march ahead—only to discover suddenly there is no one behind me."

Rusk has been personally interested and often committed
to problems affecting Great Britain and the British Commonwealth. In 1933, as a Rhodes scholar at St. John's College, Oxford, Rusk won the Cecil Peace Prize, and his Oxford experience has left a visible imprint on him. Lord Harlech, former
British ambassador in Washington, once told Rusk only half-
jokingly, "Now that Lord Beaverbrook is dead, you are the
only remaining champion of the British Empire."

Rusk has always regarded Britain and the Commonwealth
as staunch allies of the United States, but has evinced some

questionable assumptions about its cohesion, unity and unanimity. After the 1961 Communist Chinese attack on India, Rusk urged the British to call a Commonwealth conference to condemn Chinese aggression. The British managed only with considerable difficulty to persuade him that the Commonwealth has never spoken with one voice on any subject, and was highly unlikely to agree on India.

Like all Oxford men, Rusk has never forsaken his loyalty to his alma mater. At one of the CENTO meetings, an aide commented favorably on a Vietnam statement from former British Foreign Secretary, Michael Stewart. "What did you expect?" Rusk replied with a grin. "He's an Oxford man, isn't he?"

The Secretary has had strong views on China, both Chinas. He has been determined not to let Formosa fall or slide into Communist China's hands. He has been the ranking administration "hawk" on the Peking regime. He has opposed United States' recognition of Red China, and its admission to the United Nations. He has genuinely believed the Communist Chinese to be a threat to world peace. Rusk has never ceased to blame himself for failing to anticipate Communist China's entry into the Korean War, and he swore that failure would never be repeated no matter what other country was involved. Under the Rusk doctrine, China must be contained until it has mellowed into a tractable power, à la Russia.

Rusk was eloquently incisive on those points during hearings on China and Sino-American relations by the generally hostile Senate Foreign Relations Committee in the spring of 1966.

Those hearings demonstrated a notable change in the American attitude on China since the McCarthy era, a change which Rusk presumably has weighed in considering United States relations with the Peking government.

Witnesses told the Senate committee the United States should ease its opposition to China's entry into the UN, relax its trade embargo on China, even recognize it diplomatically. The Peking government, listening intently to the proposals, summarily rejected and denounced them. But it was notable that the espousal and enunciation of these suggestions to the committee brought no cries of "Communist" or "Communist sympathizer" in Washington or across the United States. The American public generally seemed to indicate, perhaps only negatively through its lack of protest, that it would tolerate some relaxation in the administration's China policy.

A new China policy paper drafted by State Department experts and advocating relations with both Chinas has been on Rusk's desk since summer, 1966. But Rusk has never really believed any change in U.S. attitude was necessary, even though he has made some statements favoring increased contacts with the Peiping regime.

Rusk started his term of office on a swell of good feeling abroad for the United States, stemming in good part from foreign hopes in Kennedy. Even the Russians had hopes for the new President—that they could take him into their camp. And until his Vienna meeting with Khrushchev, Kennedy seemed to believe he might be able to handle or at least get along well with the Russians. The Berlin and Cuban missile crises taught him differently.

Rusk has felt that the aftermath of those crises might have been more acute if the United States had not maintained with the U.S.S.R. one of his favorite diplomatic efforts—the "dialogue"—at which he has been exceedingly proficient.

Endowed with remarkable patience and an ability to retain and articulate facts, Rusk has proved a formidable negotiator with the Russians. He can outsit and outtalk Foreign Minister Andrei Gromyko, and has repeatedly done so with relish. He has never tired of repeating the United States position on any issue. He and Gromyko actually have developed a liking for each other, although there has been no evidence that either has yielded anything because of this personal relationship. Rusk has never tried to ploy the Soviets, and they seem to have confidence and respect in him. On one occasion, when a Soviet UN delegate was needling Rusk on some minor technical point, Gromyko barked, "Leave the Secretary alone." There is no instance on record that such treatment was ever extended to any other U.S. official.

Rusk the person is almost as much an enigma as Rusk the Secretary. Some of his admirers believe his humble origin and austere upbringing had much to do with his personality. For instance, on the front porch of his Washington house, Rusk has installed a sizable black pot. He said once in a radio interview [*] he had built "hundreds of fires" under it in bygone days "to fire up the family wash." Reflecting on his early background, Rusk discoursed as follows on his youth and family:

We were a rather quiet family about expressing our emotions under any circumstances. I think this was part of the reticence. Perhaps it goes with Calvinism. Perhaps it comes from the Scotch-Irish. Perhaps it comes from the tough battle with the soil in the family that had to wrest a living out of a not-too-productive soil in Cherokee County [in Georgia]. There was a certain reticence in the tradition of our families that carried into our own.

Rusk attended a Cherokee county school with no exterior walls. The outside of the building was equipped with canvas screens, which were pulled down during storms. "We were in the open air, therefore, throughout the winter," Rusk recalled. "In the winter, we were enclosed in big woolen sacks that were pulled around you. You brought your own hot brick with you in the morning and put it in the bottom of your sack."

The Secretary's early environment and family background may explain much of his caution, his reticence, his reluctance to "reach for the horizons." Contrasting Rusk with Dulles, one of his aides once said the Secretary lacks the passion of creative and visionary men: "Dulles, a totally unlovely person, made a place for himself in history, but Rusk, an incredibly decent person, will have none."

Rusk has no close personal friends in Washington, and seeks none. He has rarely had any after-hours' social contact with any of his associates. The Secretary models himself after the late General George Marshall, who believed that men in high office should have no friendships to encumber their duties. But even General Marshall's façade slipped occasionally. When Rusk was Assistant Secretary of State for the Far

[*] On Station WSB-TV, Atlanta, August 11, 1965.

East, he once marched into General Marshall's bedroom at
3:00 A.M. with an urgent problem, and a proposed solution.
"At least you have earned your keep for the day," General
Marshall complimented his aide.

Unlike other Secretaries of State, Rusk has carefully
avoided Washington's top-drawer Georgetown and Metropolitan Club sets and, what is more surprising, has been sought by
neither. His only relaxation is bridge, which he plays with dash
but seldom for money. He once said, "You must never under-
estimate a Southerner's capacity for doing nothing"—but he is
known to have ended a two-weeks' vacation, taken at the urging of his daughter, Peggy, after only three days.

Rusk takes no exercise, although he has played a duffer's
game of golf once or twice annually at the Army and Navy
Country Club with George Ball. Early in his administration,
an enthusiastic public-relations officer, hoping to portray Rusk's
"folksiness," distributed photographs of him bowling self-
consciously with some State Department secretaries. As far as
is known, Rusk has not hurled a bowling ball at a ten-pin
since that day. His idea of Sunday recreation, according to an
associate, is to put on slacks and a sport shirt and spend the
day in his office. But Rusk regularly attends the occasional cricket games staged by British Commonwealth personnel in Washington.

Rusk brought no personal entourage with him to the
State Department. John Foster Dulles' personal secretary,
Phyllis Bernau, was asked to stay on with Rusk. When she for-
sook a career for marriage, Rusk asked the departmental personnel office to assign him a new secretary. Carolyn Proctor, a
former girl Friday to an assistant secretary, was named to the
job.

The Secretary's executive assistant and closest associate is
Benjamin Read, a Philadelphia attorney and former legislative
aide to Senator Joseph Clark. Read keeps an inch-thick loose-
leaf diary of everything Rusk does, should do and know each
day. Read and Miss Proctor have been in constant attendance
on the Secretary, but they almost never see him socially.

Notably, however, Rusk has displayed a kind of imper-

sonal concern and compassion for his department's staff, and a
close watch to insure justice for those in trouble. He has demanded and obtained re-examinations of doubtful security
cases. He has stood firm against Otto F. Otepka, a State Department employee accused of slipping classified information
to the Senate Internal Security Subcommittee. He has also
been concerned about State Department chauffeurs having
nothing to do while waiting for assignments and about parking
facilities for departmental personnel. Although he obviously
did not have to, Rusk has regularly paid the nine-dollar
monthly parking charge in the department garage.

Rusk has been described as one of the most completely
self-disciplined men in Washington. He has never been known
to lose his temper, and pressure has only seemed to calm him.
He seems to dissipate pressure and irritation by puffing rapidly
on a succession of cigarettes and shuffling papers on his desk.
He has never borne grudges. Rusk has been well aware of ex-
Secretary Dean Acheson's condescending references to him
as "the little Dean," and of Ambassador Harriman's digs
about Secretaries of State "who have never run for
elective office" and "don't know their country." But no one seeing Rusk with either "the big mustache," as Acheson is known
around State, or with Harriman, would suspect there was
anything amiss in their relationships.

While Rusk has been patient almost to the point of sub-
mission, there have been limits to his patience. Kenneth Galbraith, the egotistical former ambassador to India, cracked
Rusk's icy composure frequently with dispatches from New
Delhi in which he constantly sneered at State and its principal
officers. Arthur Goldberg, ambassador to the UN, who has
been forever promoting new "initiatives" in the field of personal diplomacy, has not been a Rusk favorite. But the tolerant
Secretary has been quoted as saying that "as soon as Arthur re-
alizes the limitations of his job" he will establish a more harmonious relationship with State. Yet, Vice-President Humphrey told the Indian Railways Minister early in 1966 that
Goldberg had more influence on American foreign policy than
Rusk.

Rusk has been less tolerant of "instant historians," and there was a great deal of fast cigarette puffing and paper shuffling after Arthur Schlesinger, who had recommended Adlai Stevenson for the job, reported that Kennedy intended to replace the Secretary in 1964. "Cheap stuff," Rusk muttered to an aide who brought an advance account of the Schlesinger book. Rusk's first reaction was to draft a statement refusing to engage in "backstairs gossip" about his relationship with Kennedy. But he cooled off quickly and issued a more dignified and impersonal rebuttal of the Schlesinger story.

When he first took office, Rusk dreaded the public aspects of his job. Speech-making was torture, and a press conference was agony. Yet Rusk has become one of the most accessible Secretaries of State in recent administrations.

Realizing Rusk's dislike for formal press conferences but persuaded that the Secretary should continue airing his views on foreign affairs (even if he could not be quoted directly, but had to masquerade as a "United States official"), State's ex-Public Affairs Chief James Greenfield and his deputies Richard I. Phillips and Robert McCloskey devised a format better suited to Rusk's personality. Once a week, more or less, most of the regular State Department correspondents are invited to meet with the Secretary over drinks in a question-and-answer session. Rusk has frequently breakfasted, lunched or met for drinks with reporters, individually or in groups.

At these meetings, Rusk has been affable, easygoing and has displayed a practiced knack of evading probing questions with a touch of humor. When a network correspondent arranging a TV show on Vietnam asked Rusk if he would object to some opposition Congressmen on the same program, Rusk replied with a story about an elderly lady who dreamed a young man was bending over her bed.

"And what will you do to me now?" the grande dame quavered.

"Madam," the young man replied sternly, "this is your dream, not mine."

Rusk's guests have enjoyed such meetings with the Secretary, and almost invariably are impressed with his erudition and conversational skill. But these sessions have yet to develop any significant information which has not been made available in earlier public statements. Rusk has never been known to "leak" to the press.

Rusk has been equally at ease with diplomats. On one occasion, the Polish ambassador came in to complain about a speech made by Arthur Goldberg in Chicago, castigating the Warsaw government for its suppression of religious freedom.

Mr. Rusk accepted the official protest and then remarked, with a twinkle in his eye: "Mr. Ambassador, could you perhaps allow us some fifteen per cent of our speech-making for domestic purposes? We allow a much larger percentage for yours."

Completely disarmed, Ambassador Drozniak advised his government to regard the incident as closed.

Before Johnson increased Rusk's foreign policy authority last March, the Secretary's hesitations created a vacuum in the foreign policy field which power-seekers all over Washington were trying to fill. In justice to McNamara, Bundy, Goldberg and some others who plunged into foreign policy, however, it must be said that, more often than not, they entreated Rusk, directly or through his assistants, to play his role more vigorously.

But the Secretary stuck doggedly to his concept of duty, a reserved posture which encouraged at least a dozen men in and outside the State Department to move into the foreign policy vacuum. McNamara, with a legitimate interest in foreign policies affecting the Pentagon, has been consulted increasingly by Johnson on issues of only marginal military interest. Vice-President Humphrey has ideas on Latin America, and so had former Undersecretary of State (for Economic Affairs), Thomas Mann, but no hemisphere policy initiatives have ever come from Rusk.

Practically every Cabinet member, including Agriculture Secretary Orville Freeman, and Interior Secretary Stewart Udall, have tried their hands at conducting personal policies toward the Soviet Union. Ambassador Goldberg, latest arrival in the foreign policy vacuum, has been acting upon the unsupported theory that ambassadors to the United Nations are more effective than their Washington counterparts and has, in effect, set up a little State Department of his own in New York. "Arthur," a former presidential aide commented, "believes that if you talk to them long enough, they'll give in."

Rusk's failure or refusal to assert his primacy in the foreign policy field has produced some astonishingly contradictory developments. While the President and State were talking about "building bridges" to Eastern Europe, FBI Director, J. Edgar Hoover, was demanding the imposition of travel limits on Iron Curtain diplomats at a time when the Communists were relaxing their own. A consular treaty with the Soviets has been stymied by Congressional opposition. And the Pentagon, through its International Security Affairs Section, has often conducted a De Gaulle and NATO policy which is at odds with the State Department.

Rusk has moved serenely through all this confusion and conflict, seemingly unaffected by forays into his foreign policy preserves. He has never raised his voice to oppose policies which he knew could end only in failure. He gave Kennedy correct advice in the Bay of Pigs crisis, but failed to make his warnings forceful. He warned Johnson against branding the rebels in the Dominican Republic as Communists, but said nothing when contrary instructions went out of the White House over his signature. He opposed Johnson's impetuous decision to postpone visits here in 1965 by Indian Premier Lal Bahadur Shastri and Pakistani President Mohammed Ayub Khan, but did nothing about it. He accepted Johnson's hasty decision to meet Premier Nguyen Cao Ky early in 1966 in Honolulu and make the meeting an American-South Vietnamese affair, instead of inviting South Korea, Australia and New Zealand (which also have troops in Vietnam) as some of his departmental subordinates suggested.

Rusk once outlined his aim in a news conference: "It is the purpose of the Department of State to try and bring about what some people will call a boring situation; that is, a period of peace. I should not object if we got international relations off of the front page for a while. I see no prospect of it."

Rusk has succeeded admirably in making his tenure of office dull and commonplace. History is likely to record this as his major achievement. But before the history books of this period could be written, Rusk's aloofness and apparent indifference has created the impression, here and abroad, of a shiftless diplomacy moving aimlessly from one crisis to another. The question most often asked by foreign diplomats in Washington during the Kennedy-Johnson years has been, "Who is making American foreign policy?" There have been, depending on the year, many answers. But one thing could be said with certainty: It is not the Secretary of State.

N · I · N · E

The devil's advocate

Traditionally, the Undersecretary of State has been the workhorse of the department. While the Secretary was supposed to look far ahead at this country's roles and relations abroad, meet with the President, deal with Congress and make speeches, the Undersecretary was to oversee the implementation of American foreign policy, direct the State Department's relations with the military, intelligence and all other departments, keep an eye on its internal administration and leap into action whenever a crisis threatened to jeopardize the orderly course of foreign relations.

Formally, the Undersecretary serves as first deputy to the Secretary and takes over his responsibilities when the latter is absent. He advises and assists the Secretary in formulating, determining and carrying out American foreign policy. The extent to which he is called upon to fill these roles in a crisis depends on the President's and Secretary's confidence in him, and the President's preferences in seeking advice and taking action. Confidence and personal relations rather than formal channels determine who advises the President in a crisis.

The Undersecretary's post was created in 1919. The men who first filled it were competent but undistinguished foreign service or departmental officers. Some of their more recent successors, named as political appointees, were of similarly mediocre ability.

167

But as the United States began venturing abroad in the wake of World War I, as the thunderclouds of another war began building up across Europe in the '30s, the competence, role and responsibilities of the Undersecretary widened steadily. As a result, in modern times, a notable number of Undersecretaries have made history in their own right and not only as the alter-egos of their chiefs. William Phillips, Sumner Welles, Joseph Grew, Dean Acheson, Robert Lovett, David Bruce and George Ball have rated stars on the roll of honor of American Undersecretaries of State.

"Anybody holding this job," former Undersecretary Ball has said, "must be conscious of Sumner Welles' experiences." Welles filled the post under Cordell Hull from 1937 to 1943. What Ball had in mind, of course, was Welles' personal relationship with President Roosevelt.

Welles, a brilliant, aloof man, undoubtedly was closer to his President than any of his predecessors or successors in office. He never hesitated to use his relationship with Roosevelt to bypass the Secretary. The two often discussed major foreign policy issues without bothering to consult Hull. The President regularly wrote personal notes on current affairs to Welles, and Welles went directly to Roosevelt with intelligence summaries or foreign policy proposals which had not been seen by Hull.

Moreover, Roosevelt welcomed Welles' contributions, apparently preferring his coldly objective and analytical summations to Hull's less fluid approach to decision-making.

Because of their friendship and of his respect for Welles' abilities, Roosevelt entrusted him with some of this country's key pre-war and wartime crisis diplomacy assignments.

It was Welles who suggested to Roosevelt and helped draft a direct appeal to Hitler during the Czechoslovak crisis, in direct challenge to Hull, who opposed the appeal. Early in 1940, Welles visited the capitals of the European belligerents—Berlin, Rome, Paris and London—to explore the possibility of ending the war. Hull argued against the mission, feeling it would accomplish nothing. He was vigorously supported by the American ambassadors in the capitals concerned, led by Ambassador Joseph Kennedy in London, who complained indignantly that their jurisdictions were being invaded by "outsiders."

(In those days, special presidential emissaries were not as common as they are today. But even today's ambassadors regard the countries to which they are assigned as their private preserves and resent the intrusions of special Washington envoys on crisis diplomacy assignments.)

Welles played key parts in other major foreign policy decisions of the Roosevelt years. He helped draft the Atlantic Charter, and was the only State Department official to accompany Roosevelt to his Atlantic Charter meeting with Winston Churchill.

Welles led the American delegation to the Rio conference after Pearl Harbor, hoping to persuade all Western Hemisphere governments to break relations with the Axis powers. Argentina and Chile balked at unanimity and insisted on freedom of action. Welles accepted the compromise. Hull was furious, contending the inter-American, anti-Axis front had been damaged. But again Roosevelt sided with Welles.

In the end, it was politics that led to Welles' exit from the Undersecretary's office. Welles had no political base, while Hull was a major voice in the Democratic party. Under strong Congressional pressure, the politically astute President finally decided to sacrifice Welles and asked for his resignation. It was submitted and accepted on September 25, 1943.

The peculiar Welles-Roosevelt-Hull episode has not been duplicated since that time, and most of the Undersecretaries have managed to paper over any differences they may have had with their Secretaries and Presidents. It was widely assumed in Washington, however, that during his two-year tenure as Undersecretary (1954–56), Herbert Hoover, Jr. was often at odds with General Eisenhower and John Foster Dulles. Hoover opposed the policy of closer U.S. relationship with Communist Yugoslavia, cultural exchanges with Communist countries and the scope of some of the foreign-aid programs, particularly to India.

During one brief period of the Suez crisis, with both

Eisenhower and Dulles away from Washington, Hoover found himself in charge of the State Department. Acting in the Secretary's behalf, Hoover jeopardized this country's delicate diplomacy by delaying oil shipments to Britain and France.

If some Undersecretaries have not been notably successful, and have had only negligible influence on their Secretaries, and particularly their Presidents, the reverse has been astonishingly true in the case of others. Dean Acheson, for example, exerted a potent influence on American foreign policy as Undersecretary to General George Marshall.

On taking office, General Marshall appointed Acheson as his "chief of staff," and ordered all problems and issues addressed to him to be routed through his Undersecretary. He directed Acheson to propose policies, manage the State Department's operations and oversee its administration.

Undersecretary George Ball continued the Acheson tradition. While he held the Undersecretary's post, he was a pervasive force in the State Department. With Secretary Rusk serene in his own conception of his job, Ball was bound to leave his mark on the amorphous Foggy Bottom establishment. There was much opposition to his policies and tactics, but few denied that, almost alone in the department, he knew how to formulate ideas and to implement his own policies.

Ball's admirers have said that he was imaginative, colorful, had a keen strategic sense and an uncanny ability to express his views. His detractors argued that Ball's diplomatic activities "have all the subtlety of a sledge hammer." Critics also said that "George has never felt that there was anybody as good as he in the U.S. government," and some admitted that "he was probably right."

On January 30, 1961, Ball was appointed Undersecretary for Economic Affairs, and became—in his own words—a "lonely lawyer fallen among economists." It was not, however, until November 29 of that year that he was sworn in as the number two man in the State Department.

Ball was on the go from then on. Invariably, he was first to volunteer for any crisis job and, before anyone had time to object, he was already there handling it. He was the chief "nuts and bolts" man during the Cuban missile crisis and in the various phases of the Congo episode. Later, he chose for himself the job of supervising and reconciling the various policy differences stemming from the U.S. involvement in the Dominican Republic.

Ball was quick to fill any vacuum which appeared in the field of long-range foreign policy. With the President's and Rusk's tacit approval, Ball made himself the final authority on relations with France. There was no doubt of the higher approval, but some question always existed as to whether the President and the Secretary were presented with advance alternatives before Ball went into action.

No one quite knew what set Ball off on any given course of action. A policy speech on France (March 16, 1965) castigating General de Gaulle's criticism of U.S. policies in Vietnam "without regard to its effect on the responsible common efforts of other states" was Ball's own idea, sparkplugged by a luncheon meeting with Walter Lippmann, who argued for the French position. "It's time we put our views on the record," he told Rusk, and a few days later the speech was written and ready for delivery.

Ball, a former legal adviser to the French government and the Common Market, held strong views on both. In early 1966, he prepared what he called "a personal paper" on how to deal with the problem of Gaullism and Gaullist France. In essence, it was a declaration of war against Gaullism on the ground that the revival of national rivalries which it spawned would only end in catastrophe. When Ball's paper reached the White House, all references to "war" on De Gaulle were carefully eliminated by the President. But, undaunted by setbacks, Ball continued to advocate his French policy to the end of his stay in the State Department.

Opposition to prevailing views came naturally to Ball. While Rusk has rarely taken issue with President Johnson, Ball had few inhibitions against arguing forcefully with him. Some of the ex-Undersecretary's sharpest exchanges with the President were on Vietnam. Labelling himself "the devil's advocate," Ball consistently argued against escalation of the

American military effort there. In White House councils, Ball pressed for some attempt at negotiations each time there was a debate about increasing the size or broadening the mission of American forces in Vietnam. "Ball did not prevent escalation, but I dread to think what might have happened if there had been no George Ball," one official commented.

Ball's position on Vietnam was due in large measure to the influence of Senator J. William Fulbright, whose suggestion led to Ball's State Department appointment. At one time during the Fulbright hearings on Vietnam in the spring of 1966, Ball had accepted an invitation to testify before the Foreign Relations Committee but withdrew his acceptance after the President intervened.

In adopting the devil's advocate role, Ball apparently was attempting to reconcile the conflict of his views with his loyalty to the Chief Executive. Until mid-1965, when suggestions for negotiations of a Vietnam peace settlement were rarely voiced, Ball doggedly insisted that negotiations were the only solution for ending the war. Among his State supporters were Ambassador Llewellyn Thompson, the Soviet specialist, China expert Allen Whiting and James Greenfield, ex-Assistant Secretary of State for Public Affairs. Overruled on the negotiations issue, Ball remained silent. Within the year before he left the administration, however, Ball changed his mind on negotiations to the extent of admitting that they may not be possible as long as the Communists remain obdurate.

Ball's differences with the President extended to the White House staff. Ball had no use for McGeorge Bundy and the "little State Department" which flourished under Kennedy. After Kennedy's assassination, a young foreign service officer named Lee T. Stull, who had previously served Vice-President Johnson as a State Department briefing officer, was retained by Mr. Johnson on the White House staff. Ball saw a chance of by-passing Bundy and used Stull as a channel of communication with the new President. Simultaneously, one of Bundy's assistants noticed that the flow of State Department cables to Bundy's office had virtually ceased. An investigation disclosed that the stoppage had been ordered by Ball. Bundy had Lee

Stull transferred, first to the policy-planning staff—to brief
its members on the "LBJ style"—and later to Pakistan.

In another scuffle, Ball challenged Bundy to prove that he
spoke for the President when he opposed the famous MLF
project in policy meetings. Bundy did. In December, 1965, the
President himself scuttled the scheme.

Ball's energy and perseverance have been proverbial. A
husky six-footer, he had logged, prior to his appointment in the
State Department, 160 trans-Atlantic crossings. His aerial trav-
els became more extensive when he joined the administration.
In 1963, President Kennedy dispatched him to Pakistan, which
was angry over American aid to India and making overtures
to Communist China. Ball managed to soothe the Pakistanis
somewhat, but failed in one diplomatic maneuver.

Among the entourage accompanying Ball to Pakistan was
Army Lieutenant General William W. Quinn, deputy director
of the Pentagon's Defense Intelligence Agency and an accomplished golfer. The general managed to schedule a game with
Pakistani President Ayub Khan, and Ball promptly instructed
the officer to lose. At the seventeenth hole, Quinn was ahead
and prepared to lose on the eighteenth. But Ayub suddenly felt
indisposed and called off the match, leaving Quinn an unwilling winner.

For a man with only one kidney Ball's missions
abroad were physically gruelling. He ate and drank everything put before him, including salads in Pakistan—a practice
which made his aides blanch.

While Sumner Welles' relations with his Secretary of State
have gone down in history as an example of what they should
not be, Ball's relations with Rusk were as ideal as they can be,
given the nature of their jobs.

Ball consistently acted as the Secretary's alter-ego. At one
time, some friction was caused by reports—not entirely without
foundation—that Ball had set his mind on the number one
job. But when the President served notice that he contemplated
no change in that post, relations were adjusted to a smooth and
easy level.

Practically every evening, the two men met in the Secretary's office and talked over drinks. During these sessions, Ball constantly threw out ideas and suggestions. Because of his drive and articulation, he often initiated and carried out policies which, under other administrations, had been left to the Secretary and staffed out through regular channels.

By special agreement, Ball was permitted to enter the Secretary's office irrespective of who else was there, and vice-versa. Only the sound of three short buzzes, indicating the President was on the phone, would send Ball out of Rusk's office.

A reporter gathering material for a foreign policy story once had the unique experience of a shuttling briefing between the Rusk-Ball offices as one or the other had to keep their scheduled appointments. Each took up where the other left off, and they appeared to be completely interchangeable.

However, the cordial relationship between the two top men in the State Department could not serve as a substitute for leadership by the Secretary of State. Even in normal times, the State Department has been described as a "loose confederation of warring chiefs." It was up to the Secretary to arbitrate among them—a power which cannot be delegated to an Undersecretary, whether he is a Welles or a Ball.

Ball was succeeded in the State Department by Nicholas deBelleville Katzenbach, the former attorney general and a former editor of the *Yale Law Review*. The appointment, like that of Eugene Rostow, also of Yale, had been suggested to the President by Associate Justice Abe Fortas, a former Yale professor of law.

Katzenbach's views on foreign policy problems were not known at the time of his appointment and it is doubtful if, apart from his expertise in international law, he had given much thought to specific policies. Rusk's relations with Katzenbach have always been cordial and they are likely to be as harmonious as they were with George Ball.

In one respect, however, Katzenbach is different. He has not succeeded Ball in the role of devil's advocate. "The devil needs no advocate," Katzenbach has been saying, quoting the

President. The new Undersecretary is more likely to find his place on the side of the angels and use his legal talent and negotiating skills to promote rather than to question the President's wishes.

In the early days of his tenure, Katzenbach has concentrated on the administration of the Foggy Bottom establishment. Like all newcomers to State he has been baffled by the seeming confusion and duplication of channels and wants to do something about it. He has also been concerned with State's poor image in Congress and wants every senior official to have direct contact with the Hill rather than through "salesmen" specially assigned to the job.

Katzenbach's ambition to streamline the State Department is bound to run into difficulties. With few notable exceptions, the State Department has developed a breed of cautious professionals. The foreign service tends to believe that diplomacy is an occult science which only the initiated know how to practice. Because of an inbred assumption that the professionals are entitled to a monopoly on foreign policy problems and decisions, friction constantly develops in the channels between the State Department and the White House and other government departments.

This appears in even the most trifling matters. During Kenneth Galbraith's tenure as American ambassador to India, for example, he once suggested that President Kennedy write a personal letter to the late Jawaharlal Nehru. The suggestion was referred to the State Department, and wound up on the desk of an official who knew neither Kennedy nor Nehru. A letter was drafted and transmitted to Galbraith for review. Galbraith, whose opinion of the State Department and its staff was never high, returned the letter. It was not cordial enough, he said, "please make it warmer."

The letter then went up and down the bureaucratic ladder, each official inserting what he considered a warm phrase. With all the clearances finally obtained, the letter was forwarded to the White House, where it was summarily rejected. McGeorge Bundy composed a new epistle which was dispatched to India the same day. The result? A dozen indignant letter writers at State and a new dollop of hostility toward "outsiders."

Hostility breeds hostility. Unlike the British Foreign Office, which controls its Secret Service, the State Department still regards the CIA as its rival. In spite of Kennedy's and Johnson's directives subordinating all agencies operating in the foreign field to the State Department, some roles are hard to subordinate. After President Kennedy issued his order making the ambassador at each post the undisputed head of the country team, CIA Chief McCone had to travel around the world to direct his "station chiefs" to comply with the order.

During Kennedy's administration and the early years of Johnson's first term, State's declining role in foreign policy became daily more evident. Foreign news would come out of the White House or half a dozen other agencies and State lost its status as a news center.

As crises developed, State was tardy in supplying assessments to the White House—a consequence of the department's instinct to sit on a problem until it could determine more clearly what is happening. State's "alerting" antennae began to seem rusty. The White House began to find it difficult to extract information—as distinguished from surmises—from the department.

In an attempt to redress State's decline in the foreign policy field, President Johnson resorted in March, 1966, to an old bureaucratic device: reorganization. Ironically, the reorganization program was the brain-child of General Maxwell Taylor. It had neither been outlined by nor entrusted to State, allegedly its principal beneficiary.

The reorganization directive established an Interdepartmental Regional Group to "insure the adequacy of United States policy for the countries in their region (corresponding to the geographic bureaus in State) and of the plans, programs, resources and performances for implementing that policy." The IRG also was instructed to be "particularly watchful for indications of developing crises," and to alert its superiors at once of any sign of such developments.

But the prime result of the reorganization program was the establishment of a high-ranking Senior Interdepartmental Group (SIG), ordered to maintain a running check on all American overseas policies and projects, to assure "a proper selectivity of the areas and issues to which the United States government applies its resources." SIG also was told to deal promptly with any issues raised by assistant secretaries or any SIG member, and to rush such issues to the Secretary of State if they required higher-level handling.

The directive establishing SIG listed its members as the Deputy Defense Secretary, the administrator of the Agency for International Development, the director of the Central Intelligence Agency, the chairman of the Joint Chiefs of Staff, the director of the United States Information Agency, and the President's Special Assistant for National Security Affairs. The Undersecretary of State was named ex-officio chairman of the SIG.

As chairman, the Undersecretary was granted "the authority and responsibility to decide all matters coming before his committee, subject to the right of any member to appeal from his decision to higher authority."

The White House wanted the chairman's authority to insure that SIG would be "an incisive, decision-making body," and former Deputy Undersecretary of State, U. Alexis Johnson, wrote in the *Foreign Service Journal* (April, 1966) that it provided "no room for parochial viewpoints or bureaucratic infighting." But these pronouncements were qualified to a major degree by the escape clause under which any SIG member who disapproved the chairman's decision could appeal it "to higher authority."

The prospect was that SIG could only be successful in resolving the non-critical issues that were brought before it, and those in which SIG-represented agencies had no special interest. Equally, if SIG's State Department chairman tried to make an important decision with which the Defense Department disagreed, an immediate and injured appeal would be made to "higher authority"—i.e., the President.

Since its inception, SIG has met regularly at 4:00 P.M.

every Tuesday in the Undersecretary's conference room. In its early stages, the prime participants attended in person. Later, after curiosity was satisfied, deputies were assigned to attend SIG sessions.

Initially, SIG agendas were fairly extensive, the subjects ranging from the cost of NATO removal from France to questions of economic aid to Indonesia. The NATO payment issue produced one of the first reversals of a SIG decision. After Ball, as chairman, had decided to approve the payments, Defense Secretary Robert McNamara balked. McNamara telephoned Ball, the two discussed the issue and Ball promptly reversed himself.

The Indonesian aid problem was referred to SIG by the AID agency, which had requested a prompt decision on renewing economic assistance to the troubled Southeast Asian island state. After quickly canvassing the opinions of his SIG associates, Ball decided to renew the Indonesian aid program.

After only a few weeks of existence, the Interdepartmental Regional Group, in compliance with the terms of its duties, called SIG's attention to several incipient crises in Southeast Asia and the Far East. Ball ordered a study by the agencies most concerned with the crises. He would have done the same if SIG had not existed.

Most of the issues brought before SIG in its infancy centered on subjects in which two key government departments or agencies were involved, or at odds. None dealt with world-shaking events. Up to now, SIG has functioned smoothly and the Chairman's decisions aroused no free-for-alls. But the value of SIG will not be properly assessed until it has dealt with a controversy of bitter and tangled dimensions like Vietnam or Cuba.

To some degree, Ball's position as Undersecretary of State influenced his decisions as SIG chairman. "You can't separate Hamlet from the Prince," one official acknowledged when asked if Ball's State Department loyalties ever intruded on his supposed detachment as SIG's chieftain. Those loyalties became most apparent when SIG considered problems in which Ball had not only a State Department but a personal interest—NATO, Western Europe, France. He could afford to be more objective on other issues.

Undersecretary Katzenbach has not suffered from Ball's handicap. He has not developed policies of his own and is not likely to move on matters of importance without clearance with the President and Secretary of State.

SIG is only the latest in a series of devices designed to bring better liaison between State and Defense, as well as more efficient crisis management. The Truman administration promoted the Webb-Lovett agreement for close cooperation between State and Defense. The OCB (Operations Coordinating Board) was Eisenhower's chosen instrument for coordinating policies and it was quickly abolished by Kennedy.

Kennedy's contribution to interdepartmental harmony was the Operations Center in the State Department, presided over by a State Department man but with military men on the staff. The difficulty in staffing the Operations Center lay in the peculiar duties imposed on the chairman. A first-class man was needed for what was essentially a clerical job. The chairman had to be adept at getting information for decisions which were to be made by others.

Theodore Achilles, a distinguished foreign service officer, the last chairman of the center, had difficulty in reconciling these two aspects of his job. In the course of the original Dominican Republic crisis, after the assassination of President Trujillo, the Navy had destroyers patrolling the Windward Passage at the State Department's request. After all U.S. citizens had been evacuated, the Navy Department wanted its destroyers back, but Achilles demurred, though he had no authority over the ships. Chief of Naval Operations, Admiral Burke, was furious. "Admiral Achilles is flying his flag," he commented acidly as he insisted that the destroyers be recalled.

The Operations Center did its best work in its early days, especially during the Kennedy-Khrushchev meeting at Vienna and the Berlin crisis which came afterward. It has since degenerated into an "answering service," which traces the whereabouts of key officials absent from town. A top official described its present role as "a bureaucratic appendage." They have a lot of *Popular Mechanics* stuff," he said, "electronic equipment, fancy TV sets, but nobody uses them any more. In the latest Dominican crisis, for instance, no one thought of giving them any work."

The key protagonists in any politico-military planning are State and Defense. As long as good relations prevail between the two, there is really no significant need for SIG or any other organization to arbitrate their views. When there are high-level antagonisms like those which existed in the Louis Johnson-Acheson era, no coordinating machinery short of the President himself is likely to resolve the dispute.

Fortunately, problems have not arisen between Mc-Namara and Rusk and did not arise between Defense Under-secretary Cyrus Vance and his opposite number at State, George Ball. McNamara's orders to his staff were simple: never take issue with State when the difference is a matter of opinion. Paul Nitze, a former State Department policy-planning chief who headed the Pentagon's International Security Affairs Bureau, was in the habit of feuding with his former colleagues at State. He was told by McNamara to desist and never to disagree on the handling of foreign policy matters, unless they directly involved military issues.

Nitze is now the Secretary of the Navy and his successor, John McNaughton, has avoided open clashes with the State Department. But it is an open secret that he and his staff have been highly critical of State's De Gaulle and NATO policies. Little harm can develop from these differences as long as the two key men, the Secretaries of State and Defense, sustain a cooperative relationship.

But plans must be made for dealing with future differences and President Johnson has wisely decided that the Undersecretary of State should have a semi-final say in foreign policy conflicts. But it is a foregone conclusion that conflicts between strong-willed men in top administration echelons can only be settled by the President, and no innovations in bureaucratic organization will enable the President to shed this responsibility.

T ⋆ E ⋆ N

The astrologers

On April 3, 1963, the State Department's top officials, headed by Secretary Rusk, assembled for a meeting convoked by Walt Rostow, then chief of the department's Policy
Planning Council, to consider a remarkable document prepared by his staff. Labelled "Khrushchev at Bay," the study
asserted that "a quiet but deep crisis" was mounting swiftly in
the Soviet Union, and that Khrushchev faced eviction from the
Kremlin within a short time unless he could score a thumping
domestic or international victory to divert attention from his
burgeoning troubles at home and abroad.

Written some eighteen months before Khrushchev's dis-
missal, the study ticked off a relentless catalogue of the swell-
ing woes and tribulations pressing in on the Soviet Chairman:
too many foreign commitments, the widening split with Communist China, grave economic troubles, especially in agriculture, and "conflict" in the ranks of the Soviet Communist party
over Khrushchev's foreign and domestic policies.

The study then examined some policies the United
States might initiate and pursue with a post-Khrushchev Soviet
Union. It pointed out that after Stalin's death, we had paid little or no heed to certain "suggestive signals" from his immediate successors when they were interested in trimming the hazards and costs of the cold war, and that we had exerted no

effort to influence the successive post-Stalin leadership changes which culminated in Khrushchev's accession to power.

The study went on to outline a series of possible policy tactics and moves. It advocated relaxation of some American restrictions on trade with the U.S.S.R. to promote more commerce between the two countries. It argued that more trade might improve Soviet-American relations, assist both countries' economies—and perhaps develop some slight measure of Soviet economic dependence on the United States.

More broadly, the "Khrushchev at Bay" study suggested that the United States should initiate proposals which do not necessarily require Soviet agreement, but merely Soviet acquiescence. It should launch moves to divert Soviet energies from ideological projects abroad into programs designed to increase Soviet prestige as a peace- and home-minded country. Such moves might demand campaigns to frustrate the Soviet Union and its leaders, the study continued. The campaigns should be pursued—although not to the point of frustrating the men in the Kremlin to the verge of desperation.

In third countries, the study suggested, particularly in the underdeveloped nations, the United States must encourage resistance to infiltration and subversion attempts by Soviet and other Communists to preclude the formation of Red cadres which might attempt to seize power ten years hence.

On the tactical front, the study suggested, the United States might consider a "switch" or "counter" policy to any Soviet-manufactured crisis. Thus, if the Soviet leaders decided to stage a Berlin crisis, the United States might respond with a proposal to negotiate an agreement on German unity; if the Soviet leaders began stirring up trouble in Laos, the United States might reply with some scheme for increasing the Kremlin's economic and other difficulties in Cuba.

Distinguished for its foresight and clarity, if not for the precision of its recommendations, "Khrushchev at Bay" was a sound example of the work being done by professional Washington planners. The questions most frequently asked about that work are what happens to it, who sees it and what, if any, effect does it have on American policy? The answers are difficult to obtain and assess.

It is known, for example, that since Rostow's transfer to the White House, some of the "Khrushchev at Bay" recommendations have been adopted by the President. Expansion of trade with the Communist countries, the so-called "building of bridges," has always been part of Rostow's philosophy and has been given a new stimulus by the President.

Under Kennedy, Rostow slipped many policy-planning papers into Kennedy's reading file, with the indulgence of Mrs. Evelyn Lincoln, the late President's secretary. He has much more direct access to the President now. Mr. Johnson likes Rostow. He finds the cheerful directness of his present assistant for National Security Affairs a relief from the self-possessed bearing of McGeorge Bundy. As a result, many of Rostow's ideas have found their way into presidential speeches and decisions.

Foreign policy planning is a relatively new concept in the United States government. It is actually as old as man. The Assyrians and the Hittites planned their policies ahead of time. So did Julius Caesar. Ghenghis Khan followed a policy plan with his Mongols, and an advance policy plan guided Alexander the Great beyond Samarkand into India.

In the United States, the Rostow-defined task of governmental policy planners is "to conceive of specific objectives in particular theaters of activity and of how to move forward toward those objectives under rapidly changing operational circumstances." The objectives, the sites and the approaches, of course, are widely varied. And, generally, they are fairly prosaic and almost commonplace.

For instance, the basic State Department policy plan for India, adopted in November, 1964, called for high-priority aid, for military assistance tailored to the menace of Communist China and the anxieties of Pakistan, for tolerance of the Soviet-Indian relationship. But the paper further proposed an extension of American "alternatives" to preclude total Indian dependence on the U.S.S.R. and for the use of persuasion instead of pressures in any attempts to improve American-Indian relations.

The policy on Chile, adopted a few months later, proposed the encouragement of democratic trade unions, wider

American contacts with Chilean students and American assumption of responsibility for Chile's security in the event of an external attack.

Similarly, the Kenya policy study has recommended encouragement in developing it into a stable nation oriented toward the free world and American acceptance of Britain as the preponderant foreign power in Kenya.

Although some policy plans have been sharply pointed and direct, others were little more than bland statements of clichés. A former policy planner who had helped draft the paper on Algeria once sat down with the "country team," i.e., all the United States officials assigned to Algeria, and asked bluntly: "What are we supposed to do here?" The answers, echoing the paper, came with monotonous similarity: "We want a democratic, non-Communist Algeria." But no one suggested how to achieve that aim. The Navy attaché volunteered that Algeria was important to his service because a Soviet submarine base there would endanger the United States. Asked if he believed that danger was realistic, the attaché conceded it was not.

Virtually all of American policy planning has been predicated on the danger of Communism. Since the Castro takeover in Cuba, for example, much policy planning has been projected on the necessity of preventing "another Cuba." Most of the planning for Indonesia was hinged on the assumption that the island nation would go Communist, and elaborate countermeasures were projected to dull the effects of a Communist takeover. When the contrary occurred and the Indonesian Communist party was dismantled, the State Department was baffled—and delighted. A new U.S. ambassador, Marshall Green, had urgently advocated a hands-off policy—a departure from that of his predecessor, who urged strong U.S. support for Sukarno. The administration complied with Green's advice and the powerful PKI (Indonesian Communist party) was all but eliminated—without an assist from the U.S.

"We are ad hoc'ing," says William R. Polk, a former policy planner and now professor of Near Eastern history at the University of Chicago. "Urgent problems expel the important ones, and we are conducting policy with gimmicks. One day it is the lightweight rifle; another—the strategic hamlet, defoliation and the helicopter."

But today's policy planners deny Polk's allegation that "we have never thoroughly examined the long-range implications of Vietnam or stated clearly even to ourselves what we went there for and how we are going to accomplish it." The denial seems valid in some measure. As much if not more study has been devoted to the implications of Vietnam than to any other crisis here in recent years. Polk seems to stand on more solid ground with his assertion that the United States has not been too clear on what it wants in Vietnam, except to stop North Vietnam from molesting its neighbors.

Another weakness of recent administrations has been the high-level indifference to policy planners. As operational crises press on policy-makers and demand more time from President Johnson and his chief lieutenants, the planners have found it difficult to attract high-level attention. The President and Rusk have literally squirmed in their chairs on the rare occasions when they have consented to listen to long-range policy plans.

A study of the work of the State Department's Policy Planning Council reveals some amazingly painstaking research, carefully documented reasoning and sound conclusions. In March, 1960, for example, the council recommended a United States commitment for a new ground-level Panama Canal, to lessen this country's dependence on the Republic of Panama for the existing waterway. The author, Henry Ramsey, a Foreign Service officer, predicted that Panama's hot-tempered students would start trouble unless the canal issue was resolved—a forecast which came painfully true when the canal crisis erupted in 1964.

The Ramsey Panama paper, which had been approved as policy by Secretary of State Christian Herter, advanced these general theses:

1. The Panama Canal was a rapidly wasting asset both economically and strategically. Studies indicated that it would not be able to accommodate projected traffic in the 1980s. It was strategi-

cally obsolescent in the missile age: it could be easily sabotaged, could be put out of action indefinitely by even a conventional warhead and was too narrow to accommodate larger warships.

2. We should, therefore, begin to plan beyond its life expectancy, decide in principle upon a sea-level canal replacement which would be invulnerable to attack and accessible to ships of all sizes and utilize the interim to prepare American and Panamanian opinion for ultimate abandonment of the present canal. It is estimated that it would take ten years to construct a sea-level canal.

3. During this period and beginning immediately, we should diffuse Panamanian radical nationalism by a series of concessions and adjustments to include:

Socio-economic programs of the type later embraced within the Alliance for Progress, with emphasis on land reform and diversification of light industry; reducing the dependence of the Panamanian economy on canal revenues but increasing our "rent"; converting (after its abandonment) the present canal into a hydroelectric complex; flying the Panamanian flag in the Zone; replacing the military governor by a civilian; coordinating Panamanian-Zone policy under the ambassador in recognition of the fact that our jurisdiction over the Zone was the controlling political factor in U.S.-Panamanian relations; and taking a variety of steps to alter the *colon* attitude of the large American colony in the Zone. [One of the arguments made in favor of a sea-level canal was that it would eliminate the large American colony.] Parallel steps should be taken to influence the Panamanian oligarchy (the "14 families") to move in these directions as an alternative to violent social revolution of the Bolivian or Cuban type.

4. The paper laid heavy emphasis on the fact that radical nationalism in Panama and throughout Latin America was a fact of life which could not be eliminated by bullets or by "business as usual"; and that we must associate ourselves with the wave of the future and become involved in massive socio-economic assistance programs directed at raising the standard of living, increasing employment and opening the way for the middle class to take over government from the oligarchies, as in Mexico and Venezuela.

In late 1961, the new Kennedy administration also came around to the Panama problem and the 1960 recommendations for sea-level replacement of the canal. Additional studies were ordered by Undersecretary George Ball, who was skeptical of the project. Ball felt that some new methods of transportation, employing the hydrofoil principle, could be developed and would make a sea-level canal unnecessary. Also, the question arose later whether the canal could be built by controlled nuclear explosions without violating the nuclear test ban treaty.

Things stood on dead center until the Panama riots of early 1964 faced the Johnson administration with its first foreign crisis. Under pressure from Panama, most of the concessions specified in the Ramsey paper of 1960 were granted in the summer of 1964. A presidential commission headed by former Secretary of the Treasury, Robert Anderson, was appointed and studies started on the construction of a sea-level canal.

If there had been no riots in Panama, the Ramsey paper would have been left to gather dust in the State Department files. It can only be surmised that at least one ugly crisis could have been avoided had the policy paper been studied and acted upon before the crisis developed.

In addition to high-level indifference, State Department planners have to contend with the lack of "institutional memory" in their agency. Officials involved in crises are seldom debriefed nor are their experiences collected in a central file. One planner who tried to collect information on Angola discovered there were seventeen places where such data was stored and that each of the seventeen files contained different items of information. To remedy this situation, Deputy Undersecretary for Administration, William Crockett, established, with the aid of the Budget Bureau, something called FAIME (Foreign Affairs Information Management Effort), a system for "information storage and retrieval." But it may be several years before the desired data can be systematically stored and retrieved by computers.

"In a highly fragmented and specialized government, such as ours," says Rostow, "the Policy Planning Council remains one of the few places where there is a chance to observe and assess the nation's position along the whole front of military and foreign policy, to place what we are doing and trying to do in the long sweep of history."

Whether many persons in government are interested in placing what they are doing in the long sweep of history is another matter. Some of them share the attitude of the late Lord Keynes, who dismissed all attempts at long-range planning with the succinct observation that "in the long run, we'll all be dead."

Walt Rostow was a living refutation of Lord Keynes' dictum. Under his chairmanship, the planning staff burst with activity. The council's staff of fifteen specialists worked at a furious pace. In 1964, the council turned out no fewer than seventy-one policy papers, ranging from "amnesty and surrender in guerrilla warfare" to what the United States should do on the "Asian rimland." In handing out assignments, Rostow warned his planners he would judge their work in part by the number of fights they had. There is always danger, he told them, that since many governmental agencies must be consulted on a "country paper," the final draft may reflect so much compromise that it becomes completely colorless.

The Policy Planning Staff's output was exceeded only by the volume of memoranda and notes fired off by the chairman himself. In his four years on the council, Rostow seldom passed up a chance to express his views.

He bombarded the White House with memos and ideas on every conceivable subject. In 1962, he submitted a Basic National Security Paper listing some forty-four potential and foreseeable crises, plus proposals for more effective crisis management through a close linkage of the intelligence, planning and operational agencies. In August of the same year, he advised the President that unless there was a radical change of leadership in Peking or Moscow by mid-1963, a Sino-Soviet break in either state or Communist party relations was likely. There has been no formal break, but the split has certainly widened.

Rostow pleaded with President Kennedy to try to persuade British ex-Prime Minister Harold Macmillan to seize the leadership of the European unity movement instead of insisting upon an independent nuclear deterrent. But Macmillan charged Kennedy with repudiating President Eisenhower's commitment and said that he strongly preferred the Polaris submarines to leadership in the Common Market. Rostow also advised it was necessary to outflank General de Gaulle's appeal to European pride by more intimate consultations with individual NATO nations, in spite of the risk that the consultations would be leaked.

However, as a veteran planner has admitted, "the rarest thing in government is an idea which is new, workable and accepted," a contention endorsed by a ranking State Department official who had recently polled the department's assistant secretaries on new ideas for their areas. Every reply received was negative, the official reported. "They have too many vested interests to protect," he explained laconically.

Unlike the assistant secretaries' responses, few of Rostow's policy ideas have been negative. But it is debatable how many of them were translated into official policy. He has been given considerable credit, however, for the policy of escalating the Vietnam "liberation war" to victory. He contends that only a defeat in Vietnam will persuade the Communists to abandon further military forays against the free world.

According to his associates, a "new Rostow" has emerged since his return to the White House. The always optimistic, always articulate—his detractors say long-winded—Rostow papers have given way to terse memoranda which Mr. Johnson is said to read with interest. One Rostow paper requesting six decisions, marked with "yes" and "no" boxes, came back from the President's office with six yeses and the word "excellent" scrawled across the bottom of the page. This has been described as an all-time accolade by White House intimates.

But the cause of long-range planning has not suffered by Rostow's departure from the State Department. His successor, Henry Owen, a career civil servant and a brilliant scholar, has continued the Rostow tradition of looking over the horizon. Unlike Rostow, however, Owen does not roll with the punches; he takes his defeats seriously and clings courageously to unpopular positions.

The United States is not the only country where policy planners are tolerated but seldom heeded.

The British Foreign Office policy-planning staff consists of less than ten persons, whose papers often go to the Foreign Secretary but less frequently to the Cabinet. "About the best our chaps can expect," one foreign-office official explained, "is that their ideas, some of them at least, will get to the Foreign Secretary and occasionally to the prime minister."

Some British policy planning, the official continued, is negative in theme, "aimed at pointing out things we shouldn't do in certain places that would get us in trouble there.

"And of course our policy chaps have it easier than yours," he went on, "because we just don't have so many responsibilities around the world."

British diplomats freely acknowledge their policy planners are plagued by the unknown factor in every policy paper: the personality of the leaders for whose country the policy is drawn.

"How could you plan for De Gaulle," one British official asked wryly, "or Sukarno or Tshombe—or Lyndon Johnson?"

And like their U.S. colleagues, British planners, too, have suffered from blurred vision into the future. When Britain closed its Suez base and pulled out of Egypt, foreign office planners mentioned the chance that Egypt might seize the canal as a "low-priority possibility."

The Soviet Foreign Office, reported recently to have established a policy-planning staff, obviously faces the same unknowns as it attempts to plan for the future. And, if the Soviet ideological pattern is followed, Moscow's foreign office planners have another agency to contend with—the Central Committee of the Communist party. Soviet foreign policy plans must not only be based on the Rostow formula of "specific objectives" and how to achieve them under rapidly changing operations circumstances; they must also be tailored to the precepts of Marx and Lenin.

The intricacies of Soviet policy planning are unknown, but there is evidence of coordination among various agencies. During the Geneva atom test ban talks, Soviet officials told their Western counterparts that the Russian delegation's instructions were coordinated among the Communist party secretariat, the foreign and defense ministries and several other agencies. The foreign office seems dominant. Gromyko seldom appears with more than one military adviser in his entourage and he invariably treats him with obvious superiority.

The Communist party's presence and role in Soviet policy planning introduces an additional factor unknown to Western planners. It is as if American policy planners had to work with and clear all their plans with the Democratic National Committee.

But with all its handicaps, Soviet policy has been remarkably flexible in the post-Stalin period. Ideology may dominate foreign policy but the Kremlin sees nothing abnormal in catering to arch enemies of Communism, such as De Gaulle and Nasser.

Some of the most notable effects of Soviet policy planning have emerged in relation to NATO and General de Gaulle.

While the general kept himself in self-imposed exile at Colombey-les-deux-Eglises from 1953 to 1958, the Soviet Ambassador to France, Sergei A. Vinogradov, was a regular visitor. Vinogradov's efforts, later continued by his successor, Valerian A. Zorin, finally resulted in a significant improvement of De Gaulle's relations with the Soviets.

Unlike the British, the Soviets seem to have known how to "plan for De Gaulle" and to exploit the general's neuroses about the "Anglo-Saxons" and an integrated NATO command.

Some effects of Soviet policy planning have also been noted in formerly hostile Turkey and in wary Iran.

In transparent attempts to improve the U.S.S.R.'s relations with Turkey and Iran and thus increase the security of its southern border, the Soviet Union has been pushing exchange visits of high-level Russian, Turkish and Iranian delegations. This program has given the Soviet Union another opportunity to create whatever mischief possible in the NATO and CENTO organizations designed to deter Soviet aggression. Turkey is a member both of NATO and CENTO, Iran a member of the latter alliance.

Soviet policy planning for Turkey and Iran appears to have achieved some successes. At the moment, Soviet relations with both those countries are more amicable than they have been since the end of World War II. The Soviets have not been able to dislodge Turkey or Iran from NATO or CENTO, it is true, but they have eased Turkish and Iranian hostility toward the U.S.S.R.

Prior to World War II, long-range planning in the United States was limited largely to the military services. Only the Navy had sets of "country papers" on various foreign nations, but they contained only a few statistics and data on depths of harbors, prevailing winds and landing facilities.

The first joint Army-Navy planning began in November, 1938, after Munich. The planners were told to predicate their efforts on the Monroe Doctrine and the defense of the American continent. They were instructed to contemplate U.S. involvement in a war in Europe and in Asia, but not simultaneously. During World War II, military planning centered in the Strategy and Policy Group of the War Department, which included some civilians in freshly donned uniforms. One of the leading members of the group was Dean Rusk. Additionally, the State Department assigned such men as Herbert Feis and the late Leo Pasvolsky to plan the post-war world—in their spare time.

Foreign policy planning began in earnest in May, 1947. George Kennan recalls that after General Marshall returned from the 1947 Moscow conference convinced the Soviet Union would not cooperate with the West, he was summoned to the Secretary's office and told by Marshall:

Europe is in a dangerous sort of mess and it is not getting any better. Something has to be done. If I do not come up at once with some sound initiative, other people are going to start coming at me with various cockeyed proposals and I shall be thrust on the defensive and forced to spend my time arguing why this or that should not be done. You have ten days to consider this problem and to tell me what I ought to do. I have only one bit of advice for you—avoid trivia.

Kennan had just started working as chairman of a five-man policy planning staff in the State Department. The staff had been established by Marshall, who believed the Soviet Union was working abroad on a long-range plan while the United States was content to meet problems as they occurred. Kennan's first paper as a policy planner outlined the policy of containing the Soviet Union which he had advocated while serving as counselor at the American embassy in Moscow.

General Marshall's order to produce within ten days a plan for the rehabilitation of Europe elicited a Kennan memorandum which was the basis of the Marshall Plan. It was almost entirely Kennan's personal work.

Kennan's proposal to Marshall had special merit in that it avoided the temptation to refurbish existing programs and tie them into a package palatable to Congress and involving a minimum of political risk. The Export-Import Bank was already extending loans to European nations. Commodity credits were available, and there were funds for occupation assistance in Germany. But instead of combining what was already available, Kennan recommended a program requiring both Congressional appropriations and coordinated European action. The boldness and novelty of the plan—not just the money provided—caught the imagination and buoyed European hopes. Kennan and Marshall assumed correctly that it would be easier to evoke a response to new and sweeping ideas than to timid initiatives deliberately limited for fear of offending vested interests.

Kennan had the great advantage of being supported by a courageous President and Secretary of State. Although Truman was heading an administration believed to be on its last legs and certain to lose the 1948 election, he asked only one question when he was presented with what is now called the Marshall Plan: "Is this necessary?" When his advisers said "yes," Truman simply told them to go ahead with it.

The close Marshall-Kennan relationship was duplicated when Dean Acheson succeeded Marshall as Secretary of State and Paul Nitze became his Policy Planning Chief. Nitze's main preoccupation was the inadequacy of American forces as related to the tasks they were expected to perform. In 1949, Soviet power was increasing and Nitze called for corresponding increases in the American military establishment. His National Security Paper No. 68 called for greatly increased defense expenditures, especially in the field of conventional weapons. When Eisenhower became President, it was one of the policy papers which attracted his attention. Eisenhower endorsed and circulated the paper to the new members of the National Security Council.

Under Nitze, the policy-planning staff drafted most of the Korean War plans, seeking to contain war aims within the government's capabilities. Nitze insisted either on reducing objectives to conform with the nation's military strength, or increasing that strength. He was instrumental in raising the 1953 defense budget requests to $52 billion.

The policy-planning staff came into its own in the Dulles administration of the State Department. The first person Dulles summoned on arriving at the State Department was Policy Planning Chief, Paul Nitze, a holdover from the Acheson administration. He told Nitze he expected to spend only 10 per cent of his time running the State Department and the rest planning policy.

In 1953, Dulles appointed his own Policy Planning Chief, Robert Bowie, a Harvard scholar, who in 1966 returned to Washington as counselor of the State Department. Bowie soon became one of Dulles' intimate counselors, although the two very seldom saw eye to eye on any matters of substance. Bowie, like Nitze and Kennan before him, had unobstructed access to the Secretary and saw him several times a day. In 1953, the National Security Council's Planning Board, under Bowie's direction, produced the Basic National Security Paper, which served as a catalogue of over-all U.S. foreign and military policy. The BNSP was revised each year until the practice was abandoned and the paper itself allowed to lapse in the first year of the Kennedy administration. Rostow tried to revive the practice when he moved over to the State Department but President Kennedy simply would not sit and listen for hours to what was to him a purely academic debate.

Policy planners flourished under Dulles because of his own interest in planning, and also because the Secretary of State enjoyed the President's fullest confidence. On his side,

Dulles never took advantage of his special relationship with the President. When policy planners urged him to persuade the President to shift NATO defenses to tactical nuclear weapons, Dulles demurred. He felt his authority with the President rested on confining himself to subjects falling within his competence and would be diluted if he tried to extend his coverage.

But, within these limits, Dulles was open to new ideas. Although he was skeptical about disarmament, he agreed, on Bowie's urging, to set up a disarmament office within the State Department. Though the office failed to cover itself with glory under Governor Harold Stassen, it was able to come up with a comprehensive disarmament proposal for the 1957 London conference.

After Bowie's return to Harvard, Gerard C. Smith, a New York lawyer and former member of the Atomic Energy Commission staff, was picked personally by Dulles to succeed him. Again, the Policy Planning Chief had direct access to the Secretary and was able to influence policy in a number of ways.

Under Smith's prodding, Dulles finally retreated from his much-advertised policy of "massive retaliation," on the ground that it had about run its course. But the policy was more difficult to abandon than it had been to adopt. The President, Secretary of Defense McElroy, his deputy and the Chief of Staff of the Air Force, continued to believe in the Dulles policy at a time when Dulles himself was ready to abandon it. The Army, Navy and Marine chiefs sided with Dulles. But when Herter succeeded Dulles, and tried again to do away with massive retaliation, he found the President and the Air Force still wedded to the concept.

After Dulles' death, the power concentrated in the Secretary's office was dispersed into the geographic bureaus. The operating bureaus, always jealous of the planners, were not altogether cooperative. But the only way policy influence could have been exerted at the time was through the area chiefs.

The United States launched two important initiatives during Smith's tenure of the Policy Planning Council chairmanship. One was the proposal to establish a "hot line" between Washington and Moscow, the other a plan for Latin American rehabilitation, the same plan which re-emerged in the Kennedy administration as the Alliance for Progress.

The origin of the hot line dates back to a January 29, 1960, memorandum addressed by Smith to Charles E. Bohlen, then Special Assistant for Soviet Affairs, whose approval was necessary before the proposal could be relayed to the Secretary and the President.

The premise of the memorandum was that if "general war occurs at all during the next few years, it is more likely to develop from miscalculations than from deliberate intent." Misinterpretation of an opponent's action and the impulse to strike a preemptive blow might trigger a war. It was therefore imperative, the memorandum stressed, that any head of government, aware that a given crisis created an unusual threat of war, should be able to consult other heads of state immediately by telephone. Smith's memorandum was directed ideally toward a Washington-Moscow line, but it was thought at the time this would be impossible without plugging London and Paris into the circuit.

Bohlen, who was preparing the agenda for the May summit meeting in Paris, replied on February 16, 1960. "The proposal was excellent," he said, but "not suitable for summit discussions."

Undaunted, Smith appealed to Secretary Herter. "I suggest," Smith messaged the Secretary, "that you discuss this with the President in view of his personal involvement." But on March 7, 1960, a special assistant to Herter regretted "that after reading carefully the attached study and noting the variety of divergent opinions on the subject, the Secretary felt he was not prepared for the present to take it up with the President as you recommend."

The hot-line proposal was revived under the Kennedy administration and finally adopted by the U.S. and the Soviet Union on June 20, 1963.

Another proposal originating in the Eisenhower administration and later seized by Kennedy was the Alliance for Progress.

On June 30, 1960, Smith returned to the State Department from a White House meeting and reported that President

Eisenhower seemed receptive to a new kind of aid program —"something that would aim at social betterment and re- form"—and that he would welcome an initiative along those lines.

Within a few days, a draft was ready and submitted to the President. Shortly thereafter, it was approved. By the middle of July the President was able to announce at Newport that he would request a supplemental appropriation of $500 million to initiate the program later incorporated in the Act of Bogota and reappearing in the Kennedy administration as the Alliance for Progress.

Policy planners also played a decisive role during the 1958 crisis over the offshore islands. The Red Chinese threatened to seize the islands and bombarded them steadily from their shores. Nationalist convoys were not getting through and it seemed at one time that the islands might be starved into sur- render. The military advocated a "quick fix," if necessary, through the use of nuclear weapons if the U.S. decided to in- tervene at all. Gerard Smith represented the doves of the pe- riod and sternly warned the Secretary against the use of nuclear weapons. Dulles agreed, and somehow supplies were delivered and the islands remain under Nationalist control to this day.

Another planning concept of the late fifties was the "oceanic theory," i.e., countering a Soviet attempt to strangle Berlin by a blockade of Soviet shipping at critical points, such as the Dardanelles or Skagerrak.

The memorandum was widely circulated at the time and its authors, including Gerard Smith, believe that it contributed to the selection of the naval quarantine as a means of pressure against the Russians during the Cuban missile crisis in 1962. The core of the "oceanic" concept was that it confronted the Soviets in an area of overwhelming American conventional power, thus forcing them to look down the nuclear barrel if they desired to proceed further. It has long been assumed by U.S. planners that in the last analysis the Soviets would flinch from using atomic weapons in order to prevail in a contest of wills.

The controversial plan for the multilateral nuclear force,

intended to give the Germans and other NATO allies a share in nuclear decision-making, was also initiated in those days. Robert Bowie single-handedly sold the plan to President Eisenhower. Consideration of the plan continued under Kennedy and later under Johnson.

The history of national security planning shows that when planners have been close to Presidents and enjoyed their confidence, they have managed to produce worthwhile projects and to save their administrations from floundering aimlessly when a crisis occurred. President Eisenhower, who believed in staff work, encouraged the planners. But his successors, beset by crises requiring immediate attention, have downgraded policy planning and reduced its usefulness.

One of the results of presidential indifference to planning has been the development of mechanistic thinking about foreign policy problems and the use of "think factories" to devise shortcuts and solutions in the foreign policy field. The "think factories" feed their data into computers and seem to be more interested in winning theoretical games than in finding workable solutions, based on the knowledge and understanding not merely of bare statistics but of the psychological and historical elements involved in a foreign policy problem.

If the Marshall Plan were to be proposed today, a current policy planner has claimed, it could probably not be undertaken because of the diffusion of expertise within the government. What George Kennan with four or five assistants accomplished in less than a fortnight in 1947 would have to be "gamed out" and "staffed out" in 1966—a process that might take years. Moreover, it would be the Department of Defense rather than State that would have taken the initiative in the "staffing" and "gaming" of the project.

The Defense Department has a budget of nearly $9 million for the study of social conditions abroad, while the State Department has less than 10 per cent of that sum. This has led to such anomalies as a Pentagon-conducted Project Camelot, intended to disclose under what conditions Chile might revolt. Were it not for an alert ambassador who nipped the project in the bud, it could have resulted in Chile's severance of relations with the U.S. Another operation, code-named Simpatico, was designed to find out what made Latin Americans tick and still another—Rex Americanus—was to discover how U.S. hegemony in Latin America could be maintained forever. A project which never got off the ground was aimed at disclosing the possibilities of guerrilla warfare in Quebec after the French separatists had succeeded in overthrowing the constitutional government of Quebec province. The Pentagon's latest brainchild is a $200,000 study of "Vectors in Eastern Europe."

The uproar created by Camelot caused the President to direct that future foreign research projects should be controlled by the Secretary of State. "I am determined," the President wrote Secretary Rusk under date of August 4, 1965, "that no government sponsorship of foreign area research should be undertaken which in the judgment of the Secretary of State would adversely affect U.S. foreign relations."

The presidential injunction introduced an element of caution into mechanistic planning in politico-military affairs. But it has not suppressed it.

Vast projects of international research have been continued by the government through the Department of Defense. The State Department has remained in the background, partly because of lack of funds, partly because of its reticence to employ outsiders for the performance of tasks to which it had been assigned by the Constitution. As a result, the State Department accounts for only one per cent of the total amount spent on foreign research and intelligence.

The Defense Department's chosen instrument in the field of research is the Rand Corporation, short for research and development, a non-profit organization originally conceived in 1946 by the late General H. H. (Hap) Arnold, wartime commander of the Army Air Force. The discussions leading to the establishment of Rand took place among key officers and civilians representing all branches of the armed forces as well as such agencies as the Manhattan District and the National Defense Research Committee. But it was General Arnold who was first to see the need for the institution and the first to offer a way to finance it.

Under the original contract between the Air Force and the Douglas Aircraft Company, the newly created corporation was to receive Air Force intelligence and planning information and make reports and recommendations as warranted by research. The initial Air Force subsidy was $10 million—enough to underwrite operations until the organization could prove itself.

In the twenty years of existence, the organization has grown from small beginnings to a $21-million-a-year institution with 1,175 employees. The United States Air Force still contributes about two-thirds of the corporation's budget.

The sprawling "think tank," as it is generally known among its clients, dominates the business section of Santa Monica. Its doors are closely guarded, and security on leaving and entering the building is stricter than that observed in either the Pentagon or the State Department.

The corporation has eleven separate divisions dealing with electronics, missiles, and aircraft. Its staff includes nuclear physicists, electronic experts to whom radar and fast computers are standard tools, aircraft and missile experts, students of logistics, political scientists, economists, sociologists and mathematicians. At lunchtime some of them play *Kriegspiel*, a game of double blind chess, originally included in the curriculum of German staff colleges, in which one cannot see his opponent's pieces but can only infer their positions from comments made by a referee, who announces certain situations and prevents impossible moves.

Most of the corporation's output is classified, and it is therefore impossible for a layman to gauge the corporation's usefulness in the field of military research. The corporation claims that its first major task suggested by the Air Force in 1946 was to study the feasibility and usefulness of an artificial earth satellite—"an object then primarily of interest to science-fiction writers." The study concluded that "the vehicle has important military uses in connection with mapping and reconnaissance, as a communication relay station and in association with long-range missiles, and that a primitive satellite could be launched as early as 1952." Why, with all this prescience, a

U.S. satellite could not have been launched until the Russians had launched theirs has never been explained.

The Rand specialists also research a good many non-military subjects related to U.S. national security, and have pondered and produced studies on such issues as the cold war, NATO, De Gaulle, psychological warfare and various aspects of foreign policy. Among Rand's experts are a number of Kremlinologists, who generally resent and dismiss as "court astrologers" the specialists on Soviet affairs in Washington government agencies and offices. Rand's Kremlinologists prepare regular estimates of Soviet capabilities and intentions which are circulated throughout the government, and often are dismissed or ridiculed by the "astrologers."

One such effort, which hoisted the "astrologers'" eyebrows almost out of sight, and was later claimed to be a tongue-in-cheek hoax, was a study labelled "New Power Struggle in the Kremlin: Who Is on Top?" It was prepared for Rand by Vernon V. Aspaturian, professor of political science at Pennsylvania State University. A footnote to the copyrighted study warned that the views it expressed "should not be interpreted as reflecting the views of the Rand Corporation or the official opinion or policy of any of its private or governmental research sponsors."

Under Rand's imprint, however, the study was circulated among government experts and policy planners in Washington. As a commentary on the "mechanistic" approach to vital foreign policy problems, it deserves some attention.

The fourteen-page paper, completed in June, 1965, based its prime conclusions on a photograph published March 19, 1965, in *Pravda,* the official propaganda journal of the Soviet Communist party. The photograph, $9\frac{5}{16}$ inches by $3\frac{13}{16}$ inches, was captioned: LEADERS OF THE COMMUNIST PARTY AND SOVIET GOVERNMENT SPEAKING ON THE TELEPHONE WITH MEMBERS OF THE CREW OF THE SPACE SHIP VOSTOK-2.

The Rand study concluded from the photograph that Soviet Communist Party Secretary Leonid Brezhnev was the ranking member of the Soviet hierarchy because "Brezhnev's nose is located almost precisely at the point where a horizontal line drawn through the middle of the photograph bisects a vertical line similarly drawn."

Having reached this linear-nasal decision on Brezhnev's standing among the Kremlin's leaders, the study then turned to Alexander Shelepin, Politburo member, former secret-police and youth chieftain and one of the reputedly bright young men in Moscow. The study says:

Scrutinize the photograph very closely and examine every nuance of expression and every item or irregularity which appears suspicious. Note the sly expression, indicating more cleverness than intelligence, the squinting eyes, more Byzantine than Florentine in malevolent intent. The squinting eyes with the Byzantine slant immediately inform us that Shelepin is listening very intently—he is, after all, a professional listener, that is, a career eavesdropper.

But what is he listening to? No one in the picture is talking: observe closely that all mouths are closed. At the moment the picture was taken, one of the Cosmonauts was talking, and it was this voice that intrigued him [Shelepin]. But how?

Now, examine his right ear very closely, preferably with a magnifying glass or a projector. Note the small dark spot just above the right ear lobe which could easily be mistaken for an ink flaw to the uninitiated eye. This is actually a protuberance which is part of a secret ear plug which Shelepin, with uncharacteristic carelessness, has allowed unwittingly to visibly protrude.

Shelepin is actually the only person with an extension device who can listen in on Brezhnev's conversation with the Cosmonauts. But no one else at the table is aware of this fact.

Actually, it was not Brezhnev, but Shelepin, who unceremoniously unplugged Kosygin's extension phone in order to plug in his own secret listening device. This was an integrally designed factional windfall, since it could not fail to rouse resentment in Kosygin against Brezhnev—a resentment which Brezhnev would find difficult to explain and hence singularly disconcerting.

As far as Shelepin is concerned, the fact that he is the only member of the hierarchy privy to Brezhnev's chit-chat proves he is actually functioning as the No. 2 man. By preempting Kosygin's extension, Shelepin was indirectly preempting his telephone and hence symbolically his No. 2 position.

On the other hand, since this is a "twilight zone" preemption, this is a profound confirmation that Kosygin is de jure No. 2, although admittedly closer to the 2½ demarcation point than the 1½.

The Aspaturian study has the sly ring of a caricature, a straight-faced parody on Kremlinology and Kremlinologists, with their absorption in the placement of U.S.S.R. leaders' portraits in public and the order in which their names are published in *Pravda* reports of various official functions. And the study was so regarded by Soviet experts in Washington, reluctant to decide the order of the Kremlin hierarchy on the basis of a secret plug in Shelepin's ear or the exact position of Brezhnev's nose in a photograph.

Parodies of Sovietology and its practitioners have become highly fashionable in Washington. One such effort by a policy planner, purporting to be a secret Soviet critique of American foreign policy, was sent to key U.S. embassies abroad. From Paris came the most startling reaction. "This is a highly significant document," the embassy cabled in effect. "Can we show it to the French?" A top priority message explained—with apologies—that the document was not to be taken seriously.

Nevertheless, an entire industry has grown up around the mechanistic approach to foreign affairs exemplified in this Rand study. In addition to that corporation, the Institute of Defense Analyses, MIT and various universities have been practicing crisis gamesmanship at the behest and expense of the Pentagon.

Most of these institutions have produced fascinating studies at one time or another. General Sidney Giffin * of the Institute of Defense Analyses has cast the Cuban missile crisis and a fictional emergency over Kashmir into dramatic scenarios vastly more exciting than most movie scripts. General Giffin says the "behaviorist simulation of international relations" has enjoyed a modest vogue recently. Northwestern University is the leader in this field. It sponsors a course in Inter-Nation Simulation, employing a set of fictional states called Algo, Erga, Ingo, Omne and Utro. The names were designed to provide an unprejudiced approach to their prob-

* *The Crisis Game* by Sidney F. Giffin, Doubleday & Co., Inc., 1965.

lems by the players involved in the scenarios dealing with those countries.

Each nation has a Central Decision Maker, or chief executive, an External Decision Maker, or foreign secretary, and an Internal Decision Maker, or budget director. Each also has validators who have installed the Central Decision Maker, and each is provided with point values for economic and other assets. The game is played somewhat like Monopoly.

Whether the principle of war games applied to foreign policy planning has any validity is a matter of considerable debate. Professor Thomas Schelling of Harvard is a convinced advocate of the concept, and there are some government officials in Washington who believe it is beneficial to some degree.

"You analyze a situation in country X," said one of the officials, explaining his support of the war-games concept, "then you sit down with the Joint Chiefs of Staff people and write four or five scenarios. You project certain actions or responses against the scenario.

"Now, if a crisis erupts in country X, it may not conform with any of your scenarios, but it is likely to contain some of their factors. Suppose it falls between scenarios two and three. At least you have foreseen some of the possibilities which might involve the United States, and made possible the designation of some level of the response we might have to make."

Joint planning and war gaming within the government is preferable to entrusting the Pentagon with the responsibility for crises involving military action, this official contends, or depending on the Pentagon for crisis plans.

"Formerly, when a crisis broke somewhere abroad," he recalled, "the Joint Chiefs would go down to their lockers in the bowels of the Pentagon and haul out Plan No. 23, and that was that.

"During the 1958 Lebanon crisis," he went on, "we were shipping battle groups from Germany and the movement plans called for them to take along atomic missiles. We thus could have introduced nuclear weapons into the explosive Middle East." He rolled his eyes in consternation.

But the war-game concept in foreign affairs is not unanimously accepted. Professor William R. Polk, in a speech made September 8, 1965, to the American Academy of Political Science Association, had this comment:

> In the "game" approach to foreign affairs, problems are being reduced to scenarios, "gamed out" and thus resolved. The *Strategy of Conflict*, as Thomas Schelling called his book, pitted two antagonists against one another in confrontation. Logical responses to given moves were analyzed so that a sequence could be "played" and "escalated" to a showdown. But in the course of this, the perception of international relations, the peculiarities of the several players, were washed out so that a "world-man," who logically and coolly could understand and rightly play the game, was substituted for real and often irrational persons guided by emotions and fears rather than by the rules of the game.

All planners admit that no long-range planning, depending on often unpredictable actions over which the planner has no control, can be perfect. "We are not Utopian," the planners say, "and to us any plan that meets the actual situation 75 per cent is as good as perfect."

Even so, there is vast room for improvement in foreign policy planning as it is practiced today. Planners must be given access to all information, however secret, which bears on the problems they are surveying. They must be taken more fully into the confidence and thinking of the President and Secretary of State. A policy planner not privy to the plans or decisions made at the highest levels of the United States government simply cannot be effective. Anyone charged with planning and long-range foreign policy must know what the President wants that policy to be. The conclusions reached in "games," no matter how ingenuously devised, may not equate in any way with the aims and policies of the President and his Secretary of State.

E ⬩ L ⬩ E ⬩ V ⬩ E ⬩ N

The ultimate crisis

The situations described in the preceding chapters are typical of the crises which have confronted the United States in the past and may plague it again in the future. In the context of a world divided into two hostile camps, American Presidents perceived in these situations the seeds of an eventual threat to world peace and were therefore willing to take whatever risks might flow from moving to meet the troubles in their initial stages.

Whether the risks were worth taking in all cases is debatable. The involvement in Vietnam, Cyprus or Yemen and the techniques of handling crises only remotely affecting the national interest are subject to legitimate doubts. Only in the case of the Cuban missiles was the United States directly threatened, and the threat was parried by calm and controlled application of limited military forces. It can be argued that the danger and the stakes involved in Cuba were much higher than in Vietnam. Yet, unlike Cuba, Vietnam has absorbed a substantial part of the U.S. military establishment in a contest—not with a major adversary—but with ragged Viet Cong guerrilla bands and their North Vietnamese allies.

President Kennedy, who did not shrink from committing the necessary combat force in the face of a direct threat, was wary of committing any at all where the threat was not so obvious. In October, 1963, Defense Secretary McNamara and General Maxwell Taylor, who had just returned from Vietnam, urged the President to increase the number of U.S. military advisers there. President Kennedy immediately questioned whether U.S. combat troops would be required next. When he reluctantly agreed to increase the number of advisers to 18,000 he warned McNamara that, should this effort fail, "we must consider the alternative of getting out of Vietnam." Kennedy explained he had refused to send combat troops into Laos for reasons which remained equally valid in Vietnam. He was assured by both McNamara and Taylor that by the end of 1965 the South Vietnamese army would be able to handle the guerrillas with economic assistance alone, and that we would probably be able to bring the U.S. advisers home by then.

A year after his triumph in the Cuban missile crisis, President Kennedy had felt sufficiently confident to handle Vietnam without the need for displaying his nerve. Had McNamara and Taylor come to him with the same proposition a year before, they might have received a different answer. Immediately after the Bay of Pigs, Kennedy felt he had to prove his toughness and had agreed to a substantial increase in the number of "advisers" without question.

President Johnson, after the Gulf of Tonkin incidents, felt he had to prove his mettle even though, in retrospect, it now seems doubtful whether the second Gulf of Tonkin incident, on the basis of which the first retaliatory bombing of North Vietnam had been ordered, was actually caused by enemy action.

Depending on the personalities and circumstances involved, varying approaches have been used in major crises as well as in comparatively minor incidents, such as Cyprus, Yemen and the Dominican Republic. Over-reacting, improvisation by gifted individuals, decision-making through formal channels of the government or by specially created élite groups, pre-planning have all been applied in one case or another. The arguments as to which method was correct and which should have been used will continue as long as government exists. But one thing is certain: no one has yet devised an infallible method of handling the ultimate crisis—a direct nuclear confrontation with the Soviet Union or Communist China.

President Eisenhower was the first to recognize this predicament when, in 1955, he ordered the National Security Council to find answers to the questions troubling him. He noted that the vaunted NSC Memorandum No. 68, cataloguing contingencies facing the United States and the methods of meeting them, was silent on the subject of nuclear confrontation and he wanted the gap filled.

Specifically, Eisenhower wanted an estimate of American casualties and their likely effect on the American people. He was troubled by the fact that, in spite of the system of checks and balances, one man alone would be destined to make a decision costing millions of American lives and that the decision would have to be made in four hours, later reduced to two and one half hours—i.e., in the time it took a Soviet jet bomber to fly from the North Pole to major American cities.

What would the American people want their President to do? Eisenhower queried. Would they want him to retaliate or to surrender? "Do I lose a city first?" he asked. Or would he have to rely on the Early Warning System which, after all, might not be entirely foolproof.

Eisenhower's idea was to mobilize the country's experts in and out of the government to take a hard look at these problems. But the best conclusion the staff could come up with was that the country could never be made aware of the problem unless it faced the realism of having shelters built, children moved out of schools and the government evacuated from Washington.

As a result of the NSC study, an elaborate alert exercise was staged involving SHAPE and the far-flung commands in the Pacific, as well as an evacuation of the President and government from Washington. The alert showed that communication facilities in the Front Royal, Virginia, and Fort Ritchie, Maryland, evacuation centers proved woefully inadequate to the needs.

The debate as to whether a preemptive or a second strike would serve the country best continued to rage for over two years after the exercise. Feelings ran high for and against until, in 1958, the President finally made his decision against a preemptive strike. His reasoning was simple: no intelligence was sufficiently foolproof to avoid mistaken interpretations of enemy intentions. Also, he argued against the Air Force and the Secretary of Defense—assuming we had planned for a first strike and intelligence had failed to detect hostile movements in time, the resulting losses could well become fatal.

While Eisenhower had two and one half hours in which to make the fateful decision, the advent of the ICBMs reduced the decision time to fifteen minutes. No intelligence or early warning system could be relied upon to assess Soviet intentions in that span of time. The debate of first versus second strike flared up again with the advent of the Kennedy administration. The estimate of casualties that would result from a Soviet first strike rose to fifty million and the medical and logistical problems involved in coping with the remaining U.S. population were thought to be insurmountable.

President Kennedy was shocked at the casualty estimates. In addition, he realized that the ability to absorb the first blow with enough power left over to strike back would require enormous expenditures. It would mean keeping a large segment of the SAC aircraft aloft at all times to avoid destruction by enemy missiles on the ground. It would mean keeping missile submarines deployed at sea where they could not be attacked or neutralized. It also meant a multi-billion-dollar investment in the development of an anti-missile missile. And most certainly, it demanded a tough civil defense program, with shelters, food and medical supplies.

The alternative solution, strongly advocated by Air Force planners, was a preemptive strike by the United States. The problem was that this would require a superbly competent intelligence service capable of accurately assessing Soviet intentions and a President courageous enough to launch an attack against the Russians before they could launch one against us. Moreover, the preemptive strike strategy was politically unacceptable and, in Kennedy's view, had one fatal weakness: how could a President ever be certain that his intelligence estimates were accurate?

Officially, President Kennedy remained committed to the second strike strategy. But he never lost sight of the fact that a situation might arise where a preemptive strike, i.e., a first strike by the United States, would one day become an option confronting the President. He kept on reviewing the problem with his advisers, as Truman and Eisenhower did before him. According to some of his intimates present at these discussions, Kennedy finally decided that, under certain circumstances, the President should have the courage to order a first strike. He was said to have steeled himself for such an eventuality.

This decision, later forgotten as the danger of nuclear confrontation faded away, was part of Kennedy's belief that, to avoid war, the President must be ready for it. He was convinced, and often lectured his military advisers to the effect, that bluff would never work in confrontation with the Communists. In the 1961 Berlin buildup and in the 1962 Cuban missile crisis, Kennedy was fully prepared to carry out every step the U.S. had threatened to take.

Another inquiry closely related to nuclear confrontation was initiated by Eisenhower in the wake of the 1956 Hungarian revolt. There was a feeling of guilt in and out of the government for failing to help the Hungarian freedom fighters, and Eisenhower wanted the NSC to determine what could have been done, as well as what the policy of the government should be in similar crises.

The NSC conclusions were starkly depressing. For the first time, the government as a whole received a formal lesson in the limited nature of the tremendous military power it wielded. The NSC felt that since the Soviets could not be expected to permit the defection of any of its satellites, there was literally nothing the United States could do to help a behind-the-curtain revolt. In Europe, unmarked planes or non-U.S. "volunteers" could not be moved closer to the scene of action without risking a direct confrontation with the Soviets. The main task of the planners, the NSC concluded, was to prevent these confrontations from occurring. Should they occur, there was only one practical alternative: face the Soviets—or look the other way.

The Hungarian decision was put to the test in the early days of the Kennedy administration. With tensions mounting and East Germans crossing over to the West in ever-increasing numbers, some New Frontiersmen were tempted to encourage the East Germans to revolt against their regime.

The message that the Communists had erected the Berlin Wall reached President Kennedy on Sunday, August 12, at Hyannisport, Massachusetts, just a few minutes after he had sailed on an afternoon cruise on the *Honey Fitz*.

The message was handed to a military aide who called the Secret Service detail on board and asked them to bring the President back to shore immediately. The *Honey Fitz*, which had only gone a mile or so, was back at the pier just as the aide walked up alongside. The President never questioned the order to return. As he read the message, his first question was: "Is this our first knowledge of their action? With all that cement and stone going up, why didn't we know about it before?"

That Sunday afternoon, the President called McGeorge Bundy, Secretary Rusk and Secretary McNamara. For weeks afterward, the President and his advisers pondered over what to do about the wall, about Soviet intentions and how to help the East Germans. But the decision was the same as Eisenhower's: do nothing to encourage the East Germans to riot or revolt, and avoid anything that might give such an appearance —unless we are ready for World War III.

President Johnson seems to have dismissed nuclear confrontation with the Soviets as a possibility. While Kennedy constantly fretted about the problem, Johnson has apparently concluded he will not have to face that decision. He has seldom alluded to it in private talks or in public speeches. He has adopted Secretary McNamara's—and General de Gaulle's— conclusion that the Soviets would not attack first. The Johnson administration has accepted the diagnosis of Soviet responsibility as proved by their cautious behavior during the Vietnamese war. The time may well be past when one man in Moscow could override his colleagues and his generals and press the nuclear button. On this assumption President Johnson, who is not a speculative thinker, appears to have put the problem out of his mind.

But the problem will not die. According to current estimates, the Chinese will have delivery vehicles or missiles capable of reaching the United States by 1972 and whoever is elected in that year will face essentially the same problem Eisenhower faced in 1955. But the 1972 President's task may be easier—the Soviet Union, much more vulnerable to a Chinese nuclear attack than the United States, is likely to be on his side.

If the Vietnam war continues, confrontation with China may even come sooner. According to his close associates, Secretary Rusk has been increasingly worried lest there be more war before we can have more peace in Asia. As far back as 1964, Rusk requested a Joint Chiefs of Staff study on the possibilities of eliminating Chinese air bases by nuclear means, and his associates have recently been saying that he is willing to "go for broke" if the outcome of the Vietnam war should be in serious doubt. Rusk has never forgotten that in the Korean War he made a wrong guess about Chinese intervention and he is determined not to repeat his mistake.

Since the summer of 1966, a "new China policy" has been circulated within the White House and State Department, and timid slogans such as "containment without isolation" have been launched as trial balloons. But nowhere have there been signs that the problem of China has been receiving long-range, top-level attention except as it concerns Vietnam. "Grand designs" have become outmoded in the Johnson administration. But a long-range policy, under whatever name, is clearly needed to guide American actions and policies toward a potential enemy which, by 1972, will constitute the principal threat to the United States.

Formulation and acceptance of long-range policies in major as well as minor crises have suffered severely under the Kennedy-Johnson administrations.

The United States government in the last few years has

found crises as difficult to anticipate as they are to avoid. Some, like the Dominican crisis of 1965 and the Panamanian crisis of 1964, should not have been surprises. Warnings were raised, as we have seen, on the mood of the Panamanians as far back as 1960 and the problem simply became lost among the higher priorities of the New Frontier. Similarly, the dangerous implications of the ouster of Dominican President Juan Bosch on September 25, 1963, should have been unmistakable, and yet the State Department made no apparent effort during the next nineteen months to maintain contact with the left-wing groups which were licking wounds while planning their return to power. Ambassador W. Tapley Bennett, Jr. and the U.S. embassy staff bent their full attention to the dealings with the military junta and as a consequence lacked the empathy and the insight which might have enabled them, after the insurrection broke out, to advise the President more realistically and wisely on the character and leadership of the rebel forces. In fairness, it must be said that these failures can be attributed, at least in part, to the fact that Latin America has existed since 1960 in a state of chronic crisis. The expert talent available to work on this region has been stretched thin by the exertions of launching the Alliance for Progress, and small nations like Panama and the Dominican Republic were inevitably overlooked in a concentration upon the larger problems of Brazil and Cuba.

But the shortage of qualified personnel to deal with crises has occasionally turned out to be a blessing and resulted in keeping the United States out of troubles which it should have avoided in any case. It so happened, for example, that the Dominican explosion came to a climax on April 24, 1965, the same day that a brigade of 3,000 Pakistani troops attacked Indian positions with American tanks along a fifty-mile stretch in the Rann of Kutch. American decisions were urgently demanded simultaneously on both sides of the world.

State Department officials dealing with Southeast Asia had to compete for top-level attention with the Latin American crisis. They were frantic but could do nothing except draft a formal statement which expressed hope for a cease-fire and promised an investigation of Indian allegations that Pakistan was using U.S. tanks against India. Any other action would have required sanction of the government's top officials and literally all of them were busy trying to prevent "another Cuba" in the Dominican Republic. Neither the President, nor the Secretary, nor the Undersecretary of State would listen to briefings or read papers dealing with the Rann of Kutch, however important that particular crisis seemed to the officials directly concerned. For no other reason except that there was simply no personnel to field it, word finally came from Secretary Rusk to "let the British handle it." The British did, and by April 28, 1965, Prime Minister Harold Wilson had urged Premier Shastri and President Ayub to withdraw their military forces. By May 3, an informal and precarious ceasefire had been established.

A hit-and-miss method of handling crises has too often been characteristic of recent foreign policy. This tendency was manifested in the Dominican Republic and in the issue over Article 19 of the UN Charter. Even in the comparatively well-executed Cyprus operation it was hardly an act of statesmanship for President Johnson to issue a veiled threat to Turkey, a NATO ally, that it might have to fight alone if, as a result of its Cyprus involvement, it became the victim of a Soviet attack.

There has been much criticism of Eisenhower's formalized use of the NSC in a crisis; but some of the pitfalls of the Kennedy-Johnson era might have been avoided if a modified version of the Eisenhower procedures had been adopted.

Eisenhower came to the White House already a national hero. Kennedy and Johnson were both keenly aware that their standing in history would rest entirely upon their performances in the presidency. One aspect of Eisenhower's attitude was reflected in an observation to his friend, General Omar Bradley, after the latter succeeded him as Army Chief of Staff. "Why are you working so hard?" asked Ike. "You've already got four stars." The NSC format suited Eisenhower perfectly. He enjoyed being briefed and he liked to dispose of his decisions in the surgical atmosphere of the Cabinet room, with the issues

clearly defined in parallel columns on the paper before him
and with his subordinates primed to lay out the facts. Eisenhower's ear was quicker than his eye, and he could listen patiently and perceptively. Sherman Adams insists that Eisenhower never missed a Security Council meeting and "took this
responsibility more seriously than almost any other duty of his
office." *

Kennedy, by contrast, disliked being briefed and distrusted large meetings as a forum for honest exchanges. He
could read faster than a man could talk and oral presentations,
unless they were extremely well phrased and succinct, caused a
poorly disguised veil of boredom to settle upon his face. Kennedy felt most secure when he was discussing a problem with
the individuals who knew most about it and he was wary, particularly after his errors at the Bay of Pigs, of letting his own
viewpoint be exposed to confusion by the ill-informed interjec-
tions of kibitzers.

Often it would be only Rusk, McNamara and his deputy,
Roswell Gilpatric, General Maxwell Taylor and Bundy in an
upstairs sitting room at the White House. Occasionally, Rusk
himself would be excluded if Kennedy had already reached
conclusions in conversation with a lesser official of the State
Department. No papers went into these meetings or came out
of them, and the second and third echelons of the government,
which had access to the minutes of NSC meetings under the
Eisenhower procedure, could not acquire any full sense of
what the decisions had been and what factors had dominated
them. Kennedy never accepted the human phenomenon that it
was much easier for a subordinate to back down in good grace
from a position which he had argued strongly if his defeat
came cleanly from the hand of the President at the council
table.

The morale gap caused by cutting off the second and third
echelons from policy-making channels was widened by the
advent of Johnson, who has held himself aloof from the bureaucracy and has wrapped his decision-making in secrecy. His
hatred of newspaper-leaks is so intense that members of

* *First-hand Report* by Sherman Adams, Harper and Row, Inc., 1961.

his Cabinet, like Rusk, have shrunk from relaying the details of meetings with him to subordinates. Since he also dislikes press conferences and has held them infrequently, the lines of communication and guidance between the President and the bureaucracy have inevitably become thin and sometimes confused. Rostow, in his White House basement office, has been struggling hard to reweave the network which worked well for Kennedy, but some of the unusual men who had been willing to expose their necks in behalf of new ideas in the tolerant, yeasty climate of the New Frontier feel it wise to lie low in the Great Society. "Working with Johnson," observed one high official, since retired, "is like walking a greased log across a crocodile pond." In Johnson, the government has a leader who functions by seat-of-the-pants intuition, who alternately lauds and mistrusts his chief associates and whose pulse beats to the tempo of the breaking news. None of these are characteristics which in crisis help to unify a huge government in a taut and easy working relationship.

Moreover, Johnson has always been strictly a one-crisis man. During 1965 and 1966, his aides tried to disabuse Washington reporters of their conclusions that Johnson was totally absorbed by his troubles in Vietnam. But these persuasions did not refute the frustrations of officials throughout the government who found great difficulty in attracting the President's interest to problems unrelated to Vietnam. In mid-1966, Johnson launched a major campaign to broaden the perspective of his administration to include problems of foreign policy other than Vietnam. He told Rostow to recruit able specialists from around the country and to install them as consultants in the State Department as well as in the White House. Pointing at the Executive Office Building which stands next to the White House, he said, "If you need that space, I'll move the Budget Bureau to Bethesda."

Kennedy's buoyant personality brightened the image of the United States, and the vigor and liveliness of his administration countered a sense which had spread around the world in Eisenhower's time that the nation was becoming somewhat old and weary. But there is no evidence that a flow of new

__217__217217___217__217__217_____217_____

_____217__217__217__217__217__217__217__217__217__217__217____217_____217_____217____217____217____217____217____217____217____217____217____217____217____217____217____217____217_

concepts and new initiatives was turned loose by liberating the foreign policy machinery from the Eisenhower committee system. In fact, recent responses to developing situations, particularly as we have seen in the case of the fragmenting NATO alliance, have often seemed laggard and unimaginative. Foreign ambassadors have complained that they invariably hear different positions on the same issue from different offices in the government, or, as Dean Acheson put it, "by tapping different portions of the dinosaur." Eisenhower handled the awesome issue of civilian defense shelters against nuclear attack by exposing it to the committee system. The question was extensively studied by the NSC and a subcommittee of consultants, the Gaither Committee. The committee procedures which produced a sharp internal debate and a final decision not to make a huge investment to protect the civilian population clearly resolved the problem in better style for the nation than the on-again, off-again policies which have been pursued in Vietnam since 1960.

The "brinksmanship" for which Dulles was attacked has become an avowed element of U.S. policy under both Kennedy and Johnson. The nation has improved and expanded its military power. President Johnson has gone to war in Vietnam in order to establish the sincerity of his intentions to see his commitments through at any price. Yet he has not managed somehow to exert the subtlety and statecraft necessary to acquire for the country an international influence that is equal to its physical power. Kennedy was well on his way to becoming a world leader—Johnson has not taken his first major stride in that direction.

Critics have charged that Mr. Johnson's reactions in the field of foreign affairs are those of a politician rather than of a President of the United States. The over-reaction in Panama, the abrupt sending of Marines to the Dominican Republic, the theatrical and short-lived peace offensive have all the earmarks of politics, few of statesmanship.

What is proper for a politician is not proper for the President of the United States. The politician's promises of "initiatives" are promptly forgotten. The President's are not. A politician, like Senator Keating in the Cuban crisis, can recommend actions on the basis of surmises. A President must be sure. He cannot send Marines into a foreign country without being absolutely sure of the facts: whether they are there to save the lives of American citizens or to prevent the country from falling into Communist hands.

The case for American involvement in each crisis must be stated clearly and honestly. If there is a good national reason why we cannot tolerate a Communist government in Vietnam while we tolerate one on our doorstep in Cuba the President must state it simply without spurious ideology or trick phrases. The national interest in each case must be explained and contradictory or misleading statements avoided. Above all, the country must be convinced that before American troops are sent into battle all avenues of diplomacy have been explored to avoid or reduce the need for American military intervention.

It is difficult for a President, unversed in foreign policy and viewing it as a mere extension of domestic politics, to decide what is and what is not in the national interest. How does a President know whether the capture of Stanleyville by a gang of cannibals, or the Greek-Turkish fight in Cyprus or Mao's latest purge constitutes a threat to the national interest of the United States?

The President alone cannot make that judgment. He needs some formal machinery to channel all the information available to him, as well as assessments and recommendations from his Secretary of State. Possibly the National Security Council machinery is too cumbersome and a more flexible institution adjustable to each President's temperament could be devised. Though President Johnson shuns "grand designs," he still must establish clearly in his own mind some guideposts to a foreign policy and the means to follow them. The President's policies will be ineffective if they are not consistent. He cannot be enthusiastic about ambassadors and foreign visitors one day and bored with them the next. He cannot toss foreign policy "initiatives" into the air without following them through.

Showmanship is not enough. It is not enough to call in the

assistant secretaries of the State and Defense Departments for "get acquainted" sessions and appeal to them for "new ideas." It is up to the President to tell his subordinates what he wants them to do and ask for their recommendations as to how best to achieve it.

Similarly, the Secretary of State cannot delegate his authority by advising his assistants to "reach for the horizon." He, too, should be able to tell his associates where he wants the country to go and direct them to find the best ways of getting there.

Seldom has so much talent been assembled in the service of foreign policy as under the Kennedy-Johnson administrations. Rusk, McNamara, Ball, Rostow, the Bundy brothers, Llewellyn Thompson and a host of lesser lights have made up a team which any government in the world would be proud to call its own. The rank and file of the Department of State also compare favorably with their diplomatic colleagues abroad.

If there is one reason why a team of such brilliance and ability has not functioned more effectively, it is lack of leadership. President Johnson, primarily attuned to the domestic scene, has not yet shown his willingness to exercise it. Secretary Rusk, on the other hand, over-conscious of his constitutional limitations, has shown no inclination to step into the vacuum in order to give the country a foreign policy commensurate with its military and economic power.

The government has muddled from crisis to crisis without suffering serious damage for the simple reason that the power of the United States is still so enormous that, barring a nuclear attack, no country or combination of countries can cause it serious harm.

In Yemen, Cyprus and the Dominican Republic, even in Vietnam, the United States can lose and, in spite of what has been said, few U.S. citizens would be affected by the loss or even be conscious of it. But no such thing can be said about the ultimate crisis. A nuclear collision can come only once in the life of a nation and if the nation is to survive, its President and Secretary of State must ceaselessly and intelligently plan the methods and machinery to prevent this catastrophe.

Appendix

Mr. Ambassador,

August 28, 1964

The latest proposals that you put forward on behalf of the United States Government for a solution of the Cyprus problem have been found totally unacceptable by the Turkish Government and the reasons for this attitude have been explained to you in detail.

I have stated to you unequivocally our position in our talk yesterday. I would like now to confirm most emphatically that your latest proposals based on the precarious foundation of a lease arrangement are unacceptable to the Turkish Government and that our decision in this respect is irreversible.

Despite the clarity of our position, the Ambassador of the Federal Republic of Germany, who came to visit me yesterday, reported a conversation between Undersecretary Mr. George Ball and the German Ambassador in Washington in which the Undersecretary told him that Turkey neither accepted nor refused these proposals.

I would be obliged if you would inform your government of our stand which I felt compelled to reiterate.

I feel also obliged to draw your attention to the fact that murders and barbarous acts take place before the very eyes of the military forces of Greece which in large number have occupied illegally Cyprus and that this situation involves therefore the responsibility of the Greek Government itself.

The information we have received indicates that murderous attacks against the Turkish community are still continuing sporadically and that the claims that the economic blockade had been lifted correspond to the reality only to a very little extent.

Please accept, Mr. Ambassador, the assurances of my highest consideration.

Feridun Cemal Erkin

221

MEMORANDUM OF CONVERSATION ON NATO AFFAIRS,
November 22, 1960

Paul Henri Spaak, his assistant, André St. Mleux, David Bruce and Paul H. Nitze met for three hours at the Metropolitan Club.

Spaak reviewed the current situation of NATO. The political directive under which NATO is operating dates from the early 1950s and is out of date. The weapons situation has changed. The positions of France and Germany are quite different. The nature of the Soviet threat has changed. There has, however, been no frank and forthright discussion of basic issues either within the NATO council or among the principal political figures. General de Gaulle and President Eisenhower, for instance, have never had a serious discussion of atomic strategy.

Some leadership on the part of the United States is essential. The positions taken by the United States in recent years have largely been generalities; they haven't come to grips with the real problems. One can talk about having adequate conventional forces, adequate tactical atomic forces and adequate strategic striking forces. But how are all these things to be paid for? Choices, difficult as they may be, have to be made.

Today De Gaulle is moving toward his "force de frappe"; his plan calls for 100 supersonic bombers. The first ones should be coming off the lines by the end of 1962. The costs will be immense. France can't follow this policy and also follow a NATO policy.

At the same time, the U.S. is pressing Germany to bear an increasing share of the NATO defense cost. Germany will then be bearing the major share of NATO defense. She will then not be satisfied with a secondary position in NATO. This is a fundamental political problem for all of Europe and for the United States. How and where is it to be discussed?

The procedure of consultation through the NATO council has been working reasonably well. It is rare when the U.S. representative does not have instructions. But the effectiveness of the U.S. representative depends upon more than instructions. He must be reasonably forthright and convincing to his fellow members, without being overbearing. He should also have weight within the U.S. administration so that he can influence policy both ways—not just from the U.S. to NATO but from NATO to the U.S. as well.

The problem of De Gaulle cannot, however, be handled through the U.S. and French representatives to NATO. This requires a personal relationship between Senator Kennedy and De Gaulle. Perhaps Senator Kennedy should offer to have a private telephone line installed from his desk to De Gaulle's.

The conversation then turned to economic problems. Spaak thought NATO should play a role in the political coordination of our reaction to Soviet moves in the underdeveloped areas. The new OECD organization is to have a role in coordinating economic programs. Spaak said his experience with the neutrals Sweden, Switzerland, Ireland, etc.—persuaded him that no "political coordination" was possible in bodies which included them. Others could implement the programs provided NATO gives political coordination.

Spaak also mentioned the economic problems of Greece, Turkey and Iceland which he also felt should be dealt with through NATO.

The conversation then turned to the principal subject, the possibility that Mr. Eisenhower would put before the December meeting a proposal for a NATO nuclear deterrent. He said this was to his mind of the utmost importance, but should only be put forward in a carefully thought-out manner. The essential question was the political one of the control of such a force. If it were to be under SACEUR control, the French would say that nothing is changed thereby; they would have no more voice in the strategic decisions essential to their survival than before. Spaak thought control should be in a six or seven man body, including England, U.K., France, Germany and Italy, plus one or two rotating representatives of the other powers. Decision might be on a weighted voting, majority voting or some other scheme. Spaak agreed that the decisions to be made were probably not too complex, but it was politically essential that others besides the U.S. be in on them.

There was an extended discussion of whether a NATO strategic deterrent would be divisive or unifying. Spaak thought the latter. Spaak also was of the opinion that eventually multinational crews could be developed.

He thought a NATO deterrent was essential if a way is to be found for the French out of their problem. De Gaulle has gone as far as he can on Algeria; if he fails, we may have Fascism in the heart of NATO. De Gaullism is a man, not a political movement.

Spaak thought a NATO deterrent would help the British who are tiring of their independent deterrent role. He thought it would help the German problem.

Spaak asked Bruce and me whether it would be possible for Eisenhower to put forward a proposal that had been coordinated with the Kennedy administration. We both emphasized the point that this would not be possible. Too much preliminary work is necessary before a solid position can be worked out. We also emphasized the problem of Congressional authorization, particularly if political control over the NATO deterrent is to be put in a body in which the U.S. has a minority voice.

Spaak concluded by saying he was planning to return in February to deliver a lecture in Detroit. He would hope for an opportunity to see the President at that time.

MEMORANDUM TO SECRETARY OF STATE DEAN RUSK FROM
PRESIDENT KENNEDY

The White House
Washington
August 16, 1961

Sensitive Handling

I would appreciate it if you would prepare a memorandum on the present assignment of responsibility within the Department of State. We discussed this at breakfast this morning, but I think if we could get it down on paper all concerned on the White House staff, as well as the State Department, could have a better idea of how they should conduct their responsibilities.

John Kennedy

LETTER FROM DEAN RUSK TO SENATOR JOHN F. KENNEDY

Room 4200
111 West 50th Street
New York 20
November 22, 1960

Dear Senator Kennedy:

As a Georgia-born citizen who believes that the Supreme Court decision on integration was long overdue, I feel inclined to offer a comment on the pressures arising from the threat of certain delegations to disregard the popular votes in their states in casting their ballots in the Electoral College in December.

I trust that the threat will have dissolved by the time this letter reaches you. On the other hand, you might be forced into a position in which you would have to make a public statement on the subject. If you challenge these Southern delegations on the issue of Civil Rights, the inflamed tempers in the South (freshly stimulated by New Orleans) could lead a number of them into an irrational action which could inflict wounds on our American democracy which would require decades to heal. On the other hand, if you offer these groups the kinds of assurances which would quiet them, a large majority of your own supporters in other parts of the country would be deeply offended and your administration would take office under a cloud of cynicism which would hamper you at every turn.

If it becomes necessary for you to make a public declaration before the Electoral College meets, it might be worth considering a statement which rests upon the long-range historical and Constitutional traditions of the country rather than upon the immediate issues now involved. The American Constitutional system is one which cannot possibly work unless those who are charged with public responsibility are determined to make it work. This is because the founding fathers were concerned about the abuse of power and built into the Constitution a number of potential impasses if consensus and cooperation fail. The separation of powers among the Executive, Legislative and Judicial branches, the distribution of power between the President and the Senate in making key appointments and ratifying treaties are the best known examples of these potential deadlocks.

By long tradition, the Electoral College has become a device for registering the wishes of the voters in our Presidential elections. In many states, state laws compel electors to vote as instructed by the electorate. In some states such laws do not exist but the Constitutional traditions have been firmly established. If the Electoral College itself could become the occasion for the adjustment of political differences, a revolutionary change will have occurred in our Constitutional processes. States which now compel their delegates to vote as instructed by the electorate would, in self defense, be forced to repeal such laws in order to give their electors the freedom of action which might be required to defend their interests in the Electoral College. What has come to be a purely formal step would be transformed into an additional forum of political controversy. Citizens could have no confidence in the value of their own votes; special interests could the more readily obtain a wholly disproportionate influence at a critical point; government by the people would come to mean very little and the nation would be riven to its foundations by manipulation and intrigue.

If on this present occasion the issue can be identified precisely, on other occasions this might not always be possible. If a successful candidate for the Presidency should, while awaiting the official vote of the Electoral College, embark upon the path of negotiating political issues among the electors, he would set a precedent and enter upon a path which would lead only to the disintegration of our political institutions.

This is a brief and off-the-cuff reaction to the stories carried in the daily press about current moves by some Southern delegates. My principal thought is that an attempt to deal with such questions on their merits in connection with the Electoral College would be genuinely revolutionary and that there would be a great many in the South who would at least understand the Constitutional implications of your refusal to get into the substance of the present issue. The general line I have suggested would apply, of course, regardless of which candidate seemed to be coming up to the Electoral College in the favored position. In any vigorous democracy in which free men take their freedoms seriously, Constitutional arrangements are likely to be delicate and can survive only if there is a strong consensus about the fundamental arrangements within which differences are settled. The notion that the Electoral College meets to affirm the expressed will of the people in the several states seems to me to be one of those utterly fundamental ideas.

I hope that this letter will be useless by the time it reaches you.

Sincerely yours,

Dean Rusk

The Honorable John F. Kennedy
Senate Office Building
Washington, D.C.

SUGGESTION MADE BY DEAN RUSK, PORTER MC KEEVER AND
ERNEST GROSS, BY TELEPHONE FROM NEW YORK CITY

Since the United States delegation to the United Nations Assembly was appointed last summer, the situation in the General Assembly has changed fundamentally. First, Premier Khrushchev has made the assembly the launching pad for a major diplomatic offensive; second, the attack on the Secretary General has created a threat to the life of the very institution; and third, this has occurred in an assembly with an unprecedented number of chiefs of states and foreign ministers in attendance.

The wholly new situation calls for a re-casting of the United States delegation to provide dramatic evidence and effective implementation of the interest of all the American people and the leadership of both political parties in the future of the United Nations.

It is suggested that Senator Kennedy present the foregoing view to the President and suggest that perhaps the two career people on the delegation and perhaps at least two of the alternate delegates who are not known public figures withdraw and be replaced by such outstanding public figures as Governor Nelson Rockefeller, John J. McCloy and Thomas E. Dewey from the Republican Party, and Adlai Stevenson, Mrs. Eleanor Roosevelt and Chester Bowles from the Democratic Party.

The suggestions should be made privately and in all sincerity. If the President should act upon it, the national interest would be served and the political laurels would be at least equally spread, as Senator Kennedy's initiative would inevitably become known and the performance of the foregoing Democrats would certainly reflect credit on the party and on Senator Kennedy's leadership in selecting them.

Should the President reject the suggestion, Senator Kennedy is provided with an excellent opportunity to reveal to the American people the kind of administrative leadership he would assert in foreign policy if he were President.

DEAN RUSK'S COVERING LETTER AND MEMORANDUM
OF CONVERSATION WITH
UN SECRETARY GENERAL DAG HAMMARSKJOLD

Room 4200
111 West 50th Street
New York 20
November 30, 1960

Dear Paul:

Here is a memorandum on my talk with the Secretary General. At first glance it might seem a bit complicated, but things which are simple for most of us are complicated for a President-Elect or President of the United States.

Dag Hammarskjold could not have been more friendly and more willing to accommodate the Senator's wishes. We should give him some sort of answer as soon as we can. If the Senator can't know until Tuesday, I would suggest that someone ring the Secretary General and at least tell him that.

There was one point which I did not develop in detail in the memorandum which I ought to mention to you separately. The Secretary General is quite allergic to "phoney staging". I did not have the slightest impression that he associated this with Mr. Kennedy but rather that he was remembering some occasions in the past when he felt that he was the unwilling victim of various pieces of showmanship.

Tell the Senator I am very sorry that I won't be in New York next week but at the annual meeting of our full Board of Trustees, which is my overriding commitment each year.

Could you give me a ring as soon as you have read this?

Sincerely yours,

Dean Rusk

Mr. Paul H. Nitze
Foreign Service Educational Foundation
1839 19th Street, N.W.
Washington 9, D.C.

MEMORANDUM TO MR. PAUL NITZE

Room 4200
111 West 50th Street
New York 20
November 30, 1960

Confidential

Following our telephone conversation today, I called upon the Secretary General to discuss alternative possibilities for an informal meeting with Senator Kennedy on Wednesday, December 7. The Secretary General, who was alone, was most cordial toward the idea and expressed his desire to meet the Senator's preference and convenience in any way feasible.

The conversation proceeded upon these assumptions: (1) that the Senator would not wish to be in a situation where he would either have to meet a large number of Delegates to the UN or to make arbitrary choices in singling out a few; (2) that the Senator would not wish to be drawn prematurely into any of the issues now before the General Assembly; (3) that the Senator would not wish a meeting with the Secretary General to be elaborately "staged"; (4) that it would, however, be important that the fact of such a meeting be publicly known as an indication of the Senator's interest in the United Nations, and (5) that it would be helpful if the two could have some opportunity for an unofficial but frank talk about the UN before the new administration assumes responsibility.

If Senator Kennedy finds these assumptions generally agreeable, it would seem to follow that he would not wish to visit the General Assembly itself, either by sitting for a time with the U.S. Delegation or by taking a seat in the audience. His presence in the Assembly would be a major event, but in circumstances not easily handled by the well established procedures and customs of the UN.

There is only one point which could cause the Secretary General real difficulty in his relations with 99 member nations. In self protection, the Secretary General makes "calls" (in the diplomatic sense) outside the United Nations itself only upon Heads of State. Food or drink, however, has the magic quality of dissolving protocol and transforming a "call" into a social occasion.

The Secretary General would be happy to come to have lunch, cocktails or dinner with Senator Kennedy or would be equally happy to invite the Senator to his own home in mid-town Manhattan for any one of them. It seemed clear that, as among these possibilities, the Secretary General has no personal preference and would be glad to meet the Senator's wishes.

Still another alternative would be a visit by Senator Kennedy to the Secretary General's office in the Secretariat building, *not* in the Assembly Hall, at some such time as 5:30 or 6:00 o'clock.

The Secretary General would not, of course, ask Senator Kennedy for any commitments on policy questions. It might, on the other hand, be useful for the Senator to hear any observations which the Secretary General might wish to make about points of concern about current and future trends in the United Nations. This suggests that others present might best be only those in front of whom frank conversation can occur. The Secretary General would be entirely agreeable to the Senator's wishes as to whether the two should meet alone or in a larger group. The larger the group, the more general a conversation is likely to be.

The informality of a meeting between Senator Kennedy and the Secretary General assumes some importance from another point of view. An official call upon the United Nations by a high dignitary would raise the protocol necessity of a call upon the President of the General Assembly, now Mr. Boland of Ireland, and the President of the Security Council, who during December will be the Soviet Delegate, Mr. Zorin. Much speculation would be stimulated by a call upon one and not the other. Further, both these officials are heads of national delegations; it would be difficult to avoid feelings among other delegates that they, too, ought to be somehow involved. Mr. Boland, incidentally, has a luncheon scheduled on Wednesdays with the chairmen of the several committees of the General Assembly.

An informal meeting with the Secretary General might raise in some minds the question of notice being taken by Senator Kennedy of the U.S. Delegation to the General Assembly. The Secretary General would surely consider that this was a wholly American matter and not something on which he would have any view whatever. Presumably the question of the United States Delegation is a part of the broader question of Senator Kennedy's handling of transition problems.

It is suggested that Senator Kennedy's representative communicate directly with the Secretary General in person about the Senator's wishes and any details which might need attention.

On balance, it seems to me that the simplest alternative would be for the Senator to invite the Secretary General to lunch with him at the Hotel Carlisle. This would save the Senator certain time and would reduce any special arrangements which might arise from security or press considerations.

If the Senator concludes that it will not be possible for him to see the Secretary General next Wednesday, someone should telephone the Secretary General personally since this preliminary exploration has almost certainly caused the Secretary General to keep his calendar open on that day.

Dean Rusk

MEMORANDUM TO SENATOR KENNEDY FROM CHESTER BOWLES

November 23, 1960

Subject: *Report on Visits with Various Foreign Representatives*

Last week Clark Clifford called me in Maine to say that you had asked him to ask me to see various Ambassadors and foreign representatives who are anxious to talk with you, to explain your inability at this particular time to talk with them personally, and to report back to you any views which they might express of any importance.

This is a brief report.

1. *Ambassador Grewe, the Federal Republic of Germany*

As you may know, there has been a rumor concerning Ambassador Grewe's possible withdrawal, but I am glad to find this is denied. He is an able man, with a strong dedication to democratic, liberal principles. The Ambassador talked frankly of the situation in Germany with particular regard to Chancellor Adenauer, his Cabinet, and the question of his succession.

I had made it a point to call the Ambassador the morning after the TV debate in which the question of Quemoy and Matsu was brought up and in which Mr. Nixon raised doubts about our stand on Berlin. At that meeting I asked him to reassure his government that we would stand totally firm with regard to Berlin, and he had no reason to be concerned.

He brought up this point again and said that Mr. Adenauer had full confidence in you and your associates. The Ambassador is leaving for Berlin around the seventh of December, and said he would appreciate it if I could let him know before then whether it would be convenient for you to have Mr. Adenauer visit Washington in early February. I told the Ambassador that I knew you were very anxious to see the Chancellor. He suggested that the Chancellor was fully aware of the excessive ceremony and entertainment that went with such visits, and that such activity could be kept at the absolute minimum. He repeated what has already appeared in the press, that the prime purpose of Adenauer's visit would be to make a speech before a German-American group which has been pressing an invitation on him for some months.

2. *Ambassador Yeh of Nationalist China*

I have seen a good deal of Mr. Yeh, not only during his period as Foreign Minister—a position he held for nine years—but also during his term as ambassador. He has always been thoroughly friendly and understanding of the views that you and I have expressed. Astonishing as it seems in the context of his public statements, I think in his heart he agrees with us.

The talk was entirely pleasant and constructive. I reassured him that he need have no fears about our abandoning Formosa in any manner, or contributing to the embarrassment of his government in any irresponsible way. Indeed, we hoped that conditions might be created in which it would be possible for us to go even further in building up the economy of Formosa and expanding its cultural relations with Southeast Asia.

3. *Ambassador Carlos Sanz de Santamaria of Colombia*

The Ambassador is a very impressive individual and appears to be close to President Lleras. He also expressed the greatest gratification over your election and for the coming of a Democratic administration. He emphasized the point, however, that time in Latin America is growing very short, pressures are mounting rapidly, and that if we are to be effective we will have to take affirmative and dramatic steps during the next six months. He stressed particularly the importance of a more effective pricing system on commodities like coffee and industrial raw materials. He has imagination, and is a person who could be very helpful to us as we develop our own thinking on these programs.

The Ambassador was hopeful that in your answer to the President's congratulatory wire, you could go beyond the usual niceties of diplomatic language and express strong liberal views about the future development of Latin America and its relations with the United States. I have prepared a rough draft of a wire which I have sent to Fred Holborn, a copy of which I attach to this memorandum.

4. *Ambassador Asiz Ahmed of Pakistan*

I have always had great respect for Ambassador Ahmed, whom I first met in Asia. The Ambassador was anxious to know if we were likely to be considering any adjustments in our military association. I told him that while I could not speak for you, he could be assured that we would do nothing irresponsible, that we would carry out commitments made by the previous Administration, and that there would be no abrupt changes which would weaken our defense posture in that area or the relations between our two governments.

I told him again, however, as I have done many times in the past, that many of us hoped that more money could go into the economic development of the area and that some of the military activity in Pakistan might profitably be drawn more into the lines of internal development on the analogy of our own Corps of Engineers. He agreed, as he has on previous occasions.

He also expressed the view that attitudes in regard to Com-

munist China were moving rapidly against us and that the votes in
the UN in 1961 would probably override our objections. Much depends on Peking's behavior during the next few months.

5. *Ambassador Hervé Alphand of France*

I did not intend to see him for obvious reasons. However,
since De Gaulle looks on Mendès-France as perhaps his greatest
political adversary, and since I have a date to see Mendès-France
in New York on Friday, I thought it most discreet to mention my
plans to the Ambassador in advance, because he would almost certainly find out about them elsewhere.

The Ambassador expressed appreciation that he was informed
and said he understood perfectly the basis for the visit.

He then talked at some length about Algeria, and felt rather
hopeful that the situation would develop increasingly favorably
in the next few months. He brought up your Algerian speech, but
in a very friendly way. Indeed, he pointed out that many of the
things that De Gaulle is now beginning to do, you had suggested
three years ago.

In general, I found him to be quite moderate in his views,
and entirely friendly so far as you are concerned.

6. *Ambassador Victor Andrade of Bolivia*

I also met with Ambassador Andrade, a good friend of Clark
Clifford's, with a deep concern for Latin America-United States relations. As you know, the Ambassador is one of the oldest and most
respected in the diplomatic corps, and very friendly to the United
States.

The story that Ambassador Andrade asked me to pass on to
you followed a familiar pattern: Our economic assistance to Bolivia
has been inadequate and clumsily directed, and by associating ourselves with some members of an old and discredited regime we
have compounded our difficulties.

The tin industry, which was nationalized a few years ago, has
run into very great difficulties, and because of the government
management role, we have been unwilling to help straighten it
out. The Soviet has seized on this situation to offer a modern tin
smelting setup with technical help to operate it. The State Department is now making a belated effort to neutralize the Soviet proposal by a ten million dollar loan. Although Andrade feels this
would be helpful, he was emphatic in saying that it will not solve
their basic problems.

In the meantime, Vice-President Lechin, the left-wing, Castro
oriented Vice-President, has announced his desire to come to Washington to press you for a promise of increased assistance, using the
Soviet offer as a lever.

I told Ambassador Andrade that you were under similar pressures from many sources, that it was impossible for you personally

to get into complex situations of this kind before your new Administration takes office, that I would be glad to talk with Lechin if he should insist on coming, but I did not think I could add anything very substantial to what I had said to him, i.e., that a new Administration would review, immediately after it takes office, the problem which he described, that we would do everything possible to work out a satisfactory long-range answer, that we had a deep concern for the success of the new Bolivian government.

He appeared to be entirely satisfied by this and asked me to express his great satisfaction with your election and his hope that he would have an opportunity to meet you at some later date.

7. I have an engagement to talk with Ambassador Mongi Slim of Tunisia on Friday afternoon when I return from New York.

8. *Vice-President Radhakrishnan of India* is in this country and very anxious to see you. I am confident I can explain your difficulty, however, for we are on very agreeable terms. I am planning to see him on Friday morning in New York. I am sure I can explain your situation and the pressures under which you have been working. If anything comes up of interest, I will report to you.

9. *Ambassador Menshikov of the Soviet Union*

Mr. Menshikov has called several times for an appointment. However, my instinct has been not to see him at this particular time. If you have a different judgment, please let me know. Menshikov served in India as Ambassador for two or three years and this gives us a certain mutual background. However, I think he is a very overrated individual.

10. I have also received requests through a Chilean friend of mine who has been in contact with the Chilean Ambassador, to talk with the Cuban Foreign Minister, Roa. According to the Chilean, Roa represents a relatively moderate viewpoint in the Havana government, and would like to develop some basis for the easing of the present existing tensions.

I personally see very little advantage in talking with him now, and a good deal of disadvantage if it were known that such a meeting had been held. Indeed I would suspect that in all likelihood the Cuban government would arrange for a deliberate leak. So I have not accepted these overtures. I do feel, however, that it is interesting that this point of view exists. It may give us something to work on at a later date.

With the exceptions of Messrs. Alphand and Yeh, none of the above discussions were initiated by me, but were simply in response to calls from people who wanted to see you and were referred to me by the State Department, or came directly.

I⋆N⋆D⋆E⋆X

Acheson, Dean, 96, 217; his plan for Cyprus, 28–31; on the Cuban missile crisis, 66; his part in NATO, 97, 103, 104; and the Truman Doctrine, 142–43; as Secretary of State, 113, 138, 139–40; regarding Dean Rusk, 146, 162; as Undersecretary, 168, 170; regarding Secretary of Defense Louis Johnson, 180; regarding Policy Planning Chief Paul Nitze, 193–94

Achilles, Theodore, 179

Act of Bogota, 197

Adams, Sherman, 215

Aden, 38, 39, 41, 51, 52

Adenauer, Konrad, 97, 230

Adzhubei, Alexei, 58

Aegean Sea, 82

Africa, African, 95, 101, 123, 133, 142, 148, 151, 156

Agency for International Development (AID), 89, 177, 178

Ahmed, Asiz, 231

Aiken, George, 94, 96

Air Force, 44, 62, 63, 195, 200, 209

Airforce KC-135, 24, 25

Alexander the Great, 183

Algeria, 100, 184, 232

Alliance for Progress, 14, 186, 196, 197, 213

Alphand, Hervé, 103, 232, 233

American Academy of Political Science, 205

American Society of International Law, 11

American University, 68

Anderson, Dillon, 114

Anderson, Robert, 187

Andrade, Victor, 232–33

Angola, 187

Ankara, 4, 18, 19, 20, 21, 22, 24, 25, 27, 31

Arab world, 52, 129

Arabian peninsula, 42, 44

Argentina, 169

Arkansas, 144

Army, 4, 192, 195, 214

Army and Navy Country Club, 161

Army Air Force, 43–44, 47, 53, 199

Arnold, H. H. ("Hap"), 199

Article 19 (of the UN Charter), 93–95, 214

Asia, Asians, 71, 75–76, 90, 92, 133, 142, 156, 188, 192, 212, 231

Aspaturian, Vernon V., 201, 203

Assyrians, 183

Aswan Dam, 5, 40

Athens, 19, 20, 21, 24, 25, 27, 30, 32, 34

Atlantic, 97, 130, 173; alliance, 101, 157; fleets, 99, 100; charter, 169

237

Atomic Energy Commission, 6, 195
atomic weapons, 4, 70, 78; test ban
    talks, 190
Australia, 74, 165
Axis, the, 169
Ayub Khan. *See* Khan, Mohammed
    Ayub

Badeau, John S., 41
Ball, George, 11, 97, 149, 150, 151,
    154–55, 157, 161, 168, 179,
    180, 219, 221; acting as Sec-
    retary of State during Cyprus
    crisis, 18–35, 37; his doubts
    about escalation of war in
    Vietnam, 75; his conduct of
    U.S.-French policy, 105–10;
    his career as Undersecretary,
    170–74; along with that as
    SIG chairman, 178; his posi-
    tion on Panama, 186–87
Basic National Security Paper
    (BNSP), 188, 194
Bay of Pigs, 7, 14, 54, 65, 149,
    165, 207, 215
Beaverbrook, Lord, 157
Beirut, 4, 50
Bell, David, 9
Benediktsson, Bjarni, 118, 119
Bennett, W. Tapley, Jr., 131, 213
Benson, Ezra Taft, 6
Berlin, 15, 56, 59, 67, 110, 168,
    197, 210, 230; crisis, 108, 159,
    179, 182; wall, 211
Bernau, Phyllis, 161
Bernhard, Prince, 119
Bhutto, Z. A., 127
Big Five powers, 96
Bohlen, Charles E. ("Chip"), 13,
    60, 106, 107, 140, 196
Boland, Frederick H., 229
Bolivia, Bolivian, 186, 232, 233
Bonn, 104, 107
bonze suicides, 82
Bosch, Juan, 213
Bowie, Robert, 194, 195, 198

Bowles, Chester, 141, 145, 147–48,
    151–52, 226, 230–33
Boy Scouts, 85
Bradley, Omar, 214
Brazil, 213
Brezhnev, Leonid, 51, 116, 201–03
British Commonwealth, 157–58,
    161
British Empire, 157
British Foreign Office, 176, 190
British Supply Council, 98
Bruce, David, 145, 168, 222–23
Bruce, Mrs. David, 145
Brussels, 12
Buchanan, Wiley, 122
Buddhists, 80, 82–85, 88, 91
Budget Bureau, 187, 216
Bunche, Ralph, 48
Bundy, McGeorge, as Assistant to
    JFK and LBJ, 1–4, 6–7, 114,
    116, 120, 127, 133, 148–49,
    152, 155, 164, 175–76, 183,
    215, 219; during the Cuban
    missile crisis, 59, 66; during
    Vietnam, 79, 134; during the
    Berlin crisis, 211; his "little
    State Department," 44, 172;
    his opposition to the MLF
    project, 173
Bundy, William B., 128, 219
Bunker, Ellsworth, 43–44, 45–51
Bureau of Research and Intelli-
    gence, 80, 81
Burke, Arleigh A., 179

Cabinet, 9, 64–65, 79, 81, 85, 113,
    139, 146, 149, 150, 164, 214,
    216
Cabinet room, 2, 89
Cabot, John M., 123
Caesar, Julius, 183
Cairo, 41–42, 50–51
Calvinism, 160
Camp David, 29
Canada, Canadian, 51, 74, 94, 126,
    156

Cap Ferrat, 60
Cape Cod, 130
Capitol Hill (the Hill), 153–54, 175
Caribbean Sea, 66
Carlyle Hotel, 148, 229
Carter, Marshall S., 61
Castiella, Fernando Maria, 119–20
Castro, Fidel, vi, 55–57, 61–62, 95, 120, 135, 184, 232
Cecil Peace Prize, 157
Central Intelligence Agency (CIA), 1, 5, 39, 59–63, 65, 72, 86, 90, 176–77
Central Treaty Organization (CENTO), 4, 143, 158, 191–92
Cherokee County (Georgia), 160
Chiari, Roberto, 131
Chicago, 145, 164
Chief of Staff paper, 18
Chile, Chilean, 125, 169, 183, 184, 198, 233
China, Chinese, 62, 77–79, 93, 154, 158–59, 172, 212; Communist China and Chinese, 38, 73, 75, 77, 156, 158, 173, 181, 183, 197, 208, 231–32; Nationalist China and Chinese, 62, 72, 197, 230
Christians, 17
Churchill, Sir Winston, 128, 129, 169
civil defense, 209, 217
Civil Rights, 143, 144, 153, 224
Clark, Joseph, 161
Cleveland, Harlan, 107
Clifford, Clark, 134, 230, 232
Clifton, Chester V., 82, 130
cold war, 96, 98–99, 201
Colombey-des-deux-Eglises, 191
Colombia, 231
Columbia University, 98
Commerce Department, 6
Common Market, 12, 171, 189
Communism, 96, 122, 137, 141–42, 159, 165, 169, 181–84, 188–89, 190–91, 201, 210–11, 218; in the Middle East, 24, 26, 31, 51, 93, 113; in Cuba, 54–55, 57, 59, 66–67; in Vietnam, 72–78, 81, 84–85, 89, 91–92
Communist Party Congress, 78
Congo, 93, 94, 95, 135, 171
Congress, 9, 72, 76, 78, 94, 96, 115, 118, 132, 133, 142, 146, 153, 167, 175, 193; Congressional hearings, 154
Congress of Vienna, 122
Constitution, the, 138, 199, 225
Corps of Engineers, 231
Craig, May, 119
Crisis Game, The (Giffin), 203
Crockett, William, 187
Cuba, Cuban, 15, 56–63, 66–68, 95, 120–21, 136, 149–50, 178, 182, 184, 186, 213, 218, 233; missile crisis, 14, 34, 54–55, 59–66, 68, 108, 150, 159, 171, 197, 203, 206, 207, 210, 218
Cutler, Robert, 8, 14
Cyprus, 17–36, 37, 48, 53, 109, 156, 157, 206, 207, 214, 218, 219, 221
Czechoslovakia, 34, 96, 168
Danes, Danish, 31, 125
Dardanelles, 197
Defense Department, 65, 86, 177, 179, 180, 198–99, 219
Defense Intelligence Agency, 173
De Gaulle, Charles, vi, 1, 5, 12–14, 22, 25, 171, 201, 211, 222–23, 232; U.S. policy towards, 96, 99–111, 156–57, 180, 189–91, 211
Democratic National Committee, 191
Democratic Party, 147, 169, 226
De Murville, Couve, 106, 110
Dewey, Thomas E., 147, 226
Dhahran base, 45

Diem, Ngo Dinh, 71, 79–91
Dienbienphu, 70, 91
Dillon, Douglas, 64
disarmament, 13, 149
Dobrynin, Anatoly, 78
Dominican Republic, 9, 44, 117, 154, 165, 171, 179–80, 207, 213–14, 217, 219
Douglas Aircraft Company, 200
Douglas-Home, Sir Alec, 21
Drozniak, Edward, 121, 164
Duke, Angier Biddle, 123
Dulles, John Foster, 4–5, 8, 97, 113, 138–39, 160–61, 169–70, 194–95; his refusal to Nasser, 40; his policy in Germany, 99; his CENTO and SEATO pacts, 143; his part in the 1958 China crisis, 197; his "brinkmanship," 217
Dungan, Ralph, 121

Early Warning System, 208
Egypt, Egyptian, 38, 41, 51–52, 190
Eisenhower, Dwight D., 1, 65, 113–14, 116, 118, 122, 142, 146, 153, 188–89, 194–95, 198, 211, 216–17; his reliance on the NSC, 3, 4, 5, 6, 8, 214–15; his administration, 14, 40, 99, 138–39; his success in the Lebanon crisis, 53; on Soviet support in Cuba, 56–57, 58 fn.; his decision regarding Dienbienphu, 70, 91; at SHAPE, 97; his policy toward De Gaulle, 100–02, 108; his "open skies" plan, 149; his differences with Herbert Hoover, Jr., 169–70; his use of the OCB, 179; his support of the Alliance for Progress, 196–97; his decisions regarding the nuclear age, 208–10, 212, 222, 223

Elliott, William Y., 146
England. *See* Great Britain
enosis, 26, 27, 31
Erhard, Ludwig, 129
Erkin, Feridun Cemal, 221
Europe, Europeans, 96–97, 142, 151, 156, 157, 168, 188–89, 192–93, 210, 222; Eastern Europe, 111, 133, 156, 165; Western Europe, 14, 179
European Defense Community, 99–100
Excom (Executive Committee), 64, 65, 67
Executive (branch), 96, 225
Executive Office Building, 216
Export-Import Bank, 193

Fabian socialism, 127
Far East, 86, 101, 160, 178
Feis, Herbert, 192
Feisal, Prince, 41, 43, 45–50, 52
Felt, Harry, 90
Feria, the, at Seville, 119
Finletter, Thomas, 21
First-hand Report (Adams), 215 fn.
Foggy Bottom establishment, 170, 175
Ford Foundation, 149
Foreign Affairs Information Management Effort (FAIME), 187
Foreign Ministry, 58
Foreign Relations Committee, 172
Foreign Service Educational Foundation, 227
Foreign Service Institute, 104
Foreign Service Journal, 177
Formosa, 80, 158, 231
Forrestal, James, 3, 80–81
Forrestal, Michael, 80–81, 85–88
Fort Ritchie, 209
Fortas, Abe, 134, 174
Foster, William, 148, 149

France, French, 12, 98, 105–10, 157, 170, 171, 178, 179, 191, 199, 203, 222–23, 232; in Vietnam, 70, 73–74, 91; steel production, 97; nationalism, 99; army, 99; Assembly, 99, 103–04; NATO affairs, 100–04, 110–11
France-Soir, 105
Franco, Bahamonde, 120
Free World Alliance, 142
Freedom Award (U.S.A.), 98
Freedom, U.S. Presidential Medal of, 98
Freeman, Orville, 9, 164
Frost, Robert, 57
Fulbright, J. William, 136, 144, 149, 154, 172
Fulbright, Mrs. J. William, 154

Gaither Committee, 217
Galbraith, Kenneth, 162, 175
Gandhi, Mrs. Indira, 127
Geneva, 23–25, 29–31, 34–35, 190; conference, 76
Georgia, 143, 224
Germany, German, 4, 98–99, 100, 104–05, 107, 120, 125, 129, 156, 198, 204, 221–23; steel production, 97; West Germany and Germans, 129, 149, 156, 211; Berlin crisis, 182; occupation assistance for, 193; East Germans, 211
Ghana, 136
Giffin, Sidney F., 203–04
Gilpatric, Roswell, 65, 86, 215
Goldberg, Arthur, 79, 96, 133, 145, 162, 164–65
Goldman, Eric, 137
Goldwater, Barry, 34, 118
Gordon, Arthur, 122 fn.
Graham, Philip, 148
Gray, Gordon, 114
Great Britain, British, 12–13, 25, 29, 34, 38, 39, 42, 52, 101,

103, 105, 127, 157, 170, 184, 223; as channel of communication with Soviets, 74; Supply Council, 98; as member of De Gaulle's proposed NATO triumvirate, 100, 102; withdrawal of financial support to Greece and Turkey, 113; her ambassadors and LBJ, 125, 128–29; her ambassadors and De Gaulle, 190–91; the Cabinet, 190
Great Society, 1, 76, 216
Greece, Greek, 113, 223; in conflict over Cyprus, 17, 20, 22, 23, 25–36, 156–57, 218, 221
Green, Marshall, 184
Greenfield, James, v, 163, 172
Grew, Joseph, 168
Grewe, Wilhelm, 120, 230
Grivas, General, 31, 32, 33, 35
Gromyko, Andrei, 159, 191
Gronouski, John, 123
Gross, Ernest, 226–27
Gross, H. R., 96
Guantanamo Naval Base, 57, 66
Gulf of Tonkin, 74, 132, 207

Hague, the, 95
Haiphong, 132
Halberstam, David, 84
Hammarskjold, Dag, 94, 146–48, 227–29
Hand, Lloyd, 124
Hanoi, 70–92, 132, 135
"Hard Surface," 44–45
Hare, Raymond, 22, 23, 27
Hart, Parker J., 47, 48
Harib, 51
Harkins, Paul, 90
Harlech, Lord. *See* Ormsby-Gore, Sir David
Harriman, Averell, 79–82, 84–85, 87–88, 133–34, 148, 152, 162
Harvard, 146, 195, 204
Hassan, Prince, 38

Havana, 61, 233
Health, Education and Welfare, Department of, 64
Helms, Richard, 86
Henderson, Loy, 113
Hensley, Stewart, 86
Herter, Christian, 99, 185, 195–96
Hickenlooper, Bourke, 41, 94
High Authority, 97
Hilsman, Roger, 80–82, 84–88
Hitler, Adolf, 40, 168
Hittites, 183
Hoa, Thich Thien, 83
Holborn, Fred, 143, 146, 231
Honey Fitz, 211
Honey, P. J., 80, 88
Honolulu, 22, 84, 85, 87, 150, 165
Hoover, Herbert, Jr., 149, 169, 170
Hoover, J. Edgar, 165
House Appropriations Committee, 87–88
House of Commons, 127
House Ways and Means Committee, 78
Hue riots, 82
Hull, Cordell, 153, 168, 169
Humphrey, Hubert, 79, 133, 145, 162, 164
Hungarian revolt, 210–11
Hurd, James, v
Hyannisport, 86–87, 130, 211

ICBM, 209
Iceland, 223
Iliades, Socrates, 32
Imam, Ahmed, 38
Imam, Mohammed al-Badr, 38, 46, 49
India, Indian, 16–17, 94, 124, 126–28, 158, 162, 165, 169, 173, 175–76, 183, 213, 214, 233; Railways Minister, 162
Indian Ocean, 129
Indochina, 91, 99
Indonesia, 44, 128, 178, 184
Indonesian Communist Party (PKI), 184

Inonu, H. E. General Ismet, 23, 24, 27, 28, 29, 33, 109
Institute of Defense Analyses, 203
Interdepartmental Regional Group (IRG), 176, 178
Inter-Nation Simulation, 203–04
International Court of Justice, 95, 109
International Security Affairs Bureau, 165, 180
Iowa, 41, 94, 96
Iran, 4, 191–92
Iraq, 47
Ireland, 82, 118, 223, 229
Iron Curtain, 14, 165
Iskenderun area, 22
Israel, Israelis, 40, 41, 93, 124, 129
Istanbul, 22
Italy, Italian, 48, 49, 223

Jackson, William, 114
Japan, 142
Johnson, Louis, 180
Johnson, Lynda Bird, 119
Johnson, Lyndon B., 1–3, 5, 8–12, 16, 19–21, 23–30, 33, 37, 53, 58, 70–79, 87–88, 91–92, 94–95, 103–04, 109–10, 115, 122, 124–37, 142, 144–45, 153–55, 157, 164–66, 171–76, 180, 183, 185, 189–90, 198–99, 207, 211, 214–18; his administration, 9, 15, 22, 96, 105, 109, 111, 123, 143–44, 187, 212, 219
Johnson, Mrs. Lyndon B., 135
Johnson, U. Alexis, 177
Joint Chiefs of Staff, 4, 81, 117, 177, 204, 212
Jordan, 38–40, 42–43, 45
Judicial (branch), 225
Jupiter MRBMs, 66

Karachi, 127
Kasavubu, Joseph, 94
Kashmir, 126, 203
Kastellorizo, 31

Katzenbach, Nicholas deBelleville, 174–75, 179
Keating, Kenneth, 61, 62, 218
Kennan, George, 13–14, 192–94, 198
Kennedy, John F., 1, 3, 6–8, 11–16, 37, 39–41, 43–49, 53–58, 60–69, 71, 79, 81–82, 84–85, 87–92, 99, 108, 115–16, 121, 130–32, 140–43, 145–49, 151–54, 159, 163, 165–66, 172–73, 175–76, 179, 183, 188, 196, 198, 206–07, 209–11, 213, 215–17, 219, 222–33; his administration, 86, 94, 114, 186, 194, 197, 212
Kenya, 183
Keynes, Lord, 188
Khan, Genghis, 183
Khan, Mohammed Ayub, 16, 118, 126–28, 165, 173, 214
Khanh, Nguyen, 72
Khrushchev, Nikita S., vi, 5, 14, 19, 27, 34, 55–60, 63–69, 96, 115–16, 147, 150, 159, 179, 181–82, 226; "Khrushchev at Bay" study, 181–83
Kleberg, Richard M., 132
Knappstein, Herr Heinrich, 125
Knox, William, 58
Kohler, Foy, 57–58
Komer, Robert, 37–53
Korea, 77
Korean War, 3, 98, 99, 158, 194, 212
Korry, Edward, 133
Kosygin, Aleksei N., 116, 127, 202
Kremlin, 55, 58, 60, 63, 66, 181–82, 191, 202–03; Kremlinologists, 78, 201, 203
Kriegspiel, 200
Krulak, Victor H., 89
Kutchuk, Fazil, 22
Ky, Nguyen Cao, 91, 165

Labouisse, Henry, 34
Lambert, Tom, vi

Laos, 14, 91, 182, 203
Latin America, 14, 142, 156, 164, 186, 196, 199, 213, 231–32
LBJ ranch, 129
Lebanon, 4, 53, 204
Lechin, Vice-President, 232–33
Legislative (branch), 225
Le May, Curtis, 45
Lemnitzer, Lyman L., 81
Lenin, Vladimir, 190
Liebman, Morris, 2
Limassol, 31
Lincoln, Mrs. Evelyn, 121, 183
Lippmann, Walter, 171
Lleras, President, 231
Lodge, Henry Cabot, 82, 84–88, 90, 147
London, 25, 63, 120–21, 152, 168–69, 196; -Zurich agreements of 1959, 17, 19, 21, 28; conference, 195
Los Angeles Times, vi
Louisiana, 87
Lovett, Robert, 1–2, 113, 146, 168, 179
Lucet, Charles, 106
Lumumba, Patrice, 94–95

McCarran, Patrick, 120
McCarthy, Joseph, 137, 158
McClellan, John, 144
McCloskey, Robert, 163
McCloy, John J., 1–2, 104, 147, 226
McCone, John A., 1, 60–61, 65, 72, 85, 87, 97, 176
McGhee, George, 149, 152
McKeever, Porter, 226–27
McNamara, Robert S., 10, 30, 64, 66, 71, 72, 74, 81, 85, 87, 89–90, 105, 117, 134–35, 152, 164, 178, 180, 207, 211, 215, 219
McNaughton, John, 105, 180
Macmillan, Harold, 12, 99, 188
Maine, 119, 230

Makarios, Archbishop, 19–20, 22, 24, 27–29, 31–36
Malaya, 80, 129
Malaysian Federation, 128
Manchiet el-Bakri, 50
Manhattan District and National Defense Research Committee, 199
Mann, Thomas, 131, 164
Mao Tse-tung, 218
Marines, 195, 217–18
Maritime Union, 136
Marquess of Salisbury, 18
Marshall, George, 97, 113, 142, 160–61, 170, 192–93
Marshall Plan, 108, 142, 193, 198
Martin, Edwin, 59, 60
Marx, Karl, 190
Maryland, 209
Massachusetts Institute of Technology (MIT), 203
Matsu, 5, 230
Mecklin, John, 86
Mediterranean, 22, 26, 36, 100
Meet the Press, 106
Mendenhall, John A., 89
Mendès-France, Pierre, 232
Menshikov, Ambassador, 233
Merchant, Livingston, 148
Metropolitan Club, 161, 222
Mexico, 186
Michigan, 148, 224
Middle East, 4, 40–42, 53, 93, 101, 142, 204
Mikoyan, Anastos, 59, 116
Mills, Wilbur, 78
Mongol, 183
Monnet, Jean, 97, 98, 100
Monroe Doctrine, 152, 192
Monroe, James, 152
Morgan, Thomas E., 136
Moscow, 27, 40, 51, 55–58, 60–61, 98, 105–07, 116, 134, 147, 188, 190, 193, 196, 202, 212; "Declaration," 107; conference, 192

Moslems, 17
Moyers, William, 125, 126, 134
MRBM, 99
MRP, 99
Multilateral Force (MLF), 99, 105, 173
Munich, 192

Nassau conference, 12–13, 100
Nasser, vi, 5, 37–53, 136, 191
National Board of Intelligence Estimates, 61
National Press Club, 59
National Sanka Association, 83
National Security Council (NSC), 3–5, 7–9, 38–39, 43, 64, 89, 113–14, 133, 135, 140, 194, 208, 210, 214, 215, 217–18
nationalism, 108, 111
Navy, 4, 161, 179–80, 184, 192, 195
Nazis, 30
Near East, 184
Nebraska, 111
Nehru, Jawaharlal, 22, 126, 175
Netherlands, the, 44, 119
"new China policy," 212
New Delhi, 127, 162
New England, 82
New Frontier, 58, 65, 114, 211, 213, 216; Frontiersmen, 80, 211
New Orleans, 144, 224
"New Power Struggle in the Kremlin" study, 201–03
New York, 28, 81, 106, 135, 148, 165, 226, 228, 232
New York Times, The, 84, 86
New Zealand, 165
Nhu, Ngo Dinh, 83, 85–86, 88, 90–91
Nitzer, Paul, 54–56, 147, 180, 193–94, 222, 227–30
Nixon, Richard, 143, 146, 230
Nkrumah, Kwame, 136
Nolting, Frederick, 81–85, 87, 89

North Atlantic Treaty Organization (NATO), 1, 13, 17–19, 21, 23, 25–26, 30, 32, 36, 96–111, 128, 143, 156–57, 165, 178–80, 189, 191–92, 195, 198, 201, 214, 217, 222–23
North Borneo, 128
North Vietnam, 72–79, 126, 134–35, 185, 206–07
Northwestern University, 203
nuclear age, 55, 112, 210, 212, 223; weapons, 5, 77, 101; war, 54, 68; arsenal, 99; force, 100; U.S. umbrella, 108, 110; test ban treaty, 187; attack, 217

OECD, 223
O'Donnell, Kenneth, 130
"Operation Exodus," 136
"Operation Vulture," 70
Operations Coordinating Board (OCB), 6, 7, 179
Organization of American States (OAS), 131
Ormsby-Gore, Sir David, 18–19, 127, 129, 157
Otepka, Otto F., 162
Otis Air Force Base, 130
Ottawa, 126
Owen, Henry, 105, 189
Oxford, 158

Pacific, 208; Fleet, 90
Pakistan, Pakistani, 4, 16–17, 74, 126–27, 165, 173, 183, 213–14, 231
Palmer, Bruce, 117
Panama, Panamanians, 131, 185–87, 213, 217; Canal, 185–86
Papandreou, George, 25–30, 33–35
Paris, 22, 23, 70, 106–07, 110, 168, 196, 203–04
Parliament (British), 128
Passman, Otto, 87, 154
Pasvolsky, Leo, 192

Peace Corps, 126
Pearl Harbor, 169
Pearson, Mike, 118, 126, 128
Peiping regime, 159
Peking, 51, 78, 156, 158, 188, 232
Pennsylvania, 126, 161
Pennsylvania State University, 201
Pentagon, 4–5, 7, 16, 39, 45, 65, 78, 81, 89, 136, 139, 156, 164–65, 173, 180, 198–200, 203
Permanent Group, 101
Phillips, Richard I., v, 163
Phillips, Rufus, 89
Phillips, William, 168
Pleiku, 77
Poland, Polish, 14, 121, 123, 164
Polaris submarines, 12, 99, 189
Policy Planning Council, 181, 185, 187–88, 195
Polis, 32
Political Action Teams (PATs), 91
Polk, William R., 184–85, 205
Pope Paul VI, 135
Portland (Maine) *Press Herald*, 119
Potomac River, 124
Pravda, 201, 203
press, 58, 68, 117–19, 135, 163, 216
Princeton University, 98, 137
Proctor, Carolyn, 161
Project Camelot, 198–99
psychological warfare, 201
Pulitzer Prize, 84

Quang, Thich Tri, 88
Quarles, Donald, 4
Quebec, 199
Quemoy, 5, 230
Quinn, William W., 173

Radhakrishnan, Sir Sarvepalli, 233
Rahman, Tunku Abdul, 128
Ramsey, Henry, 185; paper, 187
Rand Corporation, 199, 201, 203
Rann of Kutch, 213–14

Rayburn, Sam, 71
Read, Benjamin, 136, 161
Red Cross, 135
Règlement de Vienne, 122
Republican Party, 147, 226
Rex Americanus, 199
Rhodes scholar, 157
Ribicoff, Abraham, 64
Rio conference, 169
Ritchie, Charles, 126
Riyadh, 45, 49
Roa, Minister, 233
Robertson, Walter, 80
Rockefeller Foundation, 146
Rockefeller, Nelson, 146–47, 226
Rome, 168
Rooney, John, 154
Roosevelt, Franklin Delano, 128, 140, 168–69
Roosevelt, Mrs. Franklin Delano, 147, 226
Rostow, Eugene, 110, 174
Rostow, Walt, 3–4, 6–7, 9, 12, 54–56, 59, 121, 133, 149, 155, 157, 181, 183, 187–90, 194, 216, 219
Royal Air Force, 51
Rumania, 14, 133
Rusk, Dean, 1, 9, 18–19, 22–25, 29, 33–34, 39–41, 45, 72, 78, 81, 84–85, 87, 96, 105, 123, 133–37, 141–66, 170–71, 173–74, 180–81, 185, 192, 199, 211–12, 214–16, 219, 224–30
Rusk, Peggy, 161
Russell, Richard, 144
Russia, Russian, 29, 59–61, 63, 67–69, 93–97, 109, 110, 116, 134, 158–59, 197, 201, 209

Sabeh, 128
SACEUR, 223
SACLANT, 99
Saigon, 22, 70–74, 76, 81–84, 87–88, 90, 117

St. John's College, Oxford, 157
St. Mleux, André, 222
Salinger, Pierre, 58
Salisbury, Lord, 10, 15
Sallal, Abdullah al, 38, 42, 48, 51
Samarkand, 184
SAMs, 60, 61
San Cristobal, 62, 63
Sana'a, 42, 51; Radio, 38
Sandys, Duncan, 18
Santamaria, Carlos Sanz de, 231
Santo Domingo, 131
Sarawak, 128
Saud, House of, 43, 45
Saud, Ibn Abdul Aziz al, 41, 50
Saudi Arabia, 38–52
Scandinavia, 130
Schaetzel, Robert, 105, 107
Schelling, Thomas, 204–05
Schlesinger, Arthur M., Jr., 96, 163
Schuman Plan, 97
Secret Service, 176, 211
Senate, 6, 64, 135, 138–39, 158, 225; Foreign Relations Committee, 72, 158; Internal Security Subcommittee, 162
Senior Interdepartmental Group (SIG), 177–80
SHAPE, 97
Shastri, Shri Lal Bahadur, 126–28, 165, 214
Shelepin, Alexander, 79, 202–03
Siberia, 62
Sigma Delta Chi, 59
"Simpatico," 199
Sino-Soviet Bank, 188
Skagerrak, 197
Skybolt missile program, 12
Slim, Mongi, 233
Smith, Bromley, 114
Smith, Gerard C., 195–97
Smith, Mrs. Stephen, 71
South America, 60
South Korea, 8, 80, 165
South Vietnam, 72–77, 80–81, 85, 90–91, 157, 165, 207

Southeast Asia, 15, 70, 72, 157, 178, 213, 231
Southeast Asia Treaty Organization (SEATO), 74, 101, 143
Soviet Union, Soviet, 13, 23, 33–34, 36, 38, 40, 45, 52, 54–57, 59, 61–62, 66–68, 73–74, 76, 78–79, 93–96, 98–99, 102–03, 107, 111, 122, 126, 129, 137, 147, 150, 152, 156, 159, 165, 172, 181–82, 184, 190–91, 193, 196–97, 201, 203, 208–12, 214, 222–23, 229, 232–33; Foreign Office, 190
Spaak, Paul Henri, 222
Spain, Spaniards, 119–20
Stalin, Joseph, 59, 99, 181–82, 191
Stanleyville, 218
Stassen, Harold, 195
State Department, v, 3, 5, 7, 13, 21, 26–27, 41, 44, 64–65, 79, 80, 85–86, 94, 102–03, 106–07, 109, 113–14, 119–20, 122, 124, 126, 129, 133, 135–36, 139–41, 149–55, 159, 161–65, 167, 169–78, 180–81, 183, 185, 187, 189, 192, 194–95, 197–200, 212–16, 219, 224, 232–33; Near Eastern Bureau, 39; "little," 44, 172
State-of-the-Union message, 137
State-War-Navy Building, 4
Stevenson, Adlai, 66, 94, 97, 145, 147–48, 152, 163, 226
Stewart, Michael, 158
Stikker, Dirk, 21
Strategic Air Command (SAC), 111, 209; alert, 56
Strategy and Policy Group, 192
Strategy of Conflict (Schelling), 205
Strauss, Lewis, 6
Stull, Lee T., 172–73
Suez, 169, 190
Sukarno, 129, 184, 190
Supreme Court, 134, 143, 224

Sweden, 31, 223
Switzerland, 223
Symington, James, 124
Syria, 33

Tagmac, General, 22
Taiz, 39
Talbot, Phillips, 39, 41–42
Tashkent, 17, 127
Taylor, Maxwell, 21, 86–87, 90, 176, 207, 215
Texas, 71, 79, 110, 119, 125, 128, 135, 153
Thant, U, 28–29, 48, 51–52
Thompson, Llewellyn, 13, 60, 67, 172, 219
Toynbee, Arnold, 11
Trinidad, 119
Trujillo Molina, Rafael Leonidas, 179
Truman, Harry, 3, 65, 91, 96–97, 112–13, 132, 139–40, 153, 210; Doctrine, 113, 142; his administration, 120, 138, 179, 193
Tshombe, Moise, 190
"Tuesday lunches," 135–36
Tunisia, 46, 233
Tuomioja, Sakari, 29
Turkey, Turks, Turkish, 4, 17–18, 20, 22–36, 66, 109, 113, 156–57, 191–92, 214, 218, 223; Security Council, 22
Twining, Nathan, 4
Tyler, William, 119

Udall, Stewart, 164
UNCDAD, 23
Union of Soviet Socialist Republics (U.S.S.R.), 107, 159, 182, 191–92, 203
United Arab Republic (U.A.R.), 5, 33–34, 38–40, 42–48, 50–52, 129, 157
United Nations (UN), 4, 13, 18, 21–22, 25, 28, 31, 34–36, 38, 48–49, 51–52, 62, 94, 145–

United Nations (UN) (*continued*)
46, 152, 158, 162, 164, 232;
Security Council, 19–20, 22,
29, 34, 95–96, 229; General
Assembly, 95, 136, 147–48,
226, 228–29; Secretariat, 229
United Press International (UPI),
86, 117
United States Information Agency
(USIA), 86, 177
University of Glasgow, 98
University of London, 80
University of Oxford, 98

Valenti, Jack, 79, 124
Van Horn, Carl, 51
Vance, Cyrus, 180
"Vectors in Eastern Europe"
study, 199
Venezuela, 186
Vermont, 94, 96, 152
Vienna, 58, 64, 135, 179
Vietnam, Vietnamese, 9, 14, 19, 53,
70, 73, 75, 80, 85–87, 89, 91–
92, 105–06, 117, 123, 125,
127–28, 134–35, 143, 154,
156, 158, 163, 171–72, 178,
185, 189, 206–07, 212, 216–
19; Viet Minh, 70; Viet Cong,
71, 73–74, 76, 81, 87, 91, 117,
125, 206; Constitution, 82, 83
Vinogradov, Sergei A., 191
Virginia, 208
Voice of America, 86
von Walther, Gebhardt, 107
Vostok-2, 201

Wall Street, 98
War Department, 192
Warsaw, 164
Washington Post, 148

Webb-Lovett agreement, 179
Welles, Sumner, 168–69, 173–74
West Point, 80
West Virginia, 145
Western Hemisphere, 54, 57, 152,
169
Westinghouse Electric Corporation, 58 fn.
Wheeler, Earle, 117
White House, 4, 7–9, 27, 44, 60,
65, 68, 71, 76, 81, 89, 94,
105, 107, 113, 115–16, 118,
120–26, 128, 131, 133, 135–
37, 139–40, 149, 150, 152,
154–56, 165, 171–72, 175–77,
188–89, 197, 214–16, 224;
Treaty Room, 124; East
Room, 133
White, William S., 128
Whiting, Allen, 172
Who's Who, 98
Williams, G. Mennen ("Soapy"),
148
Williams, Mrs. Lois, 124
Wilson, Harold, 127–28
Wilson, Woodrow, 115, 140
World Bank, 127, 133
World War I, 168
World War II, 97, 99–100, 121,
134, 192

Yale University, 98, 174; Law
School, 110; *Law Review*, 174
Yarmouth Castle disaster, 136
Yeh, George Kung-Chao, 230–31,
233
Yemen, 37–46, 48–54, 135, 206,
219
Yugoslavia, 51, 169

Zorin, Valerian A., 191, 229